****

"*THE EMERGING ORDER* SOUNDS AN ALARM
AND OFFERS WORDS
OF HOPE AND PROMISE.
The alarm is related to the Right Wing's attempted
takeover of authentic religious enthusiasm. The words
of hope and promise speak of a Second Reformation,
a Third Great Awakening, if only..."

Bishop James Armstrong
President, National Council of Churches

"IT PROVIDES THE KIND OF HISTORICAL
ASSESSMENT OF OUR TIME
THAT COULD HAVE BEEN WRITTEN ONLY TEN
YEARS FROM NOW."

Gilbert Bilezikian
Professor of Bible
Wheaton College

"*THE EMERGING ORDER* describes evangelical
Christianity's impact on the quest for freedom
in America in the 1700's and the quest for
freedom within America in the 1800's. It then
shows how evangelicalism's revival today might
produce a third period of change in the late 1900's...
IT IS AN INTERESTING, STIMULATING
AND TIMELY BOOK."

John W. Alexander, past President
Intervarsity Christian Fellowship

****

* * * * * * * * * * * * * * * * * *

"IRRESPECTIVE OF ONE'S THEOLOGICAL,
SOCIOLOGICAL, AND POLITICAL STANCE,
THE EMERGING ORDER DESERVES CAREFUL
AND THOUGHTFUL READING. ITS
PROVOCATIVE ANALYSIS OF THE PRESENT
AND PERCEPTIVE, IF NOT PROPHETIC,
VIEW OF THE FUTURE IS
EXCEPTIONALLY STIMULATING."
Floyd W. Thatcher, Vice President,
Executive Editor, Word Books

"Mr. Rifkin's breadth of knowledge and fairness in
evaluating evangelicalism are commendable. Even
though I differ ideologically from him, I found
myself rethinking many of my own assumptions
about American evangelicalism. The book
deserves a thoughtful and critical reading."
Richard V. Pierard
Professor of History
Indiana State University

"ONE IS LEFT WITH A FEELING OF HAVING
READ HISTORY BEFORE IT HAPPENED.
AND THE POTENTIAL ROLE OF AMERICAN
EVANGELICALS IN THIS PROCESS IS
MIND-BOGGLING. I HAVE NEVER READ
A MORE HELPFUL BOOK ON THE
MEANING OF OUR TIMES."
John K. Stoner
The Mennonite Central Committee

* * * * * * * * * * * * * * * * * *

THE EMERGING ORDER
GOD IN THE AGE OF SCARCITY

JEREMY RIFKIN
WITH TED HOWARD

BALLANTINE BOOKS • NEW YORK

Copyright © 1979 by Jeremy Rifkin with Ted Howard

Library of Congress Catalog Card Number: 79-10612

ISBN: 0-345-30464-0

This edition published by arrangement with G. P. Putnam's Sons

Manufactured in the United States of America

First Ballantine Books Edition: January 1983

CONTENTS

ACKNOWLEDGMENTS

The staff of the Peoples Business Commission
Noreen Banks
Randy Barber
Marylin McDonald
Mary Murphy
Dan Smith

✳✳✳✳✳✳✳✳✳✳✳✳✳✳✳✳✳✳✳✳✳

PREFACE

This book is not intended to be a critical survey of all of the contemporary currents and dispositions within modern Christianity. Rather, its focus is on the Charismatic and evangelical community and the new spiritual vitality which permeates it, a vitality which is already beginning to transform an internal spiritual revival into a major social phenomenon to be reckoned with in the 1980s and 1990s.

We believe that all of the major religious groupings will begin to reassess their own role in American life as the nation moves from the age of growth to the age of limits. For this reason, we encourage others to examine the interplay between the current evangelical awakening and the directions that the mainline Protestant, Catholic and Jewish denominations are likely to take in the years just ahead.

INTRODUCTION

We are nearing the end of an epoch that stretched across a half millennium of history. The age of expansion, with its faith in unlimited economic growth and the governing truths of science and technology, is about to give way to a new age of scarcity and economic contraction, an age so utterly different from our own that any serious attempt to give form and substance to it all but boggles the mind.

At the same time, we are in the early morning hours of a *second* Protestant reformation. This should come as no surprise since the age of expansion and the Protestant Reformation have existed in a symbiotic relationship with each other since their inception. As a consequence, the end of the prevailing economic epoch presages the end of the prevailing theological one as well. Of course, most religious observers would find such a statement difficult to fathom. They would be even more incredulous if told that it is American evangelical Christians who are playing the key role in the shift now taking place in Protestant doctrine.

Strangely enough, it is not a spirit of innovation or a mood of open rebellion that is spawning what could become the greatest change in Protestantism since its birth. On the contrary, it is in the name of orthodoxy and in the spirit of church renewal that millions of devoted Christians are giving form to a new theological construct; one whose sweep is so broad that it could well consume the theological world view of the Reformation.

Today's Christian renewal movement is a two-pronged phenomenon. First, there are the millions upon millions of Charismatics, whose belief in supernatural gifts of faith healing, speaking in tongues and prophesy represent a monumental assault on the modern age itself. For the Charismatics, these supernatural powers are beginning to replace science, technique and reason as the critical reference points for interpreting one's day-to-day existence. If this unconscious challenge to the modern world view continues to intensify, it could provide the kind of liberating force that could topple the prevailing ethos and provide a bridge to the next age of history.

While the Charismatics are generating a potentially liberating impulse, the more mainline evangelical movement is beginning to provide the necessary reformulation of theological doctrine that is essential for the creation of a new covenant vision and a new world view.

At this very moment a spectacular change in Christian theology is taking place, virtually unnoticed. The change itself is simple, but basic. The ramifications are extraordinary.

God's very first commandment to humankind in the book of Genesis is being redefined. Its redefinition changes the entire relationship of human beings to both God and the temporal world. In the beginning, God says to Adam "have dominion over the fish of the sea and over the birds of the air and over every living thing that moves upon the earth." "Dominion," which Christian theology has for so long used to justify people's unrestrained pillage and exploitation of the natural world, has suddenly and dramatically been reinterpreted. Now, according to the new definition of dominion, God's first instruction to the human race is to serve as a steward and protector over all of his creation.

It is interesting to observe that this most fundamental reconception of God's first order to his children on earth has been accepted by Protestant scholars, ministers and practitioners in just a few short years without any significant opposition being voiced. In fact, one would be hard pressed to find a leading Protestant scholar anywhere today who would openly question this new interpretation of dominion in the Book of Genesis. Yet, once the full implications of this change in doctrine begin to be felt, the Protestant work ethic that has dominated the past 600 years of the age of growth could well be replaced by a new Protestant conservation ethic, ready-made for the new age of scarcity the world is moving into. The impact of this change in ethics upon people's relationship to the world would be truly revolutionary. While it is true that the new interpretation of dominion is also being promulgated by mainline Protestant denominations and the Catholic Church, it is the evangelical community, with its resurgent spiritual vitality, that has the momentum, drive and energy that is required to achieve this radical theological transformation in American society.

If the Charismatic and evangelical strains of the new Christian renewal movement come together and unite a liberating energy with a new covenant vision for society, it is possible that a great religious awakening will take place, one potentially powerful enough to incite a second Protestant reformation.

It is also possible that as the domestic and global situation continues to worsen in the 1980s, the evangelical-Charismatic phenomena, and the waves of religious renewal that follow, could, instead, provide a growing sanctuary for millions of frightened Americans and even a recruiting ground for a repressive movement manifesting all the earmarks of an emerging fascism.

In the only other major social upheavals in American history—the American Revolution and the Civil War—it was the forces of Christian evangelicalism that provided both the initial liberating drive and the components of a new covenant vision. Whether the forces of evangelical Christianity take the lead once again and establish a forum and agenda for a radical social departure, or as has more often been the case in the nation's past, become the pawn of other political interests, is very much an open question. Certainly, in terms of structure and outreach, however, there is no other single cultural force in American life today that has as much potential as the evangelical community to influence the future direction of this country.

That influence is already being felt in the corridors of government and throughout the popular culture as sectors of the Evangelical Community have begun to mobilize their ranks in a drive to reorient the affairs of the nation. The most visible sign of the new public activism can be seen in the meteoric rise of the Moral Majority, a national organization boasting membership of some four million Americans, including over 70,000 ministers. Its spiritual leader, Jerry Falwell, a Baptist minister hailing from Lynchburg, Virginia, makes clear that his organization is non-denominational and designed to play a political role, not a theological one. Nonetheless it is only fair to point out that the Moral Majority is a creature of the evangelical revival and is made up largely of Evangelical Christians anxious to imprint their message on the political psyche of the country.

The Moral Majority caught much of the liberal establishment by surprise when it catapulted onto the national scene during the 1980 Presidential election. The secular media was at first amused, later on chagrined, and finally frightened by the prospects and power being gained so effortlessly by this new force in American politics. For the first time in this century, a part of the evangelical population had become a force to be reckoned with, and while some politicians quickly lined up to court Falwell's favor, others chose to target this new, little understood organization as the embodiment of everything sinister and dangerous in the American personality. For many unaccustomed to the evangelical way of life, the Moral Majority seemed like a corpse risen from the dead. So convinced was the liberal establishment that this brand of religiosity had been expunged from the culture long ago, they were simply incredulous by its spectacular overnight journey from obscurity to national prominence.

The Moral Majority played a role in the 1980 Presidential election. Of that fact, few political pundits would disagree. As to how significant a role, there is a great divergence of opinion. At best, it can probably be said that the Moral Majority helped elect President Reagan and helped defeat some of the many liberal politicians that had long steered the political machinery of the U.S. Congress. While the political clout of the Moral Majority is the subject of much debate, there remains even more confusion over exactly how to categorize the group of people that make it up. Many liberals mistakenly identify the Moral Majority and its leader Jerry Falwell as the voice of evangelical America, when nothing could be farther from the truth. There are nearly forty-five million evangelicals in America, and while Falwell's organization speaks for a sizable faction, it is in no way representative of the views of all evangelical Christians. The Moral Majority represents the neo-fundamentalist wing of the evangelical revival sweeping the country.

While the various wings of evangelical Christianity will be examined in detail in the body of the book, for now it should be pointed out that the neo-fundamentalists differ substantially from the mainline evangelical establishment, and even more substantially from the millions of Charismatic Christians.

The point to be made at this juncture is that the evangelical phenomenon is complex, multifaceted and often internally inconsistent, if not divisive. There is no one evangelical point of view, either doctrinally or politically. That is not to say that there aren't areas of agreement that bind evangelicals into a broad-based constituency. There is certainly a common theological thread that separates evangelical Christians from the rest of the Christian community. There is also a like-mindedness expressed in political matters, that is, up to a point. On the religious front, most evangelicals accept the Bible as either the inerrant or authoritative word of God. Most evangelicals believe in the need to "witness" for Christ and to spread the Good News, calling upon their fellow men and women to repent and accept Christ as their savior and lord. On these questions, there is little disagreement. On all other theological matters, there are differences, some minor, some quite basic, and it is these differences that give expression to the various strains within the evangelical community.

On the political front, there is a consensus, of sorts, concerning certain issues. Most evangelicals would agree with Jerry Falwell's Moral Majority on three of the key issues which have defined his national campaign. Most evangelicals are anti-abortion (pro-life), most are strongly in favor of maintaining the traditional family, most are opposed to sexual permissiveness and deeply offended by what they regard as the rise of a pornographic subculture within the country. The disagreements begin with the fourth and fifth issues on the Moral Majority docket. Falwell's supporters are in favor of a strong national defense and subscribe to a traditional laissez-faire approach to economic activity.

These positions are greatly at odds with the thinking of other evangelical Christians who would substitute military armament and free market capitalism, with the need for disarmament and the initiation of programs to more equitably distribute economic resources both at home and abroad.

While mentioned only infrequently in the popular media,

many evangelical organizations are actively pursuing the call for nuclear disarmament and are deeply committed to peace initiatives, in the hope of defusing the escalating military tensions that threaten the security and future survival of humanity. Equally impressive is the emergence of a strong force within the evangelical camp in support of a more equitable redistribution of resources between rich and poor on the earth. The issue of world hunger has become a central theme within parts of the evangelical community, and there is a growing constituency dedicating time, resources and organizational support behind outreach programs to address the urgent question of world hunger and starvation. These evangelical Christians see the question of economic justice as central to Biblical doctrine and they are gaining in influence within the larger evangelical family.

These are only a few of the particulars that unify and divide the evangelical community. The role the evangelical-Charismatic movement will play in the years ahead depends, in the final analysis, on how it interacts with the tremendous economic changes that take place as America and other industrial nations make the wrenching shift from the age of growth to the age of scarcity. As we run out of the precious stock of nonrenewable resources that allowed humankind to catapult into the vast expanses of the industrial age, the Reformation doctrine that provided the theological spark to keep the giant engines running is itself nearly spent. Of one thing, then, we can be sure. The first Protestant Reformation will not outlive the economic age it grew up with. What replaces it is a matter for debate and speculation. With the emergence of both the long-range energy crisis and the new Christian renewal movement, that discussion has begun.

This book is divided into two sections. Section One is entitled "The Great Economic Transformation." Chapters one and two of this section trace the historical development of the modern age from the rise of the Protestant ethic through the triumph of the liberal ethos. Chapters three and four explore the depth of the economic crisis wrought by the modern age and the great economic transformation that lies just ahead.

Section Two examines the religious response to the crisis of modernity and the profound economic shift occurring in the United States and the world. Chapter five surveys the scope of the current evangelical awakening. Chapters six and seven then take a brief look at the role evangelicalism has played in American history as a way of understanding the possible directions the current revival will take. Chapter eight sketches out the theological doctrine of today's two-pronged Christian renewal movement. Chapters nine, ten and eleven examine the interrelationship between the great economic transformation taking place and the evangelical awakening that is spreading across America and speculates about the likelihood of a second Protestant reformation emerging between now and the year A.D. 2000.

THE GREAT ECONOMIC TRANSFORMATION

AN ESTABLISHMENT IN CRISIS

American liberalism, the political philosophy of this nation for the past half-century, is in crisis. It is not just that liberalism can no longer implement its political agenda. Liberal principles now seem out of touch with the new realities of the last quarter of the twentieth century. Today, liberalism has lost its driving energy, an energy that once rallied our citizenry around New Deals, New Frontiers and Great Societies. As we enter the end of this century, liberalism is in eclipse. It no longer has a believable program that can motivate a nation. The liberal political community is in disarray. Its own confusion, when confronted by the cold realities of its lost status, is embarrassingly evident. Liberalism is an ideology which no longer has a coherent set of issues or even promises. Once the vigorous and expansionary political ideal of an America rising to global supremacy, liberalism is now on the defensive, identified by a cynical nation with big government, big spending and big social engineering programs that promise much and produce little.

The signs of the decline of American liberalism are everywhere; sometimes this is evidenced in public opinion polls, sometimes in the defeat of a major piece of legislation. "Is America Turning Right?" asked *Newsweek* in its cover story of November 7, 1977. While no one is yet claiming that Spiro Agnew will be proven correct—while Vice-President, he warned journalists that "this country is going so far to the right you won't recognize it"—still there is no doubt that a political climate is taking hold in America that is antithetical to liberalism and liberals.

On Capitol Hill, the liberal political coalition no longer exercises the power it did ten years ago. In 1978 alone, liberals lost decisively on key issues on their agenda, including the full employment bill and the establishment of a consumer protection agency. Both bills were heavily supported by Congressional liberal leadership and major organizations such as the AFL-CIO and Ralph Nader's Public Citizen. Organized labor's political program went down to defeat on the labor reform bill. The women's movement, failing after seven years of effort to gain ratification for the Equal Rights Amendment, had to appeal to Congress to extend the life of the legislation. The years ahead are sure to be no better. In 1982, Congress will be reapportioned in accordance with the 1980 census. As a result, Northern states, home of most liberals, will be reduced from their present majority of 225 votes to a minority of 210 votes.[1]

More important than what's taking place in the halls of Congress is the mood outside Washington, D.C. Gone, for the most part, are the liberal-left political protests of the 1960s. In their place, the once silent majority has now adopted demonstration tactics of its own to demand an end to liberal "permissiveness" and a return to the family. Marchers and picketers now carry signs that signify their new political platform: anti-abortion, anti-gay, anti-taxes, and pro-capital punishment.

The campuses are quiet. Student anxieties over the draft and racism have given way to the scramble for graduate schools and jobs. No longer are universities hotbeds of liberal political activity, a fact taken note of by columnist George Will who gave the commencement address to the graduating class of 1978 at Georgetown University. The seniors could be proud, he said, that they didn't end up loud and unruly radicals like the class of 1968. For this and similar observations, he received a rousing ovation.

Big labor, a key component of the liberal power bloc, is actually shrinking in size. In 1945, 35.5 percent of all workers in nonagricultural jobs were members of trade unions. Today less than 25 percent of the labor force pays union dues. Twenty years ago, unions won two-thirds of all organizing elections. Today organized labor loses 52 percent of all such elections. According to the Labor Department, unions lost almost 600,000 members between 1974 and 1976 alone.[2]

While campuses are dormant and organized labor is declining in membership, the taxpayer's revolt seems to be picking up steam, a political development that has completely bypassed the nation's liberal leadership. The message of the tax rebellion is decidedly antiliberal: property owners are ready to put the lid on government spending programs and liberal reforms. The implication of the tax revolt movement, says liberal spokesperson Senator George McGovern, is that: "It is unfashionable now to worry about the poor and minorities and to defend the idea that they, too, deserve an opportunity."[3]

Even within the liberal camp, "liberalism" as a political concept is falling into disrepute. "New-age" politicians like Governor Jerry Brown of California seem bent on fashioning a new political synthesis. The *style* may seem related to traditional liberalism, but the *message* is not: Government cannot solve all problems; we live in an era of limits; it is time to lower our sights and expectations. Meanwhile, an older generation of New Deal era liberals are now arguing in favor of revitalized free enterprise and fewer regulations on individual liberty. They contend that social engineering reforms of the 1960s were failures because public officials refused to recognize "the limits of social policy." Says Ben Wattenberg, a former speech writer for Lyndon Johnson and now head of the Coalition for a Democratic Majority: "There is a rejection of that mindless, boilerplate, liberalism of the McGovernites and the 1960s impressions of what the world was about."[4]

Summing up the growth of antiliberal sentiment, Cushing Dolbeare, chairman of the executive committee of the Americans for Democratic Action, remarked in June of 1978: "Seldom has the attack against liberal positions and principles been as organized and concerted; seldom have our friends and allies felt as isolated."[5]

Isolated and under attack. That is how liberals see themselves these days, and that is exactly the condition they are in. Buy why? Why has the American political climate shifted so decisively in such a short period of time?

According to conventional wisdom the American people have been exhausted and traumatized over the past two decades. Our national defeat in Vietnam—a victory by guerrilla-peasants against the mightiest technological battle machine on earth— shattered our myths about national omnipotence. After a decade speckled with assassinations, hippies, drugs, cultural change, student eruptions, black protests and sexual revolution, most Americans have chosen to withdraw into more mundane individual concerns. The rebels of the 1960s have grown up and now proclaim the politics of "self." It's no wonder; Watergate, and related political scandals, disillusioned the country about political leadership. Meanwhile, liberals promised they could end poverty, crime and a host of other social blights by tinkering with the system, and they failed. The public watched as liberals ushered in a proliferation of new legislation, government agencies and bureaucratic red tape. After it was over, the sweeping and unrealistic promises were unfulfilled. The American people, in turn, began to equate liberalism with incompetence, naivete and the squandering of public monies on every social problem in sight.

Though these social problems continue to mount, the public perceives that the liberal establishment no longer has viable solutions. What is the solution to the energy crisis? How can we revitalize our decaying urban areas? Where will new jobs come from? David Broder of the *Washington Post* writes:

> The level of frustration in this country is terribly high—dangerously high. I do not think we can just assume that people will bide their time and wait for relief to arrive from some new party, or some rearrangement of constituents between the Democrats and Republicans. There is clear danger that the frustrations will find expression in a political "solution" that sacrifices democratic freedoms for a degree of relief from the almost unbearable tensions and strains of today's metropolitan center.[6]

The economic crisis of the past decade, which began with LBJ's war-induced inflation and was transformed by the energy crisis into the stagflation of high unemployment *and* high inflation, has catalyzed the antiliberal mood of the nation. Inflation, says one writer, "is a great conservatizing issue."[7] When the average price of an American home rises about 50,000 dollars, as it did in 1978, then you can be sure that people will opt for individual security rather than liberal social reform. Lamenting the new antiliberal sentiment, political activist Tom Hayden observes: "Sometimes, it seems to me the country can't be governed now by anybody because there's no consensus. . . . The country has no glue. . . . Liberalism has no substance anymore. . . . Everybody is adrift, putting together their own ten-percent or twenty-percent of the action."[8]

As far as it goes, this rather conventional analysis of why

liberalism is in trouble as we enter the 1980s is an adequate assessment of the current state of the union. But to argue that the antiliberal climate of the nation is simply a result of Vietnam, Watergate and related scandals, failed social experiments, inflation and unemployment is to imply that what the American political system is currently experiencing is simply a swing of the pendulum from left to right. Thus, a liberal might take consolation in the fact that if we distance ourselves enough from the 1960s and if the economic health of the country improves, then the liberal consensus will again become the political doctrine of the nation.

What the liberal establishment does not yet comprehend is the hard, cold reality that American liberalism has already begun a *permanent* slide into extinction. The current public disenchantment with liberal policy and the escalating attack on liberal values is not the cause of liberalism's demise; they are reflections of a decay that has already set in.

The twilight of liberalism is upon us because the basis for liberal society no longer exists. Liberalism is founded on one overriding precondition—the possibility of *unlimited economic growth*. Liberalism, spawned during the revolutionary epoch of the Reformation and the Enlightenment, supplanted the static medieval world view with the doctrine of unlimited material expansion and the promise that humankind could realize complete fulfillment here on earth by overcoming economic scarcity. It was this revolutionary faith in the infinite supply of natural wealth that could be extracted from the earth that shaped liberalism's intense optimism about the future of the human race.

Though this optimism has been jarred considerably in the last decade and a half, the liberal maintains faith in the never-ending process of progress, namely, the continued improvement of humankind's material condition. The only barriers that exist to human progress, argues the liberal, are those in people's own minds. It is only small thinking or antiquated ideas that set boundaries to the human experience. Ultimately, all of these boundaries will fall, if we harness our energies in the right direction. Again, that direction, quite simply, is toward providing the most abundant material existence possible for every human being.

People are good, the liberal philosophy declares. It is only the social environment that makes them bad. There is only one solution to making a better social environment: that is to provide more of whatever it is that people desire. Once people's material desires are satisfied, there will no longer be any necessity for inhumanity to our fellows, for all will have what they need. More productivity will generate more wealth, which will provide more people with the material base to allow them to exist in harmony.

Liberalism, and its economic agent, capitalism, are by their very nature *expansionary*. Without sustained economic growth, neither can long exist. True, capitalism has experienced numerous economic downturns in our national history, but each time it recovered and went on to achieve even greater growth.

Even now, in the midst of our present economic downturn, the liberal establishment is busy at work attempting to prime the pumps of our technological society. Prosperity can be right around the corner again, the liberal maintains, if the proper economic adjustments are made. This time, however, liberal hopes are grounded in fantasy. The fact is, the triumph of liberal values witnessed in the West during the past 200 years was accompanied by economic expansion unique in human history. After two centuries we are now nearing the end of that expansionary period. For numerous reasons that will be discussed later in this book, American productivity is slowing steadily and by the end of this century will likely have stopped completely. Liberalism, which has always preached the doctrine of an expanding economic pie, is in decline today because the size of the pie is now stabilizing. Soon, even its present minuscule growth—America now ranks seventh among eight leading industrial nations in productivity—will level off. Two hundred years of exponential economic expansion is now giving way to permanent economic contraction. The liberal American era (or better, the American moment, for unlike Rome, our national domination of the world has lasted only a few short decades) is coming to a close.

It cannot be emphasized too strongly that we are not simply witnessing a shift in political sentiment. The decline of liberal political power is only the most superficial manifestation of a larger trend. We are embarked on a course of sweeping global change. America, as the most aggressively materialist culture on earth, will feel that change more than any other nation. Our liberal disposition is ingrained in the concept of unlimited material advance. Now we are confronted with the economic reality of a finite planet which simply cannot sustain our expansionary value system. The current decline in our liberal political values is testimony to the major social reformulations that await us. What is at stake is not just the contemporary liberal political agenda—consumer bills, welfare programs, full employment acts—although that is already becoming the first victim of our steadily contracting economy. Ultimately, the end of the expansionary economic period will usher in an entirely new philosophical ethos that will be as radically different from liberalism as the Reformation and Enlightenment were from the Middle Ages. By the year 2000, the liberal mind will be as out of touch with the new economic realities as a fifteenth-century monk were he to find himself magically transported to contemporary Manhattan.

Two philosophical/political paradigms seem already to be emerging as postliberal ethics. Both embody, in radically different ways, a psychology that reflects the coming age of scarcity. One envisions a future where Hobbes' war of each against all comes to dominate the world. The other leads to a new epoch where cooperation between human beings and between the human race and nature become the prevailing norm.

The question of which alternative future will come to dominate American life will be answered, in part, by the theological response to the decline of the liberal ethos.

In the only other major economic shifts in American history—the movement from colonialism to independence and from agrarianism to industrialism—the forces of evangelical Christianity generated both the initial liberating drive as well as the outlines of a new covenant vision. Today, America is experiencing the stirrings of a new spiritual revival just at the time the economy is beginning to shift from the expansionary ethos of industrial development to the contracting ethos of the steady state. If history is any guide, this religious awakening is intimately bound up with the wrenching changes going on in the economy.

Before examining the dynamic between America's new religious revival and the profound economic transformation taking place, it's important to examine the nature of the liberal ethos, which is at the root of our present predicament.

THE LIBERAL ETHOS AND THE AGE OF EXPANSION

THE COMING OF MODERNITY

About once a year, the serious newspaper reader will come across a story headlined, PRIMITIVE STONE-AGE TRIBE FOUND LIVING IN BRAZIL, or some other Southern Hemisphere location. Most often these people are hunter-gatherers who dwell in caves and have never been stumbled upon before. Caught in a time warp, they are our living ancestors and a startling reminder of who we were not so very long ago. Not only do they live the life of pre-modern people, but they view the world around them in a most un-modern way. Often they have no word in their vocabulary for work; no concept of private property or the rights of the individual; their sense of time, undistorted by machines, is elongated and cyclical; their gods are everywhere, in the trees, the snakes, the river. For them, life has not changed in tens of thousands of years.

The occasional discoveries of these tribes jar us into a renewed awareness that people have not always thought about themselves and their environment as we do now. In fact, the beginning of modern liberal thought in its broadest sense—humanist, rational, reductionist; obsessed with time, efficiency, production, consumption, wealth, change, growth—is no older than a scant twenty generations at most. The great liberal epoch of the Age of Reason and the Enlightenment burst onto Western society just 300 years ago. The concept of progress, that peculiarly modern notion that the human condition will continue to improve as our power over the environment increases, is no more than two centuries old. It is a testimony to the power of liberalism that few individuals in modern Western society can even conceptualize a philosophical system that presents a decisive alternative to the liberal doctrine.

Even socialism, often thought of as a competing ideology to liberalism, bases its most critical assumptions—such as its glorification of economic growth and its total reliance on science and technology—on traditional liberal-humanistic values. This has not, incidentally, always been the case. Early nineteenth-century socialists organized the working class as a force in opposition to the coming industrial age. But Karl Marx, and his theories of "scientific" socialism, changed all that. According to Marx, oppression was not inherent in industrialism, itself. The problem was simply one of transferring ownership of the means of production from one class to another. For Marx, and most socialists since, all technology and science were neutral. What is of critical importance is who controls the productive forces and toward what ends. From the mid-nineteenth century on, Marx's vision has become not only the dominant, but nearly the only theory of socialist economics. Today the Soviet Union barters for American technology to increase their productivity, glories in meeting ever-expanding production quotas and is facing pollution problems as bad, or worse, than ours. Meanwhile, that other world giant, the People's Republic of China, has launched an ambitious drive to become a fully "technological" state by the year 2000. In the name of this lofty goal, Coca-Cola bottles will soon be littering the grounds around the Great Wall.

No one would dispute that socialism is, in other respects, different from liberalism, especially in its views on private ownership of capital and the role of the individual in society. Still, it is a difference of degree, not of kind. The belief that one's purpose in life is defined in terms of material progress and that the ruthless exploitation and subjugation of nature is essential to achieve that end is as much a part of the philosophy of life in Moscow and Peking as on Wall Street.

Though today they reign triumphant, liberal values are no more natural to the human condition than are the values of the hunter-gatherer. Rather, they are the product of an immense struggle, at once religious, economic, political and philosophical, that began some five centuries ago.

From A.D. 500 to A.D. 1500, medieval Christian doctrine governed the world of Western Europe. Unlike the moral relativism and situational ethics of our own day, medieval society was governed by a set of absolutes from which, in theory, no deviation was countenanced. All secular authority flowed from God, through his agent on earth, the Catholic Church. Not surprisingly, the primary characteristic of this theocentric world was its static nature. Social change was not the norm, as it is now, but the rare exception, for each innovation had to be measured against long-standing religious tradition to test whether it represented heresy or was in keeping with God's word.

There was no conception of economic growth and progress. The human purpose was not to "get ahead" or to amass wealth but to seek salvation. Society was viewed as an organic whole, a kind of divinely directed moral organism in which each person had a part. The individual had no sovereign meaning and few rights as he does under the liberal state. In medieval society, the emphasis was on duties and obligations that were prescribed by God. John of Salisbury, a twelfth-century writer, described the typical conception of the medieval commonwealth:

> Those men who preside over the rites of religion should be honored or revered as the soul of the body. . . . The prince takes the place of the head, subject to God alone and to those who act as His representatives on earth. The senate corresponds to the heart, from which proceed the beginnings of good and evil deeds. The offices of eyes, ears and tongue are claimed by the judges and the governors of the provinces. Officials and soldiers correspond to the legs. Those who are always about the prince are likened to the sides. Treasurers and warders . . . are like the belly and intestines, which if they become congested with excessive greed and too tenaciously keep what they collect, generate innumerable incurable diseases, so that ruin threatens the whole body. . . . Tillers of the soil correspond to the feet . . .[1]

In medieval society, making money was not a sign of accomplishment, but rather a form of antisocial behavior. Theologians during the Middle Ages argued forcefully that commercial pursuits and the accumulation of goods were barriers to salvation that corrupted the soul by focusing attention on the profane, rather than the sacred afterlife. Accordingly, rules were imposed and enforced that hindered any chance for substantial economic growth in society. Lending money to make more money—usury then, banking now—was forbidden as immoral activity, since the usurer does no work himself, but simply profits from this neighbor's misfortunes. The market system of pricing goods to gain the maximum price the market will bear, was unknown. During the Middle Ages, prices were fixed and regulated by guilds and governments on the basis of what was considered a "just" price.

Theoretically, every aspect of economic life was governed by moral principles in keeping with God's will. Competition was subordinate to group activity. Property rights were not sacrosanct and property owners had to justify their possessions. This is not to deny, of course, that the feudal system was brutally harsh on the peasantry, allowing a handful of nobles to live the good life while the Catholic Church confiscated huge amounts of economic surplus for its own aggrandizement. But it is also true, as sociologist R. H. Tawney has argued, that before the advent of liberalism, people called avarice and greed in high places by their right names and "had not learned to persuade themselves that greed was enterprise and avarice economy."[2]

For fully one thousand years, the Catholic Church and the political institutions of feudalism held sway over the life of Western Europe. For those who lived during this epoch, it seemed inconceivable that the theocentric order of the Middle Ages would not continue to dominate all aspects of existence until the judgment day when all history would end with the return of God to earth. But then came the Reformation, and suddenly the Western world view was radically, and irreversibly, altered.

THE REFORMATION

Our Lord and Master Jesus Christ, in saying; Repent ye! intended that the whole life of believers should be penitence. This word cannot be understood of sacramental

penance, that is, of the confession and satisfaction which
are performed under the ministry of priests. It does not,
however, refer solely to inward penitence; nay, such
inward penitence is naught unless it outwardly produces
various mortifications of the flesh. The penalty thus continues as long as the hatred of self, that is, true inward
penitence, continues, namely; until our entrance into the
kingdom of heaven.[3]

Few of us are familiar with this passage. In fact a casual
reading of it is sure to generate little if any thought and even
less interest. Yet this rather esoteric sounding ninety-three-word
paragraph has probably had a greater impact on every one of
our lives than any other idea of the past 500 years.

In 1517 a little unassuming priest nailed this thesis to the
church door in Wittenberg, Germany, and changed the course
of history.[4] Martin Luther's doctrine tore through the veneer
of legitimacy that had surrounded the Catholic Church of Europe since its coronation as the official Church of the Holy
Roman Empire under King Constantine in A.D. 300.

Luther's proclamation directly challenged the three underlying assumptions from which the Church derived its power
and authority over the Christian world: first, that Church authority was equal to Biblical authority in translating God's will
in matters of doctrine and policy; second, that individual salvation could be earned in this world by a combination of good
works and papal intervention; and third, that the Church represented the exclusive priesthood of God's chosen apostles on
earth.[5]

Before Luther's bold frontal attack, Church doctrine, for
the most part, reflected the writings of St. Thomas Aquinas.
Aquinas believed that although men and women's will had
fallen from grace after their revolt from God in the Garden of
Eden, their minds had not. Therefore, St. Thomas concluded
that God had purposely spared the mind so that people could
use their own reasoning power to transcend their fallen state
and find their salvation in Christ. Luther disagreed. Personal
salvation could never depend on an individual's own reason.
Salvation, to Luther, was not something people could earn. On
the contrary it was purely a gift from God.[6] To believe otherwise, "reasoned" Luther, is to believe that men and women
are somehow on the same level with the Divine. For Luther,
there was only one way to secure salvation: through *faith* alone.

Only by recognizing one's complete and total powerlessness and depravity could an individual even hope for salvation. Even then, God made the decision of who would be saved and who damned, regardless of a person's virtues. This, of course, had the effect of undermining the Church's central role in the life of every believer. If salvation depended only on individual faith and God's grace, then the Church's sacramental system, with its emphasis on good works as a means of earning one's way into heaven, was irrelevant. And if partaking of the sacraments couldn't earn you a place in God's kingdom, then of what value was the Roman Church?

By challenging the Thomistic doctrine of grace through reason and good works, Luther was also challenging the authority of the priesthood.[7] Up to that time it was simply assumed that the Pope was God's designated intermediary on earth and that the priesthood could help each individual to better understand God's will and therefore "earn" his or her place in heaven. Again Luther said no. Papal authority and the priesthood were not blessed with some superpower to act as intermediaries between people and God. Since all were fallen, all were sinners, and therefore all equal in the eyes of God, salvation could only come from God, and not through imperfect intermediaries or people's good works. As to authority, even priests were imperfect, because like all men and women they were sinners. The only unimpeachable authority, therefore, was God's will as made accessible to *all* human beings through the Bible. Moreover, since all people were imperfect and sinners, the Church's translation of Biblical doctrine was no more authoritative than that of the average person who looked to it for his own salvation.

Luther undermined the authority of the Church. He replaced the notion of the exclusive priesthood of the Church with the notion of the universal priesthood of all believers. He undermined Church doctrine by proclaiming the Bible (not the Pope) as the ultimate authority in determining God's will. And, finally, leaving nothing whatsoever to human authority alone, he argued that doing good works or exercising superior reason were all futile exercises; salvation did not depend on human accomplishments or abilities but only on God's grace.

Thirty years after Luther nailed the handwriting on the wall, John Calvin, a French cleric, refined the new heresy into popular doctrine and mobilized the masses for an assault right into the heart of the Church's inner sanctuary.

Leon Trotsky, the great Russian revolutionary, theoretician and strategist, said of Calvin's ideas that they were as revolutionary as the theories of Marx. Both Calvin and Marx developed an all inclusive deterministic view of human beings, nature and history.[8] For Calvin, every act of life was predetermined by God Almighty; for Marx, economic necessity was the determining factor. Like Marx, Calvin was no armchair intellectual. Both men took their ideas out into the real world, and each was equally "determined" to transfer their theories to practice. Both, in their own way, succeeded in changing the course of history.

Calvin agreed with Luther that people could not achieve salvation through good works, but only by God's grace.[9] But, reasoned Calvin, since God's decision is in no way influenced by what each person does or fails to do in this world, and since God obviously saves some people but not all, then the question of salvation must, in fact, be predetermined.[10]

Of course, the big question then was how does one know if one is numbered among the elect or the damned. Calvin addressed the question of proof of election with a new theory which, in practice, has become so deeply imbedded in the character structure of modern humanity that the residual effects are still felt in every single action and institution.

Calvin argued that no one can ever really know if he's been saved or damned because only God knows this, and it's not ever fully revealed. But since the world and everything in it exist to serve the glory of God, those who have been saved will "naturally" fulfill all of God's commandments with the ultimate zeal and enthusiasm. They will do so, not because it will gain them a place in heaven (this question has already been decided), but simply because God *wills* it. Moreover, everyone has an obligation to believe they are chosen. That belief, according to Calvin, must be constantly renewed through the performance of God's will in the world. Constant performance and resistance to the temptations of the devil are a kind of partial proof or at least a sign that one can look to for hope that he has been saved. Parenthetically, the chief temptation of the devil is idolatry of the flesh. Sensual pleasures, music, art, dance and all other forms of enjoyment were looked upon as evil diversions, designed to seduce the individual away from the proper performance of God's will.[11]

All in all, Calvin's answer to the big question of proof of salvation was pretty inadequate, but its very "tentativeness" served to create an ever-present, vigilant asceticism in the lives of the true believers. With Catholicism, the individual could at least store up credits or merits through good works and secure a place in heaven. The Church even offered some important loopholes for the individual sinner who sought to mend his ways. Confession and the priest's absolution were always available to those who wanted to wipe their personal slate clean and try once again to earn his way back into God's good grace. With Calvin's doctrine, none of this made a lick of difference.[12] Instead, the individual was forced to live from moment to moment constantly reassuring himself against his own gnawing doubts by constantly performing God's will. Even a momentary lapse from a total ascetic commitment could undermine one's personal belief and confidence that he is one of the elect.

Calvin replaced the *external* order imposed by the Church on each individual with an *internally* imposed order of far greater magnitude and scope. Every action at every moment of a believer's life had to conform with God's glory. All personal conduct must, therefore, be perfectly controlled and ordered. Lapses, respites, doubts, were all signs of nonelection and therefore to be resisted. Not only does one have the responsibility to perform God's will constantly, as if he were one of the chosen (whether he is or not), but he must also perform to the utmost of his ability, because to do less is to compromise one's responsibility to carry out God's will in this world.

Calvin's doctrine transformed the unsystematic and somewhat casual way of life of the average Catholic serf into the methodically planned and rigorously executed life of the new bourgeois man and woman. Self-control replaced church control as the modus operandi.

We all know people who are compulsive workaholics, fanatically busy, extremely ordered, and very self-controlled. When asked why they do it, they generally shrug their shoulders and say, "I just don't know." The reason they don't know is that after 500 years, the transcendent value of Calvin's concept of "calling" has been lost amidst the steady secularization of society. The outward manifestation of Calvin's doctrine, however, continues with an almost independent existence.

The ideas of the Reformation radically changed the con-

ception of people's role with respect to nature, society and
God. In so doing, the Reformation theology set the stage for
capitalist development and the emergence of the liberal ethos.

THE PROTESTANT REFORMATION, THE SPIRIT OF CAPITALISM AND THE EMERGENCE OF THE LIBERAL ETHOS

John Calvin lived at that precise moment in European history
when the fuedal economic system of the medieval age was
beginning to give way to a new economic order. As mentioned,
the medieval era had been characterized by a nongrowth steady-
state economic structure. The Catholic Church, which was so
very much a part of that structure, provided a theological doctrine ideally suited for medieval economic life. The Church's
emphasis on a hierarchical structure of authority that fixed
relationships between the people, the Church and the secular
world, with rigidly prescribed behavior patterns provided a
"way of life" that was immune to the notion of "change." While
there were no big suprises to life—except the occasional excitement generated by a crusade or small natural disaster—
neither was there a great deal of undue anxiety about what the
future might bring. The social and personal life of the average
Catholic serf was as regular and steady as the economic environment he lived in.

By the sixteenth century, however, the feudal societies of
Europe were being seriously challenged by an emerging new
order. Intercontinental and oceanic trade routes were opening
up, new inventions like the printing press and the mechanical
weaver were making their debut, and port cities were expanding
their populations. Alongside these early signs of capitalist development came the Reformation theology of John Calvin. The
Reformation provided both the liberating energy necessary to
challenge the old feudal system and the covenant vision necessary to establish the new capitalist order.

As we have said, Calvin believed that, while everyone was
either elected or damned at birth, each person was, nonetheless,
duty bound to consider himself chosen and to reject any and
all doubts about his election. Overcoming doubt, said Calvin,
could only be achieved by "unceasing activity in the service
of God." The key word here is unceasing. The slightest relax-

ation in one's calling or work would tend to undermine a person's self-confidence and raise serious doubt as to whether or not he had been elected to salvation in the first place. Calvin's new man and woman, then, were like hamsters on a treadmill, frightened to death that if they slowed their pace of activity even for a moment, they might, in fact, fall off the wheel altogether. Before that time, in medieval and other cultures, work was defined quite differently. Human beings, like the other animals, would put out just the amount of energy they needed in order to provide for their bodily needs. Then they rested. People's worklife corresponded to the prerequisites of a steady-state economy—the same prerequisites that manifest themselves in a natural ecosystem.

Calvin, on the other hand, believed that any time lost in relaxation or rest was a loss to the glory of God and a sign of nonbelief. For the first time, then, a new principle of work was established. The individual was to labor at his optimum at all times. The effect was the introduction of the concept of *efficiency* into the economic life of society. Ways must constantly be explored to increase one's output. Therefore, any effort that improved one's "calling" or work, was considered worthy of God's approval.

The concept of calling, then, took on a new and expanded role. It was no longer good enough to continue to do whatever one did in the world the best way one knew—this was Luther's notion of calling. Even if one worked at 100 percent capacity, as long as he was doing the same task in the same manner as before, he could not possibly be increasing his productivity. While he would be busy all of the time, he still wouldn't be serving God to the fullest. Maximum output, contended Calvin, was as important as maximum input. To improve efficiency and output, people had an obligation to aspire to more productive callings in life, argued Calvin. It was not a very big jump from this notion to the notion of *specialization of labor*.[13] After all, the basic principle behind specialization is the idea of increasing efficiency. Calvin, then, had rather unconsciously provided two of the four elements essential for capitalist organization and development. He also would more consciously provide the other two as well.

With the Reformation person producing more than he needed to sustain his own natural physical needs, what was to become of the surplus? Calvin provided the answer. Since the surplus was never intended for the benefit of the individual but only to serve the glory of God, it would be sinful to lavish it on one's carnal appetites. On the other hand, there was nothing sinful about the surplus itself. How could there be, since it was produced to serve God's glory. Therefore, the only proper thing to do with the surplus was to reinvest it into one's calling in order to continue to improve the output and provide even larger surpluses for God's glory, and so on. Here the notion of *capital formation*, the key ingredient of capitalist development, was given birth.

It might be added, at this point, that the idea that the product of one's labor was designed to serve God's glory and not people's appetite fit neatly with later capitalist theories that saw labor as merely one of several purely utilitarian factors in the production process. Instead of people serving God, however, they began to serve the capitalists instead.

To summarize, Calvin's doctrinal reformulations led to the introduction of efficiency, specialized calling and capital reinvestment in the economic process. His tightly structured theological doctrine established the guiding principle for the fourth crucial element of the capitalist system as well, the *rational production mode*. The modern industrial process depends on rigorous calculation and planning. So did Calvin's view of people's role in the world.

For Calvin, chaos was synonymous with evil. Chaos bred anxiety which was a sign of men and women's fallen nature. Overcoming anxiety and fear, the hallmarks of one's fallen nature, could only be achieved by ordering every single aspect of one's daily life. The result was something like perpetual activity. Calvin produced the person of order, the rational person: the machine person for the machine age.

Of course, very few business executives or assembly-line workers believe they are performing efficiently to serve the glory of God. Fewer, still, would buy the idea that they were specializing in a particular field because it produced proof of their election to heaven. And there's probably not one person in a hundred who would accept the idea that they should resist their own lustful consumer appetites and plow all their surplus back into new investments—not just because the rate of return might be good, but because God would be served.

While it is true that the transcendent value behind the Protestant ethic and the rise of capitalism has all but disappeared, there is no doubt that the effect of the doctrine on redefining work in an industrial era still exists and still affects every single American.

Of course, it is only fair to say that it was never Calvin's intention to provide a theological rationale for the emergence of modern capitalism. Quite the contrary. Calvin was committed to restoring the Christian community to the kind of simple purity that characterized the faith in the early days after the crucifixion of Christ. Today's world would no doubt stand just as condemned in his eyes as the secular world he so fervently fought against in his own day.

Calvin believed that the secular world should be guided at all times by God's laws. In his own city of Geneva, Calvin was successful in creating a virtual theocracy. While he never held public office, Calvin was instrumental in advancing social legislation which would still be considered progressive by twentieth-century standards. According to the registers of the city of Geneva, Calvin was the driving force behind "the regulation of hours and conditions of labor; restrictions of the tasks imposed upon women and children; control of inflationary prices of bread, cheese and wine; the right to organize for unskilled and guild labor; public investment in business enterprise to relieve unemployment; adoption of orphans as wards of the city"; and countless other laws.[14] Unfortunately, as is often the case with great reformers, the spirit and intent of Calvin's doctrinal beliefs were soon twisted to suit the needs of others.

In the end it was Calvin's emphasis on the importance of engaging in worldly activity as a sign of election to the kingdom of God that helped usher in a new social class, the bourgeoisie. It was the bourgeoisie, seeking to justify and spur on their own desire for material accumulation and social power, who transformed the religious doctrines of Luther and Calvin and formulated a revolutionary new philosophy of society—liberalism.

The bourgeoisie of the sixteenth and seventeenth centuries rebelled against the constricting tradition of feudalism. They were not interested in perpetuating an organic, static society that allowed no place for their class interests in the social order. The bourgeois was, above all else, an "economic man" who saw only positive personal and social good as a result of making money. A trader or merchant by profession, he felt constrained by medieval regulations and a value system that denied the virtue of pursuing wealth for its own sake. In opposition to mercantilism, the bourgeois argued for free trade and production, the necessity of usury, and the establishment of laws to protect individual profits and property from government and Church interference. Ultimately, the bourgeois triumphed; medieval society was replaced by the industrial revolution, urbanization, the age of science and technology, capitalism, and the other components that form contemporary society. But this massive transformation from one economic reality to another could only be realized by overthrowing all previous conceptions of human beings and society. Reformation theology provided the bourgeois class with the ideological dynamite it needed to launch one of the most victorious revolutionary movements of history.

During the time of the Enlightenment, one of the more popular songs in Great Britain was a tune entitled, "The World Turned Upside Down." Its lyrics were a metaphor for the monumental changes that had taken place during the transition from the Middle Ages to modernity. The bourgeois philosophy of liberalism had truly turned the world upside down. Virtually every concept held sacred and natural in the feudal order was replaced with its diametrical opposite by the new order. The entire basis of society shifted from obligations to rights and from the community to the individual.

Step by step, as liberalism developed, the God of the Reformation theologians was pushed further and further back from center stage and eventually was banished from the scene altogether. Early liberal thinkers were not atheists, far from it. But for them, God was no longer personally involved; rather, he was the creator who simply set the universe in motion at some distant time in the past, and then went off to conduct other business. He did not, in other words, interfere in the affairs of the human race. As befitted the thinking of a new class bent on pursuing economic interests, liberals held that people were absolutely alone, free to create their own meaning and establish their own values. Theocentrism disappeared; in its place was substituted anthropocentric humanism, the belief that the individual human being is the measure of all things. The moral order based on the absolute interpretation of God's law was replaced with rationalism, moral relativism and utility. The vertical values of spirit gave way to the horizontal pursuit of wealth.

The old order had disparaged temporal life, maintaining that the only important task for men and women was to seek salvation by obeying God's will. Liberalism decisively broke with this tradition, and for the first time in history sought to prove that the individual could fulfill his role and achieve ultimate satisfaction right here on earth. This assumption has led to all of the great sweeping reforms of the past three centuries. Politically, for instance, liberalism's secular humanism brought about constitutional government founded upon the belief that the individual is sovereign, every member of society is created equal, with equal rights such as freedom of speech and expression. All of these various rights and freedoms flow naturally from the liberal emphasis on the dignity and centrality of the individual.

As the history of liberal doctrine has been formulated, the individual rights we ascribe to liberalism today are merely extensions of a greater concern—materialism. Material economic growth is the precondition for liberal philosophy. Without growth and material abundance, liberals have argued from the Enlightenment down to our day, people could not be free. *It is only by surmounting scarcity that human beings fulfill their potential.* As philosopher Bertrand de Jouvenel has argued, modern political thought has been dominated since 1500 by a "hedonist and productivist" approach to life. By placing people at the center of the universe, liberals by necessity have established a civilization that "takes pride in its capacity to satisfy ever more fully all desires . . . and where political systems aspire only to achieve the same objective: to dispense satisfactions more fully."[15] The cornucopia is the perfect symbol of liberalism's promise.

Faith in the liberating power of materialism carries with it one critical assumption, the belief that the earth possesses unlimited abundance. The formulators of liberalism, the men of the Age of Reason and the Enlightenment, had no doubt that the earth would yield more wealth than could possibly be used. All that was required, they argued, was to discover the right intellectual and social "tools" that would free its abundance. From the beginning, that has been liberalism's purpose. Though current resource depletion and environmental devastation now challenge the view that there will always be more, three hundred years ago, liberals had good reason to foresee a future of unlimited wealth. In the 1600s, the New World, the greatest frontier known, was just opening up for exploitation. By the beginning of the next century, industrialism had begun. Wherever people looked it seemed that the world held more—more wealth, more property, more productivity, more knowledge to be used in the service of humanity. The obvious contrast with the unchanging order of the Middle Ages was proof to all persons of reason that the new age was superior to all that had come before.

Many individuals contributed to shaping the new world view. But none were more important to the formulation of the tenets of liberalism than the triumvirate of Francis Bacon, the prophet of the science of nature; John Locke, the prophet of the science of human nature; and Adam Smith, the prophet of the science of economics. Their views have been substantially modified in the intervening years, and a good deal of the particulars of what they argued are unacceptable to contemporary liberals (as, for instance, much of Karl Marx's philosophy would be to the Soviet Politburo today). Still, their basic argument, and especially their secular, humanist, materialist world view, remains the dominant ethos of our own times.

SCIENCE

In July 1978, the world was shocked to hear of the birth of the first human baby conceived in a test tube. While a handful of theologians and ethicists expressed a degree of misgiving about the development of a technology that appears uncomfortably close to Huxley's *Brave New World,* the vast majority of Americans, and virtually everyone in the scientific community, heralded the artificial birth as a triumph of modern science. As a researcher at Wayne State University in Michigan told a newspaper reporter, "I think that one cannot stop the progress of research. Nature is there for us to unravel."[16] This kind of attitude, so pervasive in our modern scientific establishment, finds its roots in the writings of Francis Bacon (1561–1626) over 350 years ago.

Science did not begin in the sixteenth century, of course. The Egyptians, Babylonians and others in the ancient world turned their eyes toward the sky to plot the stars. Early Greek science produced a number of fascinating inventions, including a working model of a steam engine. But until the modern era, science was simply one of a number of ways of contemplating the world. Traditional science sought knowledge for understanding. No one felt compelled to do something with it. Science was a kind of metaphysics, an attempt to answer the big questions of human existence by ascertaining the nature of good and evil, right and wrong and how to lead the moral life.

With Bacon, all of this changed. Living as he did during the period of transition from medieval life to modernity, Bacon, like all Enlightenment thinkers, was disgusted by what he considered the superstition and wrong thinking of the past. The ancient Greeks, Bacon wrote derisively, "assuredly have that which is characteristic of boys; they are prompt to prattel but cannot generate; for their wisdom abounds in words but is barren of works."[17]

Bacon had no use for the traditional science which contented itself with simply stating hypotheses. The hypothesis must be proved, or it is simply "contentious learning."[18] For Bacon, and all scientists of the modern era since, the purpose of science became "the enlarging of the bounds of human empire, to the effecting of all things possible."[19] Knowledge for mere understanding is useless, he asserts. There is only one proper goal for science: power. Time and again, Bacon hammers away at his theme of developing a system of knowledge that will give people unlimited power over their environment. "The command over all things natural," he writes, "—over bodies, medicine, mechanical powers and infinite others of this kind—is the one proper and ultimate end of true natural philosophy."[20] Used properly, science could establish "a line and race of inventions that may in some degree subdue and overcome the necessities and miseries of humanity."[21] Thus science is valuable to the extent that it produces economic increases.

To Francis Bacon, the first and last word of human experience stated simply is: to be human, we must be in control. Action, not contemplation, is the goal; any action that leads to greater control over nature is beneficial. How can we establish control in order to "effect all things possible"? By developing a "Novum Organum," a new tool, a new philosophical approach to the world of nature that will discard religious faith, spiritual revelation and emotion, because they can tell us nothing about the workings of the world. We must seek only knowledge which is both useful and certain.

The universe has a rational order, Bacon maintained, that can be easily and completely understood, if we merely adopt the proper methodology. In order that we may understand, we must distance ourselves from nature, place ourselves outside of it so that we can more easily manipulate it. We must, in other words, be *alienated* from the rest of the world so that we can deduce the order of nature. The mind itself must be "from the very outset not left to take its own course, but be guided at every step, and the business be done as if by machinery." [22] Admittedly, this process can be "laborious to search, ignoble to meditate, harsh to deliver, illiberal to practice, infinite in number, and minute in subtlety." [23] But the results of such an investigation are certain to yield greater power.

Though the process has subsequently been modified, Bacon is describing the roots of the scientific method. Along with other thinkers of this period, especially René Descartes (1596–1650), Bacon foresaw the possibility of unraveling nature by ignoring its complicated and seemingly mysterious whole and reducing each aspect of the natural order to a mathematical equation. Mathematics teaches us that the whole can never be greater than the sum of its parts. Thus, scientific reductionism holds that the totality of reality can be ascertained simply by measuring and quantifying all of its various components. Descartes developed this theme further until he had philosophically reduced all of nature to a machinelike entity which could be engineered and improved upon by rationalism—logical, objective, and disinterested thinking. Thinking rationally, Descartes claimed, "we can thus render ourselves the masters and possessors of nature." [24]

What Bacon and Descartes theorized, Isaac Newton proved. By developing a mathematical method that described mechanical motion, and showing how that method could be applied to all natural phenomena, Newton gave the human race the ultimate power to work its will on the world. Science, in turn, became value-neutral, because its purpose was simply to discover the true relationship of things and use that knowledge rationally to bring about ever greater prosperity for humankind. With this quantitative approach to the world, questions of ultimate truth or ends become meaningless because they cannot be scientifically determined. Equally important, knowledge arrived at through means other than rational methods is rejected as irresponsible and subjective. Taken together, Bacon's theories of the purpose of knowledge and Newton's mathematical discoveries ushered in the new age of science.

With the coming of the scientific age, nature, once seen as divine, magnificent and mysterious, was transformed into so much quantitative physical phenomena moving through the universe, all subject to certain physical laws. Desacralized and reduced to mathematics, the world became nothing more than material for manipulation. There was no longer any ultimate purpose or metaphysical significance to nature, any more than there is a purpose to mathematics. Nature simply exists, and has value only to the extent that people use it. In the end, nature becomes simply a factor in the economic process to be used as efficiently as possible. There are no bounds to our ability to exploit the bits of matter in motion that comprise what we call nature for the simple reason that there are no bounds to the discoveries that can be made by the rational human mind using the scientific method. Our power over nature, contend liberal scientists from Bacon to the Nobel Laureates of our own period, knows no limit. If this view robs nature of all intrinsic beauty or meaning, it has at least provided the motivation that launched three centuries of rigorous economic development that continues to our own day.

Or, as that scientist at Wayne State University said when asked about the manufacture of human beings in laboratory test tubes, "... one cannot stop the progress of research. Nature is there for us to unravel."

GOVERNMENT AND SOCIETY

There was perhaps never a mind wiser and more methodical, or a logician more exact than Locke; and yet he was not a great mathematician. He could never submit to the fatigue of calculation nor to the dryness of mathematical truths, which at first present no sensations to the mind; and no one has proved better than he that one can save the geometrical spirit without the aid of geometry.[25]

—Voltaire

Francis Bacon and Isaac Newton developed a scientific method that reduced nature to a machine whose workings could be rationally understood through mathematics. John Locke (1623–1704) did the same thing for government and social relations. For Bacon, the purpose of science was to learn how to control nature. For Locke, the purpose of government was to allow people the freedom to use their newfound power over nature to produce wealth.[26] Thus, from Locke's time to our

own, the social role of the state has been to promote the subjugation of nature so that people might acquire the material
prosperity necessary for fulfillment. "The negation of nature,"
Locke declared, "is the way toward happiness." People must
become "effectively emancipated from the bonds of nature."[27]

A spokesperson for the emerging middle class, Locke sought
to justify the economic claims of his constituents against the
remnants of feudal authority. To do that, Locke needed a powerful weapon to challenge the status quo. He found that weapon
in reason. Using reason, Locke turned his efforts to fashion a
"new way of ideas." By the time he finished his inquiry, he
had formulated virtually all of the major social beliefs of liberalism that continue to our own day. He was truly the founding
father of liberal values.

Like most intellectuals of his period, Locke was deeply
impressed with how scientific rationalism had made sense out
of a formerly incomprehensible natural world. But why, he
asked himself, were the affairs of human beings so chaotic?
The answer, he concluded, was that the natural laws of society
were being violated because the social order was built upon
irrational traditions and customs that originated from the theocentrism that had ruled the world for so long. With the aid of
reason, Locke set out to determine the "natural" basis of society. He immediately concluded that religion could not form
the social foundation simply because, by definition, God is
unknowable. How can the unknowable be the proper basis for
government? And so, in a monumental break with his philosophical predecessors, Locke argued that while religion could
rightly be a private concern of each person it could not serve
as the basis of public activity.

Having removed God from the affairs of people as Bacon
had removed Him from nature, Locke was left with human
beings, alone in the universe. No longer was the human being
to be considered as part of a divinely directed organism. Now,
men and women became just what Bacon and Newton had
made of nature, mere physical phenomena interacting with
other bits of matter in the cold, mechanical universe. This being
the case, on what basis could a social order be formed? Here
Locke provided an argument that was dear to his class. Once
we cut through useless custom and superstition, argued Locke,
we see that society, being made up solely of individuals creating
their own meaning, has one purpose and one purpose only—
to protect and allow for the increase of the property of its

members. Pure self-interest thus becomes, in Locke's mind, the sole basis for the establishment of the state. Society properly becomes secular, humanist, materialist and individualist because, Locke maintains, reason leads us to conclude that this is the natural order of things. By the laws of nature, each individual is called upon to act out his role of social atom, careening through life, attempting to amass personal wealth. There is no value judgment to be made here; self-interest is simply the only basis for society.

But won't this constant and unmoderated scramble for personal affluence result in a savage war, each person against the other, with some members of society being victimized in the process? Not at all, says Locke, for human beings are not naturally evil or fallen, but inherently good. It is only scarcity and lack of property that make them evil. As people are naturally acquisitive, it is therefore only necessary to continue to increase the wealth of society and social harmony will continue to improve. Had Locke written just 100 years before, he might well have concluded, as Hobbes had, that the only way to keep self-interested people in line was by vesting absolute authority in one person in society. But Locke could argue that government rested on the consent of the governed because by the time he wrote, science was already promising unlimited abundance from nature, and the exploitation of America's incredible riches was in full swing. With the discovery of America, the land available for cultivation, alone, immediately increased some 500 percent. High quality timber, gold, silver and new crops like tobacco and corn were all available in quantities previously unimaginable. Locke had good reason for believing that scarcity was on the verge of being banished forever from human experience. People need not fight among themselves because nature has "still enough and as good left; and more than the unprovided could use."[28] People can have liberty of action because their self-interest would not conflict with others. Locke, then, became the philosopher of unlimited expansion and material abundance.

Still, are there no limits at all to the amount of wealth individuals can amass? After all, philosophers from Aristotle to Aquinas had argued that beyond a certain point, property became a barrier to happiness. Not so, argues Locke. In a state of nature, he admits, it is true that primitives can only accumulate a limited amount of property from the bounty of nature. If a primitive attempts to take more property than his crude knowledge will allow him to consume, then it will spoil and possibly rob other members of the community of their own chance for accumulation. But in a commonwealth founded upon reason, where money is the medium of exchange, an unlimited amassing of property is permissible, indeed natural, for that is the purpose of money. Since money cannot possibly spoil, it is impossible to possess too much of it. Obviously, some individuals will amass more property than others, but this too is natural, for the world was given to "the use of the industrious and rational." He who applies reason the best will benefit the most.[29]

Locke does not stop here. The ownership of property (value extracted from nature) is not only a right in society; man also has a duty to generate wealth. In an environmentalist's nightmare, Locke writes, "land that is left wholly to nature . . . is called, as indeed it is, waste."[30] Nature is only of value when we mix our labor with it so that it will be productive:

> He who appropriates land to himself by his labour, does not lessen but increases the common stock of mankind. For the provisions serving to the support of human life, produced by one acre of inclosed and cultivated land, are . . . ten times more than those which are yielded by an acre of land, of an equal richness lying waste in common. And therefore he that incloses land and has a greater plenty of the conveniences of life from ten acres than he could have from a hundred left to nature, may truly be said to give ninety acres to mankind.[31]

Using this early version of the "trickle down theory" (the more one makes individually the more society benefits collectively), Locke goes on to declare that a person should "heap up as much of these durable things (gold, silver, and so on) as he pleases; the exceeding of the bounds of his just property not lying in the largeness of his possession, but the perishing of anything uselessly in it."[32] Reading Locke from our present-day concern with ecology, one has the unnerving feeling that he would not be satisfied until every river on earth were dammed, every natural wonder covered with billboards and every desert converted into parking lots. So rigidly productivist and materialist is Locke that he condemns American Indians as a handful of people living in one of the richest lands in the world, idly refusing to exploit their riches: "A king of a large and fruitful territory there feeds, lodges and is clad worse than a day-laborer in England."[33]

With Locke, the fate of modern man and woman is sealed. From the time of the Enlightenment on, the individual is reduced to the hedonistic activity of production and consumption to find meaning and purpose. People's needs and aspirations, their dreams and desires, all become confined to the pursuit of material self-interest. Though liberalism shattered the closed society of the Middle Ages, it substituted an open social order that can only be defined in materialist and acquisitive terms. The success of the liberal ethos in the past three centuries has been directly correlated with the ability of science and technology to extract from labor and natural resources ever greater material productivity. It is productivity itself that liberalism holds out to people as their ultimate meaning.

LIBERAL ECONOMICS

In 1776, Thomas Jefferson combined Locke's principles of liberalism with a strong dose of Reformation theology and fashioned the Declaration of Independence. That same year, across the Atlantic in Great Britain, Adam Smith built upon Locke's broad outline an economic philosophy for liberal society. In giving full development to the virtues of rational self-interest, Smith ushered in the age of capitalism.

The very title of Smith's manifesto, *The Wealth of Nations*, is evidence of his primary concern. His basic goal was to design an economic theory that would most efficiently promote economic expansion, the desirability of which he had not the slightest doubt.

Smith championed the cause of a growing class of manufacturers who saw their interests stifled by government monopolies and the closed ranks of the mercantilists. Just as Locke had promoted the social interests of the bourgeoisie merchants and traders, Smith appealed to "natural laws" based on Newtonian-Baconian science to legitimatize the economic interests of the new industrial entrepreneurs.

In *The Wealth of Nations*, Smith argues that just as heavenly bodies in motion conform to laws of nature, so too does economics. If these laws are observed, economic growth will result. But government regulation and control of the economy

violated these immutable laws by directing economic activity
in unnatural ways. Thus markets did not expand as rapidly as
they could and production was stifled. In other words, any
attempt by society to guide "natural" economic forces was
inefficient, and for Adam Smith, efficiency in all things was
the watchword.

An inquiry into the laws of economics, Smith declared, will
lead us to the inevitable conclusion that the most efficient
method of economic organization is "laissez-faire," the notion
of leaving things alone and allowing people to act unhindered.
Smith, like Locke, believed the basis of all human activity is
material self-interest. Since this is natural, we should not condemn selfishness by erecting social barriers to its pursuit. Rather,
we should recognize people's desire to satisfy themselves for
what it is—a virtuous activity that, in fact, benefits everyone.
It is by each individual operating egoistically that scarcity may
be overcome by surplus:

> Every individual is continually exerting himself to find
> out the most advantageous employment for whatever cap-
> ital he can command. It is his own advantage, indeed,
> and not that of society which he has in view. But the
> study of his own advantage naturally, or rather neces-
> sarily, leads him to prefer that employment which is most
> advantageous to the society.[34]

Smith explicitly removes any notions of morality from economics, just as Locke had done with social relations. Any
attempt to impose morality on economy simply leads to a violation of "the invisible hand," which Smith asserted was a
natural law that governs the economic process, automatically
allocating capital investment, jobs, resources and the production of goods. People could use reason to understand this law,
Smith allowed, but just as human beings cannot control gravity,
they cannot improve on the "invisible hand." Since nothing
can be more efficient than this "natural" force controlling the
rational market, wealth can best be produced only through free,
unfettered trade and competition among rational, acquisitive
individuals. Since the purpose of economics is a continually
expanding market, anything which promotes growth is to be
welcomed.

Believing that men and women are basically egoists in pursuit of economic gain, Smith's theories subordinate all of hu-

man desires to the quest for material abundance to satisfy physiological needs. There are no ethical choices to be made, only utilitarian judgments exercised by each individual pursuing material self-interest.

By its very definition, then, capitalism makes crucial assumptions about the world. First, capitalist theory from Smith to the current President's Council of Economic Advisers assumes that nature is generous beyond limit. Because people naturally engage in a lifelong free-for-all as they pursue their economic self-interest, nature must constantly yield the necessary amounts of new wealth in order that the acquisition process may continue.

Second, capitalism assumes that each individual's rational pursuit of his self-interest leads to undeniable social good. With capitalism, the big questions about human purpose need not be asked. The question, "What is the social good?" can only be answered with the reductionist reply, "The social good is whatever results from each person's quest to fulfill his own materialist desires." There can be, by definition, no larger purpose than that dictated by each individual's ego. Nor is there any basis from which to determine which desires should be satisfied and which not. All desires are reasonable, and capitalism will seek to meet them through the cornucopia resulting from economic growth.

Third, because capitalism is a theory to maximize material self-interest and accumulation, the economics of Adam Smith are concerned only with those individuals alive at this moment, not the generations that lie in the future. If a person's entire life is rooted in the pursuit of self-interest, he cannot take care of others at the same time. Nor should he, argues Smith. Thus capitalism explicitly disregards the future in favor of today. Just as today's social interest is realized when each person looks after only himself, the interests of tomorrow's generations will likewise be guaranteed in the same manner. As long as the current generation succeeds in creating economic expansion, succeeding generations will benefit.

Finally, because capitalism argues that the sole purpose of economics is to expand constantly, anything negative that results from that relentless growth is regarded as a mere "externality." In other words, if as a result of industrial production the environment becomes polluted, this is simply regarded as a side effect of the economic process. It does not call into question the process itself, because capitalism's only purpose is to foster the most efficient economic growth possible. Here, efficiency is defined as that which maximizes short-term growth and profit.

CONTEMPORARY LIBERALISM

The great, pioneering thinkers of the Enlightenment all shared a common belief that they had discovered irrefutable principles which would serve as the basis for the complete transformation of society. Reason led the fathers of liberalism to conclude that since all people are born equal, it is the social environment that essentially determines their actions. Alter the environment and governing institutions to conform with "natural law," and people would begin to develop their own natural perfection. Some of the most optimistic philosophers of the eighteenth century speculated that if the natural order of things were observed in all human matters, a fully emancipated society, filled with fully realized human beings, would result within a generation. During the French Revolution many thought that the end point of history had been reached. One philosopher even predicted that it would be possible to raise an entire generation of Newtons in France.

Since the Enlightenment, of course, liberal philosophy has gone through many permutations. Though early Enlightenment thinkers argued that they had discovered certain immutable principles, succeeding generations of liberals always strove to update the liberal doctrine so that it would fit developing social trends.

During the last several centuries there has been a constant attempt by liberal thinkers to find the ethical base for liberalism. Since God's word was no longer the test by which every act, even thought, was to be measured, what would be the ethical tests for modern man and woman? Bacon, Locke and Smith sought that base in the abstract concepts of reason and natural law. By the nineteenth century, these concepts had been further refined. Jeremy Bentham, a leading liberal thinker whose influence continues in most present-day liberal social programs, agreed with Locke that the true basis for all human conduct should be rooted in utilitarianism. According to Bentham, people act from two motives: to secure pleasure and to avoid pain. In other words, all human beings seek happiness. Therefore, argued Bentham, the role of those in power is to secure the greatest happiness for the greatest number. "Any action may be said to be conformable to the principle of utility when the tendency it has to augment the happiness of the community is greater than any which it has to diminish it."[35] Bentham went so far as to "scientifically" develop an exact mathematical equation that could chart the relative degrees of pain and pleasure involved in various matters, the better to allow legislators to enact those measures most conducive to spreading happiness. For Bentham, utility was everything—if cockfighting produces more observable happiness in the participants, then it is preferable to listening to Mozart, and government programs should reflect that fact. Just a generation after Bentham, another leading liberal thinker, John Stuart Mill, modified utilitarianism somewhat to include not only the quantity of happiness but also the relative quality. The ideas of men like Bentham and Mill are the basis of contemporary social policy.

Bentham's was just one attempt to find an ethical foundation upon which liberal principles and programs could be built. Other attempts have focused on evolution, pragmatism, logical positivism, situational ethics, and so on. Every one of these attempts, no matter how much they seem to have strayed from the original thoughts formulated in the revolutionary epoch of the Enlightenment, has returned over and over again to the one essential component of all shades of liberal philosophy—*material growth*. Throughout its three centuries of development, it is this component that has been unswervingly subscribed to by all thinkers who share the liberal humanist "conception that involves contempt for man's inner life to the advantage of his sociological life, contempt for his moral and intellectual life to the advantage of his material life."

Modern liberals have tended to distance themselves somewhat from the pure self-interest and hedonism advocated as being "natural" to the human condition by Enlightenment thinkers. Adam Smith confidently predicted, at the birth of the industrial revolution and modern capitalism, that unfettered individual competition and self-interest would naturally lead to the benefit of all in society. Today's liberal surveys the track record of capitalism since Smith's day and realizes that "free enterprise" can lead to monopoly, concentrated economic and political power, huge discrepancies of wealth and inhuman working conditions. The liberal is therefore more than willing to step into the economic arena as a referee. He advocates such things as trust-busting, corporate taxes, environmental pollution standards, pension funds and OSHA regulations. Similarly, the liberal places less emphasis on property rights and relatively more on human rights. Still, the liberal does not condemn private property; he simply wants to see more people own some. So while the liberal is willing to compromise the "invisible hand," he is unwilling to move beyond the original conception of capitalism, that private ownership of capital, operating within the market economy, fulfilling the desires of people on the basis of supply and demand, is the best system possible. If there are problems in the system, the liberal says, let us correct those abuses; there is no need to replace the entire system with an alternative. The liberal believes that all of the correct principles for society have been articulated; we have only to fulfill their promise through the proper adjustments.

In other arenas of social life, the modern liberal has made similar modifications of liberal doctrine, always maintaining the underlying principles while attempting to moderate the inherent harshness of the game. In essence, what the modern liberal is attempting to do is to take principles which were first enunciated over 300 years ago as the doctrine of a single class, the bourgeoisie, and extend them to all members of society. This results partly from the humanitarian inclinations of the liberal and partly from the realization that to maintain the social stability of the system, it is imperative that *all* members of society be brought into the promised heaven on earth. The fear being that if they are not, social upheaval and revolution could result. Thus, liberalism no longer emphasizes the rugged struggle among individuals, but substitutes for it the concept of "pluralism," wherein large constituencies battle among themselves to fulfill their own political and economic agenda. Blacks, women, corporations, senior citizens, and so forth compete as *special interests* for larger pieces of the expanding economic pie. The modern liberal rejects outright individual hedonism in favor of the material betterment of the group or constituency; the idea being that human beings are social animals capable of cooperation.

From these examples it should be clear that while today's American liberalism—the liberalism of welfare programs, government regulations, civil rights legislation—might send John Locke and Adam Smith back to their desks to hammer out new theory, the ideology of the Kennedys, the McGoverns and the Udalls retains the fundamental assumptions of classic liberal philosophy, namely, that it is material progress that defines what a person is and what he can become. The modern liberal, of course, will object to "gross materialism" for the obvious negative effects it has on the environment and social relations. But here we are not speaking of conspicuous consumption, which is how the liberal seems to comprehend the concept of "materialism." The massive overconsumption of the middle and upper classes is merely a symptom of a deeper disease. That disease is materialism in its truest sense: it is the set of ideas that holds that the human being is inherently perfectible, and that this perfectibility rests solely on the ability to generate and consume ever greater material wealth; that the function of science, capitalism and the state is to provide every person with the knowledge, tools and freedom necessary to fulfill all basic material drives; that political and social rights are extended to ever greater numbers of people to allow them the opportunity to take part in the drive for material betterment; that the greater the number of people involved in the process of generating new wealth, and the greater the collective yield of their individual efforts, the greater the likelihood of overcoming war, hostilities and avarice and creating a harmonious social order. Thus, the liberal believes that it is possible to start with individual material self-interest and still end up with collective peace and happiness. After three centuries, liberalism continues to argue that there is no higher value in the universe than the individual and his desires—not all desires, but those that fulfill his material and physiological wants. The modern liberal may not be as conscious a materialist as were the fiercely secular thinkers of the Enlightenment, but a materialist he is.

It is this very unconsciousness about his underlying beliefs that prevents the liberal thinker from seeing the possibility for qualitative social change. For today's liberal, just as for the men and women of the Enlightenment, all phenomena in the universe are merely quantitative. With liberalism as our guiding ethos, things change quantitatively but nothing is ever truly transformed. With all life reduced to an update of Bentham's utilitarianism, the grand and sweeping vision of human liberation enunciated during the Enlightenment becomes, in reality, a one-dimensional portrait of a humanity that has freed itself from "priests and superstition" only to become the slaves of mere things.

Liberalism then has historically offered two sets of values to humanity as a kind of package deal. To all human beings, liberalism has upheld the hope that each person could become, in a sense, a god on earth, flowering into his full potential. But in order to reach that point, it is necessary to first produce the palace of abundance. In the process, the materialist values tend to dominate human existence because they lie closer to liberalism's philosophical center than do humanist beliefs. Liberalism's heart lies with humanism, but its head is governed by materialism. In the final analysis, the head governs the heart. The necessities of economic growth must take precedence over the value of the individual, for liberalism cannot imagine a free individual without material accumulation, any more than medieval thinkers could envision human existence without the transcendent power of the Almighty.

Breaking from the closed system of the Middle Ages, the faith in the boundless possibilities of the future must have seemed a heady thought. But in a world without material boundaries, there is never any logical place to halt one's economic activity. There is always more to be done before the secular paradise can be realized. Thus, in the name of human fulfillment humankind is encouraged to take part in a race that can never be ended. There is always one more lap before the finish line. Even so, until recently it appeared that there was no limit, at least, to the speed and endurance that could be attained along the way.

AMERICA: THE CENTURY OF GROWTH

The twin forces of the Protestant Reformation and liberalism found their promised land in America. As already noted, Enlightenment thinkers such as Locke and Smith saw in the New World the real possibility of banishing scarcity from the earth.

America was a storehouse of natural treasure, a vast continent of wilderness frontier, with available resources of every description, open spaces that could be claimed by any settler, fertile land and a relatively mild climate.

Then, too, there was no entrenched class or social force in America that could resist economic expansion and rapid social change. The original inhabitants of the land, the Indians, proved little match against the might of the European settlers.

Yet, even with these advantages, economic growth began slowly. America's industrial revolution did not really reach its

stride until after the Civil War, at least a half-century behind
Great Britain. This was in part due to the very availability of
land; in America each person could own his own farm. Also,
in the early years there was a great deal of doubt about the
usefulness of manufacturing. Farming was considered a more
noble and socially useful occupation. The most articulate
spokesman for this view was Thomas Jefferson:

> Those who labor on the earth are the chosen people of
> God, if ever He had a chosen people.... Generally
> speaking, the proportion which the aggregate of other
> classes of citizens bears in any state to that of its hus-
> bandmen, is the proportion of its unsound to its healthy
> parts, and is a good enough barometer to measure its
> corruption.[36]

Whatever the cause, the industrial revolution was slow in
coming to our shores. In 1815, while cities and factories were
swelling in Great Britain, just 1 percent of the American population was involved in manufacturing, and fewer than 10 percent lived in cities of 2500 people or more.[37] But by the time
of the Civil War, all that had changed dramatically. Population
increases had swelled the work force from 1.9 million at the
turn of the century to eleven million in 1860. As labor shifted
from agriculture to manufacturing, new machinery and production methods, such as the development of interchangeable
parts, boosted worker productivity by over 50 percent above
that of the laborer of 1800. By the end of the Civil War,
America had entered a new era of productivity and economic
expansion.

The entire country became consumed with the notion of
economic growth. Massive expositions, such as the Centennial
of 1876 in Philadelphia, paid homage to machines of every
sort. Mythical production workers such as Paul Bunyan and
Joe Magarac became popular folk heroes. Robber barons and
industrialists became household names.

This burst of economic activity lasted until 1929. During
this period America was transformed from a land of small towns
to a nation of factories and huge urban centers. A few figures
testify to the vast changes that took place. In 1865, for instance,
just 16,000 tons of steel were produced; by 1929, 56 million
tons. The use of energy in the manufacturing processes grew

exponentially as well; the 16 million horsepower used nationally in 1865 balloned to 116 billion by 1930.

Individual consumption of electricity also increased dramatically. In 1882, the first power plant was built in New York. In 1907, just 8 percent of all nonfarm homes in the state had electricity, but by 1929, 85 percent of all nonfarm homes had electricity. From virtually nothing the use of electricity grew to 9 billion kilowatt hours by 1929.

As Robert Heilbroner observed, "By the time we had turned the corner into the twentieth century, robber barons had already invested huge amounts of capital in new machine technology and erected giant corporate empires. In 1870, the average iron and steel firm employed fewer than 100 men; in 1900, over 400. During the same period, average output per firm jumped from under 4,000 tons per year to nearly 45,000 tons, and the capital invested in an average company rose from $150,000 to almost $1 million." In 1929, the average worker was producing about four times as much as his grandfather living at the end of the Civil War. Per capita income advanced fourfold as well. That same year the Gross National Product, the market value of all the final goods and services produced by the economy in a year, had reached 100 billion dollars, ten times the GNP of 1865.

The stock-market crash of 1929 and the ensuing Depression brought this dizzying rise to affluence to an abrupt end. Production fell by nearly 50 percent from 1929 to 1933, and unemployment increased eightfold.

Until the crash, government had played a small role in the economic system. Unfettered free enterprise was still the rule of the day. But the Depression of the 1930s brought F.D.R. to power, and with him, government commitment to increased economic growth, a commitment that continues to this day. Supported by the economic theories of Lord Keynes, the federal government made sustained economic growth its most important goal.

With the new corporate–government partnership sealed, the post–World War II years became an era of almost unbelievable production and consumption. Between 1929 and 1971, the GNP per capita increased by a staggering 194 percent. The average American household in 1970 received an annual income about three-quarters greater than it did in 1950.

This enormous growth was spurred on by several converging factors. Chief among these was the ridiculously low cost of natural resources during this period. From the end of World War II to the 1970s, the cost of oil, gas, coal and most other raw materials remained virtually unchanged, which means in real terms that they actually *declined* in price. The availability of inexpensive petroleum, for instance, initiated a host of post–World War II industries, such as plastics, the petrochemical industry and the manufacture of synthetic materials for clothing.

The spectacular postwar economic expansion can also be attributed to the fact that American industry escaped the war damage free, while most of the other industrial giants suffered massive destruction of plant, equipment and economic infrastructure. The war had another effect as well. Between 1941 and 1945 it spurred a host of technological innovations, the most important of which involved the auto industry. Following the war, the automotive industry exploded across America. This, in turn, spawned a myriad of related developments: highway construction, surburban home building and the development of shopping centers. Other industries experiencing similar growth immediately following the war included the airlines, television, pharmaceuticals, photocopying and computers. Growth rates of 15 to 30 percent a year in these key industries were not uncommon in the late 1940s and early 1950s.

Along with this astounding postwar productivity, the population boom brought millions of new producers and consumers into the marketplace and helped usher in the growth of giant multinational corporations and the opening up of new markets abroad.

The economic explosion of the 1950s and 1960s created a kind of "growthmania" in America. As one Presidential economics adviser put it, "if it is agreed that economic output is a good thing, it follows by definition that there is not enough of it." Says William Ophuls:

> Growth is the secular religion of American society, providing a social goal, a basis for political solidarity, and a source of individual motivation; the pursuit of happiness has come to be defined almost exclusively in material terms, and the entire society—individuals, enterprises, the government itself—has an enormous vested interest in the continuation of growth.[38]

By successfully focusing all of its attention on economic expansion, liberalism has not had to confront the thorny political problem of redistribution of wealth and power. As one prominent economist candidly remarked: "Growth is a substitute for equality of income. So long as there is growth there is hope, and that makes large income differentials tolerable." In other words, as long as the economic pie continues to grow, and each person's slice continues to increase, the demands for redistribution of wealth will be effectively muted. This is critical for liberalism because the hard fact of the matter is that in spite of tremendous economic expansion over the past thirty years, there has been no significant domestic trend toward equalization of income. Today 1.6 percent of the population in America holds over 30 percent of the wealth, while twenty-five million people remain at the poverty level.

Yet, income redistribution is never discussed because all of our hopes are pinned on economic growth. Indeed, since 1945, the solution to virtually every social problem we have is growth and more growth. As Herman Daly has put it: "The way to have your cake and eat it too is to make it grow."

This growth principle of liberalism is used to justify America's international position as well. According to a World Bank study conducted a few years ago, nearly 800 million people subsist on a daily equivalent of eighty cents in what the Bank calls "absolute poverty." (Interestingly, this is roughly the same number of people who existed in the world 200 years ago when the age of economic expansion began). The 1974 world average GNP per capita was only $26.60 a week. The scope of world misery is beyond comprehension. Yet, the liberal solution to the problem of worldwide poverty is for the rich to consume more, not less. Says Dr. Paul McCracken, former chairman of the Council of Economic Advisers, "The action most urgently needed in the world economy is for the strong economies to be willing to accept higher levels of living." Or, as researcher Herman Kahn has noted, "If you wish to make the poor rich rapidly, the most rapid way to make them rich is to increase the gaps. The most efficient method we have ever found of making poor people rich rapidly is having a lot of very rich people around." Through economic growth, he claims, "the richer the rich get the richer the poor get."

As long as the economic-growth statistics have continued their steady climb, the liberal ethos and capitalism have been relatively secure. Were the system to suddenly slow down or stop growing altogether, the ideology we have lived under for so many years would be in real trouble. That is just what is happening today.

At the birth of the contemporary industrial age, one of the leading liberals of the Enlightenment, the French aristocrat, the Marquis de Condorcet wrote:

> No bounds have been fixed to the improvement of the human faculties;...the perfectibility of man is absolutely indefinite;...the progress of this perfectibility, henceforth above the control of every power that would impede it, has no other limit than the duration of the globe upon which nature has placed us...[39]

When Condorcet wrote these words, he could not imagine the possibility that one day the globe would no longer be able to support humanity's quest for material progress. Yet, less than two centuries later, we have reached the point that Condorcet and all other liberals throughout history have thought so implausible. The slowing of our mighty industrial machine already reflects the fact that we have strained the biosphere, upon which all life and wealth rests, to its limit.

3

LIMITS TO GROWTH

NONRENEWABLE RESOURCES

In 1973 the Arab Oil Producing and Exporting Countries announced a dramatic price hike, quadrupling the cost of crude oil for an energy-dependent industrialized world. The historic significance of that decision is still not firmly grasped by most Americans.

America, like most highly industrialized economies, is almost totally dependent on oil. Our entire economic system has been built on an oil energy base. In fact, the cheap and seemingly abundant supply of domestic and imported oil over the past 100 years has been largely responsible for our increased prosperity. Of the three major ingredients in the production mix—natural energy resources, human labor and machine capital—oil energy resources have been considered the least costly and therefore most relied upon to increase real wealth.

Our reliance on energy resources to maintain an unparalleled standard of living is reflected in consumption statistics. With only 6 percent of the world's population, the United States consumes approximately one-third of the world's energy.[1] When brought down to the level of the individual consumer, the figures on energy use are even more awesome. As ecologist Lester Brown points out in his book, *The Twenty-Ninth Day*, for most of the time man has been on earth, his individual energy intake was largely limited to the "two or three thousand calories that each person consumed daily as food." Today, says

Brown, per capita consumption of energy per year in the United States equals the equivalent of twelve tons of coal.[2]

The quadrupling of oil prices by the Arabs in the early 1970s forced the realization that the supply of oil was becoming increasingly scarce. The overnight price jump, however, did not appreciably change America's energy habit—or for that matter, the habits of any of the rest of the industrialized countries. While there have been attempts to lessen our dependence on oil energy sources, it could hardly be expected that the United States economy would radically reorient its entire energy-based economic system overnight to accommodate the new realities posed by the depletion of the world's oil resources.

The United States economic machine continues to use gargantuan amounts of petroleum, half-refusing to acknowledge that the end of the petroleum age has arrived. Yet, whatever the standard or expert opinion to which one turns, there is no doubt that the oil spigot is about to run dry.

According to a study, directed by M.I.T. professor Caroll Wilson involving experts from fifteen countries, "the supply of oil will fail to meet increasing demand before the year 2000, most probably between 1985 and 1995, even if energy prices rise 50 percent above current levels."[3] A similar study made by the influential Trilateral Commission—an international organization made up of the most powerful business and political leaders of the Western nations—is only slightly more optimistic. It concludes that oil demand will begin to surpass supplies by the early 1990s.[4]

Writing in the *Bulletin of the Atomic Scientists*, economics expert Emile Benoit calculates that at present consumption rates, existing oil reserves will be exhausted by the year 2000. Even assuming the discovery of new oil reserves totaling four times the present available stock (which is an unrealistically inflated estimate), the net reprieve of such a discovery would extend our oil reserve only an additional twenty-five years or so before the end of the oil line was reached.[5]

It's hard for most of us to imagine that the usable oil on this planet will be gone in the next twenty years or so. After all, it took nearly three billion years of natural evolution to create this tremendous stock of energy. Nonetheless, there are only enough ultimately recoverable oil reserves left to provide each person with 500 barrels. This means, says Lester Brown, that the average American, driving a full-size automobile and averaging 10,000 miles per year on the road, would use over forty barrels per year, or his entire share of the remaining oil, in just twelve years.[6]

Even though the existing supply of oil reserves—both domestic and worldwide—continues to shrink, energy demands in the United States are expected to double in just twenty years, if our energy use continues to grow at a conservative rate of 3.5 percent per year. At the same time, world energy use is expected to quadruple by the year 2000.[7]

With worldwide petroleum reserves running out, the energy companies, politicians and others have been beating the drums for a transition to alternative energy sources. Implicit in their public utterances is the assumption that there still exists an unlimited quantity of other energy resources and that all that is needed to continue our present economic growth rate is the wherewithal to cross over to these alternatives as soon as possible. They acknowledge that such a crossover will require some sacrifice in terms of capital expenditure, and greater technological ingenuity to effectively extract these energy supplies. However, they never, for a moment, doubt their long-held belief that "usable," productive energy exists in unlimited quantities. A close examination of each of the energy alternatives contradicts this central assumption.

Take, for example, coal. At current coal-consumption growth rates of 4.1 percent per year, it is generally recognized that there are enough coal reserves in the world to provide energy for 135 years. Of course, if, as expected, the United States and other countries begin to turn increasingly to coal to replace the fast depleting oil reserves, that absolute time span would be reduced to well under 100 years.[8] More important still, the external costs associated with extracting and harnessing coal energy make it impossible to entertain even the prospect of mining a fraction of the remaining reserves. First, it takes large amounts of water to mine and produce usable coal. That water is simply not available in the quantities that would be required. According to one highly regarded survey, "If all the coal mines, power stations and liquefaction or gasification plants now projected were to be built, they would require for their operations, exclusive of reclamation, between three and four times the *total* amount of water now used throughout the entire country."[9] With most of the United States already experiencing a critical long-range shortage of water supplies, there is no way to provide the astronomical water needs that would be required to mine the existing coal reserves.

Second, the environmental dangers associated with burning massive amounts of coal make it prohibitive. According to a National Academy of Sciences study, "the primary limiting factor on energy production from fossil fuels over the next few centuries may turn out to be the climatic effects of the release of carbon dioxide."[10] Increased use of coal results in the emission of massive doses of carbon dioxide into the atmosphere. This carbon dioxide layering creates a warming or "greenhouse" effect by blocking the radiation of heat into space. The NAS report says that carbon dioxide levels in the atmosphere could well double in the next seventy-five years, "raising temperatures at the midlatitudes by 3 to 6 degrees centigrade and that near the poles by about 9 to 12 degrees centigrade."[11] The traumatic effect on plant and animal life on the planet would be devastating. The entire ecological balance of the earth would be completely jarred. Among other consequences, the polar ice caps would melt, raising ocean levels worldwide, and causing almost all major port cities around the globe to drown. Dramatic changes in world temperature would result in the wholesale extinction of much of our existing plant and animal life. The speed of the change alone—seventy-five years or less—would eliminate the possibility of evolutionary adaptation. (It would take millions of years for most plant and animal species to adjust genetically to such quantitative changes in the earth's temperature.)

The NAS is not alone in its concern. Many reports over the past several years have come to the same conclusion. Worldwatch Institute argues that if current emission rates of carbon dioxide continue for several more decades, the resulting worldwide temperature increase will produce climatic changes "perhaps on a scale approaching that with which the Ice Age came and went."[12]

Shale oil extraction shares similar problems with coal. It is true that several Western states—Colorado, Wyoming and Utah—contain large shale deposits. As with other sources of energy, however, the real value of the shale depends on the cost necessary to extract it. Like coal, shale extraction requires huge amounts of water in excess of what's available. The critical shortage of water is particularly pronounced in the Western states where the shale deposits exist. Added to this cost are the other costs of mining and processing. The fact is, the energy required (in terms of costs) to retrieve shale oil in a usable form is so high that the net return of energy is minimal. Even with the most advanced technological extraction processes now available, it is estimated that shale could meet only about 2 percent of the current energy-consumption needs of the United States.[13]

For several years, the hope for an energy alternative rested with nuclear power. That hope, also, is beginning to fade. Extraordinarily high production costs, combined with severe health and safety concerns, have greatly reduced the number of nuclear power plants being built. Projections for nuclear energy growth are now "less than one-third of what they once were in many countries." In the United States thirty-six new nuclear power plants were ordered in 1973. By 1974 the number had fallen to twenty-seven. In 1975 the orders dropped to four, in 1976 to two, and 1977 back up only to four.[14]

Deflating the "cheap energy" myth of nuclear power, a Congressional report made public in 1978 states:

> Contrary to widespread belief, nuclear power is no longer a cheap energy source. In fact, when the still unknown costs of radioactive waste and spent nuclear fuel management, decommissioning and perpetual care are finally included on the rate base, *nuclear power may prove to be much more expensive* than conventional energy alternatives such as coal.[15]

It is estimated, even at current rates, that worldwide expansion of nuclear power plants will within twenty years generate enough fissionable material in international transit to make 20,000 atomic bombs. With nuclear material crisscrossing the globe daily, the chances of hijackings for military and terrorist purposes are better than good. There is simply no way to adequately police that level of transportation. Even with extraordinary policing effort, the likelihood of an occasional accident causing the release of deadly radiation must be taken for granted.[16]

Then, too, there is the still unresolved problem of nuclear waste disposal. As hard as it may seem to believe, with all of the attention placed on nuclear research and development and billions of dollars spent to erect existing plants, the scientific community, the energy companies and the government have not yet figured out how to get rid of the waste. Harvey Brooks of Harvard University, who heads the National Academy of Sciences committee on the question of nuclear waste disposal, declared: "I would predict that should nuclear energy ultimately prove to be socially unacceptable, it will be primarily because of the public's perception of the waste disposal problem."[17]

To put the magnitude of the waste disposal problem in perspective, *Science* magazine estimates that disposal of just the volume of military wastes alone could cost as much as "what it costs to put a man on the moon."[18] That's just for openers. When you add future projected commercial waste disposal to the mix, the figures become mind-boggling.

Today, there are approximately 2500 metric tons of nuclear waste in storage—the cumulative by-products of sixty-four nuclear reactors. By 1985, when the Nuclear Regulatory Commission projects 136 reactors, the waste in storage will increase to 25,000 tons (an increase of ten times the present problem).[19] The prospects begin to look frightening when one stops to consider that even with today's relatively small amount of nuclear waste, there are reports of radiation leakage, and still a safe method to dispose of the material has not been found. Radiation leaks have been discovered at the United States government nuclear reservation in Richland, Washington. Over 500,000 gallons of liquid, radioactive waste has leaked from tanks stored at the facility. In June 1978, the state of Kentucky closed down its nuclear burial site at Maxey Flats in the wake of an EPA study showing that "radioactive particles were migrating offsite." Similar leakages have been reported at burial sites in Oak Ridge, Tennessee, Ocean City, Maryland, and near San Francisco, California.[20]

Even if United States nuclear power continues to level off, it will be necessary to find new burial sites as often as every two or three years after the turn of the century to accommodate all of the waste. This in turn will necessitate strict monitoring and around-the-clock armed guards on each site for thousands of years to insure against leakage into the biosphere.[21]

Of all the alternative energy sources being contemplated, solar energy appears to have the fewest drawbacks, although even it is far from adequate—that is, if adequate is defined as maintaining anywhere near the present energy levels and growth rates of advanced industrial societies.

Solar energy is diffuse, unevenly distributed and unavailable at night, and it varies with climate, the seasons and geography on the planet. For all these reasons solar power does not lend itself to massive centralized systems of collection and dispersal—the kind of energy grids that our highly industrialized economies call for.[22]

Because solar energy is relatively diffused, it requires a tremendous capital expenditure to collect, store and transform it to productive uses. Erecting massive solar panels in the sky will cost tens of billions of dollars and require a great deal of energy input. The net energy gained is, then, not likely to be as great as many of its enthusiasts contend.[23]

As with other forms of energy, there is also a heat problem to contend with. Ecologist William Ophuls points out that:

> In practice, the process of taking energy from one area for use in another would create local and regional heat imbalances; moreover, with major development of artificial solar heat collection the earth's albedo (reflectivity) would be changed, and the global heat balance would be substantially affected because solar radiation formerly immediately reflected back into space would be absorbed and added to the global heat inventory.[24]

Nonetheless, solar power will be relied on more and more, despite its drawbacks, simply because the alternative forms of energy are so unacceptable. Indirect power from the sun, in the form of wind and water, have already become increasingly important. Among the large-scale proposals under consideration are the construction of giant windmills located in the Plains states and the building of many new dams to generate hydroelectric power. A West German company is already studying the feasibility of building a new fleet of clipper ships for international transportation, and there is even talk of damming up the Grand Canyon to provide a new source of hydroelectric power. Still, even with the full utilization of all of these solar energy plans, the amount of energy generated could not approximate the energy levels currently consumed in the United States. For example, today hydroelectric power supplies about 5 percent of our energy needs. Even if every possible avenue were exploited to harness additional energy in this fashion, it would be impossible to generate more than 10 percent of our present energy demands—demands which, at current growth rates, will double in twenty years.[25]

Dr. Emile Benoit of Columbia University very accurately identifies the present energy dilemma. For the past several hundred years says Benoit, industrialized societies have been living off the capital stock of highly concentrated energy that took three billion years to accumulate. Now that this rich, stored energy is about to be depleted, it will be necessary to live more and more within the present inflow of diffused solar energy. In other words, the material advances of the past several hundred years result from the use of three billion years of energy capital accumulated in the form of oil, natural gas, coal, and so forth. There is no way, either to replace that accumulated energy capital, or to continue to expand materially at the rate we have during this past historical period.[26]

Energy resource depletion is only the beginning of the story. The planet is fast running out of almost every major non-renewable mineral necessary for the maintenance and growth of highly industrialized economies. Each year the United States economy alone uses nearly "40,000 pounds of new mineral supplies per person for our power plants, transportation, schools, machine tools, homes, bridges, medical uses and heavy equipment."[27]

America is chiefly responsible for gobbling up the remaining stock of the earth's precious minerals. According to the United States Department of the Interior, the United States economy produces or imports 27 percent of the world's bauxite production, 18 percent of the world's iron ore production and 28 percent of the world's nickel.[28] In order for the rest of the world to reach a par with the American standard of living, it would have to consume up to 200 times the present production of many of the earth's nonrenewable minerals (this assumes a doubling of world population between now and the year 2000). While catching up with the United States' standard of living is the goal of most developing nations, it is obviously a pipe dream.[29]

A United Nations study conducted by Nobel Laureate Wassily Leontief concludes that even at present rates of growth in the international use of nonrenewable minerals:

The world is expected to consume during the last thirty years of this century from three to four times as many minerals as have been consumed throughout the whole previous history of civilization.[30]

It's not hard to understand, then, why so many experts predict that within seventy-five years, or less at current consumption rates, the economic needs of the planet will have "exhausted presently known recoverable reserves of perhaps half the world's now useful metals."[31] Dr. Preston Cloud, a geologist at the United States Geological Survey, is one of those experts. Testifying before the Joint Economic Committee of the Congress in 1978, Cloud said that some of the minerals on the endangered resource list by early in the next century include copper, gold, antimony, bismuth and molybdenum.

Domestically, by A.D. 2050 the United States will have run out of extractable quantities of tin, commercial asbestos, columbium, fluorspar, sheet mica, high-grade phosphorus, strontium, mercury, chromium and nickel.[32]

Increased reliance on foreign imports of most key minerals, combined with intense worldwide competition for the remaining scarce reserves, will raise prices and the bargaining leverage of the mineral exporting countries—just as was the case of oil for the OPEC nations.[33]

Despite the overwhelming statistical evidence presented in the United Nations, Congressional and academic studies, reports and hearings, there are still a few souls who cling to the theory that at existing growth rates there are enough nonrenewable resources to provide for all the world's population forever, or at least for a good long time into the future. Their underlying assumptions, however, are without merit.

For example, it is often remarked that the entire planet is composed of minerals. Of course, what is overlooked is that only a tiny fraction of that amount is usable or potentially extractable. Assume, for the sake of argument, however, that the entire weight of the earth was potentially convertible to productive energy—which would leave us all walking on thin air. At a current 3 percent growth rate in the use of ten leading minerals, we would literally mine the equivalent of the entire earth's weight within several hundred years.[34] That's not a very long time when one stops to realize that human beings have been on earth for over 34 million years and that the earth itself has existed for 4 billion additional years.

Others argue that manganese nodules mined from the seabed could provide us with a new source of nonferrous metals. According to some experts this source could provide "copper equal to a quarter of current output, nickel equal to three times current output, and manganese equal to six times current output." These same experts believe it's possible to quadruple these figures sometime in the future. Again these figures appear impressive until they are placed within the context of exponential growth.

At current rates of consumption increase, the demand for copper will be ninety times the current level in just 100 years, for nickel, twenty-eight times the current level and for manganese, seventeen times the present level, virtually wiping out whatever short-term advantage, measured in years or decades, might accrue from these additional deposits.[35]

Finally, some people continue to believe that existing reserves of nonrenewable minerals can be maintained indefinitely by either replacing more scarce minerals with less scarce and/ or by efficient recycling of existing minerals. Substitution, since most major metals are fast diminishing in supply, is of relatively little advantage in the productive process. As William Ophuls points out, "substitutes (like aluminum for copper) are on the whole less efficient than the material they substitute for, and more energy is therefore required to perform a given function." Then, too, some minerals because of their unique properties are simply irreplaceable.[36]

Recycling is often envisioned as the answer to mineral resource depletion. While more efficient recycling is going to be essential for the economic survival of the planet, there is no way to achieve anywhere near 100 percent reprocessing. Recycling efficiency today averages around 30 percent for most used metals. It also creates additional pollution and requires ever greater amounts of energy "to collect, transport and transform" the scattered material. Like metal substitution, recycling, within the context of existing exponential growth rates in mineral use, buys only a small, almost irrelevant, period of extra time—a few decades, maybe fifty years at most.[37]

RENEWABLE RESOURCES, POPULATION AND LIMITS TO GROWTH

The concept of renewable resources is a bit misleading. It conjures up the notion of never running out. But just as with energy resources and minerals, we are beginning to discover the concept of absolute limits in regard to so-called renewable resources—plant and animal life.

Cropland, grazing land, forests, food strains and fisheries are rapidly becoming scarce. The consequences for the continuation of human life on the planet are ominous.

The gene pool of life has evolved over several billion years.

In that time some ninety-eight million species of plant and animal life have appeared on earth. Today, there are between three and ten million species of plant and animal life coexisting in a delicate web of interdependent relationships.[28] That interdependence is the basis upon which the entire life order of the planet is sustained—including human life.

Now, that life order is literally being decimated by the onslaught of modern civilization. It is estimated that during the dinosaur age, animal species became extinct at a rate of about one per thousand years. Between 1600 and 1950, the period of the industrial revolution, animal species were dying out on the average of one per decade. Today, according to the International Union for Conservation of Nature, one animal species disappears, irreversibly, every year. Ecologists have estimated that beginning sometime around 1980 and the year 2000, nearly one out of every six species of plant and animal life on the planet will vanish. This would mean, according to Thomas Lovejoy of the World Wildlife Fund, the absolute obliteration of over 500,000 species of life. This wholesale genocide amounts to 17 percent of the world's remaining plant and animal life. Its effect on the gene pool, evolutionary development and human survival is incalculable because the magnitude of the losses over such a short time span is unparalleled in history.[40]

One of the few species that is not diminishing in numbers is Homo sapiens. In fact, it is the enormous growth of the human population itself over the past half-century that is putting such enormous strain on the carrying capacity of the earth's ecosystem. The worldwide rush for industrial development—to provide for the needs of an increasing population—is chiefly responsible for the tremendous dislocation and destruction of so much of the rest of the animal and plant kingdom.

Human population statistics are indeed staggering. Every day 333,000 new babies are born. Even allowing for the fact that 134,000 deaths occur every twenty-four hours, the net increase to the world population per day now stands at nearly 200,000. This means that there are seventy-three million more people in the world each year.[41]

The magnitude of population growth statistics can only be truly grasped by means of historical comparison.

It took two million years for the human population to reach one billion. The second billion took only one hundred years. The third billion took only thirty years, between 1930 and 1960. The fourth billion took only fifteen years. Between 1960 and

1975 the world's population grew at a rate of 2 percent per year, going from 2½ billion to 4 billion people.[42] At current growth rates, the world population will double once again, making the population 8 billion by the year 2010, and 16 billion by the year 2045.[43]

The survival of the future human population will depend on effective husbandry of plant and animal life. Yet, the world's available productive crop- and grazing land is diminishing each day both in absolute terms and in terms relative to growing population needs.

Between 1950 and 1975 the world output of food nearly doubled. At first glance, this would appear significant, except that in the same time period the world's population increased by two-thirds. In the early 1900s world food demand increased by around four million tons per year. Today food demands are increasing on an average of thirty million tons per year. That's because global population is surging forward with an additional seventy-three million people each year. At the same time, the worldwide distribution of food is so uneven that "the one billion people in the affluent parts of the world consume half, and the other three billion get the other half."[44]

The food production and distribution problem is exacerbated by the massive urbanization of the world's population. In 1950, around 29 percent of the global population lived in urban areas. Today it is 39 percent. The United Nations predicts that if current migration rates continue, by the turn of the century 49 percent, or half of the world's population, will live in concentrated urban environments of over 100,000.[45] Most urban dwellers will live in fewer than 100 cities across the planet, with populations of up to sixty million (eight times the size of New York).[46] This will place impossible demands on agricultural production, transportation and distribution mechanisms worldwide.

The crush of humanity in cities will be devastating. Even in the highly industrial United States, scores of major cities like New York, Cleveland, Detroit, Newark and Chicago are already facing the prospect of bankruptcy over the next decade. Disruptions and breakdowns in vital police, sanitation, education and other social services are already beginning to take place. For the major cities of the developing world, the picture is a hundred times more grim. Edward Goldsmith, in an article entitled "Settlements and Social Stability," capsuled the future prospects for cities of Africa, Asia and South America:

Urban populations are still increasing—South Asia alone, at the rate of three hundred thousand a week. If urbanization continues in both the industrial and nonindustrial world, social chaos, epidemics, and famine are imminent on an unprecedented scale, as cities simply break down and cannot provide the basic necessities of life for their inhabitants.[47]

In the next twenty-five years, the world demand for food will double, according to most forecasts. That means that ways must be found to double worldwide agricultural output. The prospects are not good. Some economists argue that a more equitable distribution of existing production would solve the problem. It is true that maldistribution is a major contributing factor to starvation. One out of four people on the planet—or 1.2 billion—are either undernourished or on the borderline of starvation.[48] Yet in 1974 world grain production was about 1,200 million tons, "or enough to supply about 2,900 vegetable-equivalent kilocalories per person per day." (Two thousand two hundred kilocalories are considered essential for subsistence survival.)[49] While hundreds of millions of people àre starving, the average American child this year will consume as much of the world's resources as twenty children born in India.[50]

Redistribution, then, is essential. But, it is illusory, most experts argue, to believe that even with massive redistribution, world food production can be doubled in less than twenty years. The reasons are many.

Approximately 10 percent of the earth's surface is cropland.[51] Much of it, however, is lost each year as a result of the steady encroachment of industrial development. In the United States alone, "more than one million hectares of arable cropland are lost to highways, urbanization and other special uses" each year, according to a study reported in *Science* magazine. While the study goes on to say that such losses are partially made up by the addition of 500,000 new hectares of cropland per year, most often the new acres under cultivation represent poorer quality farmland with a lower yield potential.[52]

With strip mining expected to increase dramatically in the United States over the next thirty years, even more cropland will be lost. Illinois is already losing 6,000 acres of agricultural land to strip mining each year.[53]

Worldwide, efforts to expand the area of cultivated land has led to farming in areas of increasingly poor quality—hillsides, semiarable land and other marginal space. The result has been an actual fall in per hectare yields over the past several years.[54]

Here in the United States the squeeze on agricultural profits has forced many farmers to abandon long-range conservation methods in favor of short-term, over-exploitation of existing cropland. To increase yield on more marginal lands, farmers are increasing the use of chemical fertilizers and pesticides. This, in turn, depletes the soil and decreases the resistance to pests. To cut losses from soil erosion and pests, farmers increase the dosage of chemical fertilizers and pesticides, resulting in even greater soil erosion. This vicious cycle is repeated over and over again on farms across America. As a result, nearly four billion tons of sediment are washed away in the United States each year.[55] This washout clogs and pollutes rivers and lakes, thus diminishing the supply of available water needed for crop irrigation. The Council for Agricultural Science and Technology says that, "a third of all U.S. cropland was suffering soil losses too great to be sustained without a gradual, but ultimately disastrous, decline in productivity."[56] In dollar terms, the costs of replacing nutrients lost through soil erosion would have amounted to 1.2 billion dollars in 1974 alone.[57]

The world's grazing land is also being severely threatened. Grassland provides the fuel for draft animals that are used to cultivate one-third of the world's cropland.[58] Overgrazing, to provide for the needs of increasing population, is leading to massive soil erosion and causing the supply of livestock in many areas of the world to dwindle. The strain put on both crop- and grazing lands to produce more than their natural capacity is turning whole regions of the world into deserts, barren of life.

The United Nations estimates that seventy-eight million people presently live in barren desert lands.[59] In the Sahara, over 650,000 square kilometers of grazing and farm land have been lost to desertification over the past half-century. North of the Sahara, over 100,000 hectares of land become desert each year.[60] The United Nations says that, "16 billion dollars worth of potential agricultural production is lost each year in the world's arid and semi-arid zones because of past and current desertification."[61] While massive irrigation projects might reverse a small fraction of the losses, there is simply not enough water available to reclaim most of the land that's turning into desert. Water from underground is already being extracted faster than it is being replenished. With increasing emphasis on the mechanization of agriculture, greater amounts of water will be needed. Yet the United Nations Food and Agriculture Organization says there will be a critical shortage of water worldwide by the year A.D. 2000. Even if the entire world were to decide to use existing water supplies to irrigate wherever possible, it would still be possible only to irrigate some 20 percent of the arable land. A decade ago, experts were looking to desalinization of ocean water as the answer. Today, these hopes have diminished. The costs involved in production and transportation make it prohibitive on a large scale.[62]

Another factor in the loss of productive land is massive worldwide deforestation. According to the findings of ecologist Lester Brown, in almost every country experiencing mass population growth, deforestation is occurring on an unprecedented scale.[63] Deforestation, in turn, increases flooding, land slides, soil erosion and desertification.

Economists are now predicting a "timber famine" by the year 2020. Some estimates are more pessimistic, and forecast critical world shortages by the mid-1980s.[64] The effect on national economies will be as devastating as the losses in nonrenewable energy sources and minerals.

The industrialized nations are absolutely dependent on wood to provide everything from building materials to paper products. Wood is equally important for the nonindustrialized nations. Nearly half of the people on earth cook and heat with firewood.[65]

In many Third World countries virtually the entire population is dependent on timber as its chief energy source. The average Third World person requires between one and two tons of firewood each year to survive. Because population growth now outstrips the generative capacity of regional timberlands, massive deforestation is taking place. This is particularly true in Central America, Northwestern South America, the Middle East, South Asia and Northern Africa. According to Worldwatch Institute, "the poor must hunt for wood, sometimes spending entire days gathering just enough wood for one person to carry." In West Africa families are now spending 25 percent of their income on firewood. In some areas deforestation has become so acute that people are turning to dry cow dung as a fuel substitute. As a consequence the cropland is denied the fertilizing nutrients of the manure, and agricultural yield decreases still further.[66]

For all these reasons, there is less available productive land to feed more mouths. This results in an increased reliance on mechanization to improve both crop and livestock yields. Unfortunately, mechanization usually means sacrificing quality for quantity. Chemically treated food crops and livestock are less valuable in terms of nutrition and are a major factor in the increase in human diseases, from heart ailments to cancer.[67]

It's no wonder. An article entitled "Technique and Animals," in *Science* magazine, graphically illustrates the relationship between increased mechanization, loss of nutritional value and disease. The article points out that half the country's antibiotics are fed to farm animals to counter diseases that would not occur in the first place were it not for the tremendous strains mechanization imposes on the animal's physiological development. The following are examples of the effect that mechanization has on livestock:

> Calves raised for veal ... suffer anemia and weakness from their low-iron diets; also, because they are fed no roughage, they resort to licking off their own hair. ... Pigs chew each others' tails off. Chicks have their beaks cut off so they will not peck each other. Pigs and chickens even resort to cannibalism ... the mortality rate is as high as 20 percent on some farms, and many more deaths occur in the course of transporting animals for fattening and slaughtering. ... Ventilation and temperature control on the trucks are haphazard and losses in transportation alone amount to $1 billion a year—equivalent to a four-mile-long freight train filled with carcasses.[68]

Reliance on a handful of genetically bred super-strain food and animal crops also reduces the essential variation in the plant and animal gene pool that is necessary for evolutionary development and the proper balancing of local ecosystems. Now that cloning of food strains and animals is about to become a reality, genetic variation will cease to exist at all in most major food crops and livestock strains. Imagine one type of wheat with hundreds of millions, or billions, of genetic carbon-copy twins growing all over the world. Or one type of cow with millions of genetically identical twins. With no genetic variation whatsoever, only one alien strain of bacteria or virus could wipe out the entire wheat and cattle population of a nation or the planet.[69]

Above all, mechanization of agriculture depends on the use

of increasing doses of nonrenewable energy resources. It normally takes a tenfold increase in nonrenewable energy resources to double agricultural yield.[70] Therefore, to provide enough food for a doubled world population in only a score of years—even assuming people are no better fed than today—would require a tenfold increase, worldwide, in productive energy to provide both chemical fertilizers and fuel for modern farm machinery. But our stock of fossil fuels is running out, and prices on the remaining supplies continue to rise. Consequently, the cost of agricultural production continues to climb as well.

In a world made increasingly dependent on capital-intensive, energy-intensive agricultural production for survival, options for the future become increasingly limited, regardless of the choices one makes.

If we are approaching the absolute outer limits of land productivity, what about the ocean as a resource for our food needs. This thinking was fashionable a few years ago—but is no longer. The oceans are no more a cornucopia for the future than the land. For the most part the oceans are biological deserts. Most nutrients of value are to be found near the surface or in coastal marshes. Even under ideal conditions, marine biologists say it is unlikely that we could count on more than doubling or tripling our current production of nutrients from the oceans.[71] However, ideal conditions no longer prevail. Because of a combination of years of over-fishing, oil spills and the dumping of industrial wastes, the oceans are becoming barren of marine life. According to *International Wildlife* magazine:

> The [international] fish catch per person is down 11 percent over the last seven years. And prices of almost all forms of seafood are rising. All but three of the thirty fisheries in the Northeast Altantic, which supply Western Europe, are now overfished; the picture in the Northwest Atlantic is equally grim.[72]

THE GREAT MYTH OF PROGRESS

For thousands of years human beings harbored the belief that the world was flat. Even as evidence to the contrary continued to accumulate, they refused to let go of their long-standing conviction, a conviction that provided them with a reference point from which to look at and judge the world around them.

Modern man and woman harbor a conviction that is equally fallacious. We cling to the illusion, despite evidence to the contrary, that human physical activity in the world is constantly creating "more order and greater material value." We are unwilling to relinquish this conviction because it allows us to define and cope with the world around us.

The age of materialism has been characterized by the notion of progress. Reduced to its simplest abstraction, progress is seen as the process by which the "less ordered" natural world is harnessed by people to create a more ordered material environment. Or to put it another way, progress is creating greater *value* out of the natural world than that which exists in its original state. Science, in this context, is the methodology by which people learn the ways of nature so they can convert them into principles or rules which are consistent with human goals. Technology, in turn, is the application of those rules to specific needs in order to transform the natural process into forms of greater value, structure and order than exist in the primal state.

The ultimate tragic dimension of modern existence lies in the way humanity has literally turned upside down the incontrovertible fact of life that man is subject to nature rather than nature subject to man. The irony of this is bound to bring a faint smile of amused acknowledgment to even the most hardened of beings, even while the consequences of the folly now threaten the very existence of life on this planet.

The fact is, the assumptions upon which modern man and woman base their sense of meaning, purpose and direction in the world is false. Not just partially false, but 100 percent false. Progress, science, and technology have not resulted in greater order and value in the world, but their opposite. This is not a purely philosophical or sociological observation. Were this the case, the merits of the argument could at least be debated, perhaps even ignored or dismissed. After all, over the centuries there were many philosophical arguments put forth to question the theory that the world was flat. Not until the great naval explorers circumnavigated the planet did humankind finally, and then only reluctantly, give up its long-standing conviction. The same holds true with the modern notion of progress.

The modern world view completely and utterly contradicts the second major law of thermodynamics—a law which has guided the entire age of physics. Like a giant blind spot, we have refused to understand the profound implications of this law even as we have selectively applied it in order to create the modern technological society.

The first law of thermodynamics is that "the energy in the universe is constant." That is, it can neither be created nor destroyed. It is a fixed commodity. The second law of thermodynamics, and the one which has been so narrowly understood, is that "the entropy of the universe is constantly increasing."[73] What this means, essentially, is that the earth's matter and energy are constantly being converted from usable to unusable forms by "combustion, wear and tear and rendering into waste." Dr. Georgescu-Roegen of the University of West Virginia puts it this way:

> Thermodynamics divide energy and matter into two qualities—available to man for his life purpose, and nonavailable. Matter or energy, while remaining continuously constant, may change its quality, but—and this is an important point—always by the degradation of available into nonavailable form.[74]

Matter and energy in a form that is usable or accessible is referred to as low entropy. Matter and energy in an inaccessible or unusable state is called high entropy. For example, pieces of coal in a mine are in a low entropy state. That is, they can be extracted and burned. Once they are burned, however, the energy is converted into carbon dioxide and dispersed into the atmosphere, making it unavailable or inaccessible for further productive use. This dispersed, unavailable state is high entropy.[75] In the natural world, according to the second law of thermodynamics, everything is constantly moving from a low-entropy to a high-entropy state, or from an ordered to a disordered condition. This is an ironclad law without exception or qualifier, say the physicists. Any process, then, that speeds up that natural progression from order to disorder, from low entropy to high entropy, only shortens the time line to ultimate chaos in the world.[76] Herein lies the fatal catch-22 of modern society. The purpose of modern industrial technologies is to find more efficient ways to harness and expend matter and energy that exists in a low-entropy state.

Dr. Barry Commoner, in his seminal work, *The Poverty of Power*, sums up the relationship between the *scientific principle* of thermodynamics and its *technological* application in modern industrialized society.

> The chief practical purpose of thermodynamics is to learn how energy can best be harnessed to work requiring tasks. These tasks—the work that people do—are all intended to, and usually do, generate order from disorder (building barns from heaps of lumber, or sky scrapers from piles of sand, cement and metallic ores). . . . What people do, then, is to use energy to reverse, in highly specific, localized ways, the overall decay of the universe toward disorder.[77]

Industrial technology, then, creates temporary order, but at the expense of *speeding* up the overall process of moving from low entropy to high entropy. In other words, the more we exploit and expend the low-entropy matter and energy around us in the natural world in order to create a more efficient order in a concentrated time span and place, the greater the overall chaos we ultimately create in the larger world.

The second law of thermodynamics, therefore, contradicts the modern notion of progress. The world is moving inextricably from a state of more order to less order, from more value to less value. While technology gives the illusion of reversing the process at any particular moment in time, it is really doing just the opposite. That is, technology is no more than a means of speeding up the process of moving from low entropy to high entropy or from value to waste, or from order to disorder—whether it's burning a piece of coal or making paper out of a tree.

The physical proof of this is all around us. It's called pollution. Pollution is not, as popular opinion holds, a simple by-product of industrialization. Pollution is the sum total of energy and matter that has been transformed from a low-entropy to a high-entropy state. When we think of pollution nowadays and its effect on the biosphere of life, we are likely to conjure up images of decay, fragmentation, waste and disorder. That, according to the second law of thermodynamics, is exactly what it is: energy and matter that have been transformed to a high-entropy, unusable, and dispersed state.[78] For example, coal burned up as energy creates carbon dioxide which is dispersed into the atmosphere. Since the amount of matter and energy in the universe can neither be created or destroyed, but only transformed from an ordered to a disordered state, pollution is the constant physical reminder that, for all our notions of progress, modern civilization has merely succeeded in buying itself a short joyride of several hundred years. We have had fun and lived well by speeding up the entropy process—and creating a temporary semblance of order—at the expense of moving the world faster to its ultimate physical demise. Herman Daly, testifying before the Joint Economic Committee of Congress, put it succinctly: "The entropy law tells us that when technology increases order in one part of the universe, it must produce an even greater amount of disorder somewhere else."[79]

Now we will have to pay the price for our misconceived notions about material progress, science and technology. We are now forced to live in a world in which the high-entropy consequences of our behavior—pollution—threaten our very survival. The second law of thermodynamics teaches us that in the long run, there is no such thing as getting something for nothing. In entropy terms, says Dr. Nicholas Georgescu-Roegen:

> The cost of any biological or economic enterprise is always greater than the product. In entropy terms, any such activity necessarily results in a deficit.[80]

POLLUTION

Pollution, the high-entropy, disordered state of matter and energy, is closing in on us from all directions with exponential speed and force. As we desperately attempt to create new technological lines of defense to ward off the impending chaos, we merely find ourselves further isolated into smaller fortresses, our efforts only adding to the chaos. We are warned to stay indoors as air quality alerts become more frequent. We are afraid to go to work because the chemicals we come in contact with could cause cancer and death. We consume our processed foods with little relish, wondering to ourselves which of the ingredients are poisonous to our systems. The scientific truths and technological tools that were supposed to bring us an artificial world of increased security and comfort are now spawning a level of intense anxiety that is precariously close to gelling into mass social hysteria. That anxiety is well founded. Consider the facts.

There are currently about 50,000 chemicals being produced or manufactured in the United States. In 1975 alone, United States corporations produced 155 billion pounds of 8,000 different synthetic-organic chemicals worth 25 billion dollars. The long-term effect of introducing these thousands of chemicals into the environment is barely known, because only a tiny fraction of them have ever been studied. It takes the Environmental Protection Agency three years, at a cost of a quarter of a million dollars, to study the long-term toxicological effect of just one chemical.[81] At this rate it will take 150,000 years and 12½ billion dollars to study the effects of the chemicals now on hand. And, every twenty minutes, new chemicals are being introduced into the biosphere.

Our society is fast turning into a virtually synthetic chemical environment. For example, take pesticides. Since 1940, the amount of pesticides used in the United States has doubled about every eight years. This year well over one billion pounds of pesticides will be manufactured and dispersed throughout the United States.[82]

In just thirty-five years, we have transformed our economy from the iron age to the synthetic age. *Modern Plastics* magazine estimates that between 1980 and 1990, "the volume consumption of iron, which still marks our age, will have been surpassed by that of synthetics." The rate of increase in the production of plastics per year is staggering—a whopping 15.9 percent. At this rate, the United States will achieve a 2800 percent increase in the use of synthetics by the year A.D. 2000.[83]

In the movie *The Graduate,* there is a famous scene where a businessman takes Dustin Hoffman into a quiet corner and whispers into his ear a little career counseling advice: "plastics." He knew of what he was talking. Today plastics—a derivative of our increasingly scarce supply of petrochemical fuels—are intimately intertwined into the entire fabric of American life. The list of plastic products that we rely on seems endless. It's hard to imagine that this revolution in product design has been with us for little more than one generation.

The synthetic world of chemicals, plastics and pesticides is far removed from the natural world that Homo sapiens and other forms of life were biologically designed to live in. The dramatic speeding up of the entropy process and the resulting

waste pollutants are having a profound and irreversible impact
on the delicate balance of complex relationships that exist between all forms of life in the natural ecosystem. The multiplier
and accelerator effect on the entire life system as a consequence
of even the slightest technological tampering can be mind-
boggling. A small isolated example is instructional.

In a small village in the Borneo jungle, health workers
decided to spray the straw huts with DDT in order to control
the mosquito population responsible for the spread of malaria.
The lizards that normally inhabit the walls of the huts consumed
large doses of the DDT and died. The village cats, in turn, ate
the dying lizards and themselves died. The cats' demise resulted
in an infestation of rats into the village. The lizards' death left
the straw-consuming caterpillars free to multiply (the lizards
feed on the caterpillars), and eventually they gobbled up the
straw-thatched roofs of the village huts.[84]

Imagine, then, the possible consequences to the ecosystem
and its effect on life in an advanced industrial economy where
billions of pounds of pesticides and chemicals are regularly
dumped into the environment in which we work and live.

Natural and industrial solid waste (matter and energy transformed from low- to high-entropy states) has become a monumental problem in modern economies. In his book, *Murderous
Providence: A Study of Pollution in Industrial Societies,* Harry
Rothman points out that, "if the American people and their
solid wastes were spread evenly over the United States there
would be in each square mile of the nation 56 people surrounded
by 54 tons of rubbish which would include: 3 junked cars, 26
discarded tires, 8,500 bottles, 17,000 cans, one ton of plastics
and 8½ tons of paper." By 1980, it is projected that each American will generate eight pounds of solid waste every twenty-
four hours for a total of 340 million tons per year.[85]

The problem of solid waste is becoming so acute that the
League of Cities says it's now the second most costly municipal
service, immediately behind education, "but ahead of such
expensive services as police and fire protection." In 1976,
according to the EPA, our cities spent over 4 billion dollars
on solid waste disposal and at current rates of increase that
figure will continue to rise dramatically, very shortly becoming
the single most expensive public service item for the nation.[86]

There are currently over 10,000 landfill sites stretched across
the United States that are used to dispose of commercial wastes.
According to the EPA however, 90 percent of this waste is not

disposed of in accordance with minimum public health standards. Glops, glues, and sludges, which are terms scientists use to refer to "waste streams" composed of many types of toxic, acidic and flammable elements, now pose a major health threat to human life in the United States. Birth defects, mental retardation, fatal diseases, miscarriages, have all been traced to exposure to commercial waste streams that have leaked or run off poorly managed commercial waste landfills.[87]

Now there is growing evidence that corporations are turning to organized crime to illegally dump their solid wastes rather than pay the extra costs required to dispose of them according to EPA guidelines. For example, in January of 1978, Newark police caught a truck driver dumping an 8,000-gallon tank of waste into a sewer in the middle of the night. Incidents of this kind, say law enforcement officers, are beginning to appear more frequently all over the country, suggesting a pattern involving major underworld involvement.[88]

If the grave dangers posed by solid waste were all we had to contend with, the survival task before us would be formidable enough. But added to the overall pollution crisis are the even more frightening problems associated with air pollution—those wastes which are dispersed every day as tiny particles in the atmosphere around us.

Once again, the magnitude of the problem can probably best be appreciated by taking a look at one specific example. Scientists at the Brookhaven National Laboratory in New York undertook a two-year study of the effect of sulfur dioxide emitted into the atmosphere from power plants in Ohio, Illinois, Indiana, Michigan and Wisconsin. According to the study, the sulfur dioxide, which travels to the East Coast via the westerly winds, results in approximately 21,000 premature deaths each year.[89]

It is estimated that the damage to material and property alone due to air pollutants runs around 3 billion dollars per year.[90]

Perhaps the two most disturbing effects of the buildup of air pollutants are acid rain and the destruction of the ozone layer. Gene Kelly might think twice before singing in the rain nowadays. The likelihood is that wherever you are in the United States today, the rain that falls on you is going to be poisonous corrosive acid. The increasing acidity of the rain is largely due to the burning of fossil fuels in industry, automobiles, et cetera, which emit massive amounts of sulfuric acid into the air. Says

Leon S. Dochinger of the United States Department of Agriculture, "[acid rain] is perhaps the most serious environmental dilemma of this century."[91] Acid rain is destroying soil, crops, forests and sea life. It is even eroding metal and stone-constructed buildings. Geologist K. Lal Gauri of the University of Louisville, an expert in stone restoration, warns that great world structures like the Parthenon, the Colosseum and the Taj Mahal are already in various stages of decay due, in part, to acid rain.[92] In Sweden, studies show up to 15 percent reduction in forest growth by the year 2000 because of the deadly effects of acid rain. In the Unites States acid rain, according to some studies, has reduced cotton yields by 33 percent and tomato harvests by 21 percent.[93]

Gene E. Libens of Cornell University and Norman Glass of the EPA report that the rainwater in the eastern part of the United States has become so acidic over the past fifteen years that the acid content is now one-third nitric acid, two-thirds sulfuric acid.[94]

In New York's Adirondack Park, acid rain is held responsible for killing off nearly 90 percent of the fish in some 200 high-altitude lakes. Much of the acid rain has been traced back to smelters as far away as Ohio.[95]

Competing right alongside acid rain is the destruction of the earth's ozone layer by synthetics, plastics, chlorinated fluorocarbons and other polluting elements. The ozone is a small protective layer high up in the biosphere—some thirty miles—which screens out much of the sun's ultraviolet rays. Without that effective screen, all complex forms of life would die. A recent report by the National Academy of Sciences estimates a future depletion of the ozone layer of up to 16.5 percent as a result of the pollutants that industrial society is dumping into the biosphere.[96] While the general public is under the impression that only the fluorocarbons in aerosol sprays are responsible for the ozone destruction, new scientific studies are identifying other responsible chemical elements, ranging all the way from bromine used in the manufacture of plastics to chlorination used in water supplies and sewage treatment . . .[97]

The environment we have created may now be a major cause of death in the United States. Cancer, heart and lung disease, accounting for 12 percent of deaths in 1900 and 38 percent in 1940, were the cause of 59 percent of all deaths in 1976. . . . Growing evidence links much of the occurrence of these diseases . . . to the nature of the environment.[98]

This is the conclusion of a top-level federal government task force composed of representatives of the EPA, the National Cancer Institute, the National Institute for Occupational Safety and Health and the National Institute of Environmental Health Sciences.

Pollution, caused by our highly technologized industrial society, is now, for the first time, reversing the established trend of rising statistical increases in life expectancy in America. Even though medical and health care costs have shot up from 76 dollars per person in 1950 to 552 dollars per person in 1976, and now account for almost 9 percent of our Gross National Product, life expectancy has leveled off and shows signs of decreasing.[99] The problem, argue many medical experts, is the tremendous rise in all forms of pollution at every level of human existence. The high standard of living we have experienced in this highly advanced industrial environment is the trade-off we're now paying for in terms of spreading disease and death.

The deadly effects of pollution on the human physiology are staggering. In New York City most taxi drivers have such a high level of carbon monoxide in their blood that it cannot be used for blood transfusions to persons with heart ailments.[100] Nationwise, auto emissions alone kill 4,000 people and are responsible for four million sick days.[101]

Recently scientists told a Senate subcommittee that it is no longer possible to find uncontaminated milk to feed to infants.

> Human breast milk increasingly contains pesticides, residues and other carcinogens. Infant formulas contain harmful lead deposits . . .[102]

Several government reports in the past several years conclude that 60 percent to 90 percent of all types of cancers in the United States are caused by man-made environmental factors, ranging from food preservatives and additives, to toxic chemical substances.[103] Secretary of Health, Education and Welfare, Joseph Califano, shocked the nation's work force in late summer of 1978 by announcing the results of an extensive study showing that between 20 percent and 40 percent of all cancers are work related—the result of contact with an entire range of metals, chemicals and processes that are essential to the continuance of our industrial output. Because there is usually a twenty- to thirty-year lag time between exposure to chemical carcinogens and contraction of the cancer, it is estimated that as many as one out of every three Americans alive today will get cancer in their lifetimes. In fact, since most of the sharp rise in industrial and commercial uses of synthetics, pesticides and other chemical substances took place after World War II, many medical experts are predicting a virtual runaway epidemic of cancer by the mid-1980s.

Cancer is by no means the only major disease resulting from the pollutants of industrial society. The United Steel Workers Union reports that "more than a half-million workers are disabled yearly by occupational diseases" of all kinds.[104]

PROSPECTS FOR THE AMERICAN ECONOMY

The evidence is overwhelming. We are exhausting, in absolute terms, our store of fossil fuels and minerals and depleting our available crop- and grazing land, forests and fisheries. Exponential growth rates in population worldwide, and the corresponding escalation in consumption demands, are placing unparalleled strains on the world's fragile ecosystems. We are literally devouring our planet, spewing out massive wastes in every direction.

Millions of human bodies are being packed together in several hundred giant urban ghettos scattered across the planet; billions and billions of pounds of deadly, toxic wastes are oozing out of the ground and hovering over the earth in thick layers of darkened sky.

This frightening process of erosion and decay is already well advanced. It's visible to the naked eye. Still, some economists, and most corporate planners and heads of state, continue to talk of exponential economic growth rates, as if there were no absolute limits to the carrying capacity of the earth's natural system. Simple arithmetic, however, should convince even the most skeptical of observers, that the outer limits of the age of material expansion are about to be reached. It is the weight of statistics, not the arguments of philosophy, that already dictate the end of the liberal ethos and the concept of unlimited growth.

According to a study done for the United Nations by economist and Nobel Laureate Wassily Leontief, in order to maintain just a moderate rate of global growth over the next few decades, it will take a fivefold increase in mineral consumption and a fourfold increase in food consumption.[1]

To meet the needs of world population growth in the next thirty years we would have to "build houses, hospitals, ports, factories, bridges and every other kind of facility in numbers that almost equal all the construction work done by the human race up to now."[2]

In order to maintain existing rates of industrial growth in the developed world, industrial production would have to double every ten years. Projecting just fifty years ahead, this would mean an increase in resource consumption thirty-two times larger than that of today. Just 100 years from now, at existing industrial growth rates, resource requirements would be a thousand times greater than they are today.[3]

In terms of individual standards of living, if the United States maintains its current 3 percent per year per person growth rate for 150 years, average income would increase 100 times. Dr. Carl Madden, former chief economist for the United States Chamber of Commerce, testifying before the Joint Economic Committee of Congress, asked: "How can the earth yield energy and materials to meet such fantastic standards, or how on earth (literally) will a family manage to absorb them?"[4] Indeed! Obviously the answer to Dr. Madden's question and all of the statistical projections based on present growth rates is a resounding "No Way!" The planet earth cannot absorb that kind of sustained growth, under any circumstances.

It has been generally estimated that humanity's impact on the world's environment is growing at between 5 and 6 percent each year. If we assume, as some of our corporate and political leaders do, that it is possible, with the right combination of incentives, programs and arrangements, to continue existing growth rates—namely no substantial slowdown in economic growth—then the overall environmental impact on the world would be four times as great as today by the year 2005, and sixteen times as great by the year 2033. Consider the effect we now experience in terms of pollution and the massive destruction of our natural ecosystem and imagine a sixteen times increase in net impact in just fifty-five years. Environmentalist William Ophuls comments: "The intense stress on the world's ecosystems . . . could not be supported . . . nor do we appear to have the resources to support the levels of demand for food, minerals, and energy implied by such figures."[5]

There is absolutely no way to maintain existing growth rates. We have run up against the fixed limits of the ecosystem of the planet earth. Since the 1973 oil price rise, economic growth has been declining in all of the advanced industrial nations. From 1972 through 1976 the industrial economies grew at an annual rate of 2 percent (in real terms), well below the average 5 percent growth rates of the previous twelve years.[6] The initial decline in growth rates is traceable to the upward adjustment of oil prices, reflecting the realization that this precious energy resource is running out.

The industrial nations are more than 90 percent dependent on fossil fuels.[7] Therefore, it's obvious that the rise in the price of oil and other energy resources has had, and will continue to have, a profound effect on rising costs, mushrooming inflation and the long-range slowing of economic growth. In fact, escalating inflation, spawned by resource scarcity, is the key economic factor responsible for a slowing down of the world's long-range growth trend.

> Unless the battle against inflation is fought with more courage and originality than it has been up to now, we, the people, are moving closer and closer to taking our destiny into our own hands. The rage of the 1960s then may be child's play against the fury of the 1980s.[8]

These are the words of syndicated columnist Sylvia Porter. Her feelings are shared by tens of millions of Americans who repeatedly name inflation as the most serious problem facing the country. There are many reasons given for the inflation problem, all of which have some truth to them. Government spending, especially high military budgets, administered prices, set by huge corporate monopolies, and wage demands by organized labor are among those more often bantered about. Ironically, the chief cause of inflation, and the one which, in the long run, is unamenable to orthodox government manipulation, is energy and mineral scarcity. Depletion of all forms of nonrenewable resources means rising prices. Today, American industry is forced to exploit ever poorer grades of material resources in order to meet existing growth needs. The additional costs incurred in extracting inferior-grade resources adds to the overall inflation rise. For example, nearly half the petroleum in Texas is also used up in the process of extracting and transporting new oil finds. The net energy yield of only 50 percent contrasts sharply with the cost of extracting Mideast oil from the Persian Gulf. There, the amount of energy required to extract oil is extremely low because much of the crude oil lies in pressurized pools just below the surface—making it easily accessible.[9]

Economic statistics demonstrate the increased cost of mining lower and lower grades of energy. In 1960, for every dollar invested in energy production, 2,250,000 BTU's of energy were produced. By 1973, the same dollar investment yielded only 1,845,000 BTU's—an 18 percent drop in productivity.[10]

As the nation turns increasingly to coal and shale production, even greater amounts of energy will be needed to produce comparable energy yields, further raising costs, prices and inflation.

The rising cost of energy production is placing tremendous demands on industry to finance new capital to support new production technologies. These capital needs are enormous. A new petroleum factory costs 500 million dollars, a nuclear power plant up to 2 billion dollars.[11] As Dr. Barry Commoner points out, these kinds of costs can only be met by huge corporate entities, like Exxon, Mobil and Gulf. The energy-chemical complex in this country, says Commoner, now dominates the United States economy:

It owns $181 billion in assets, or 29 percent of the assets (and sales) of the 500 largest corporations in the United States. The sales of these companies represented 18 percent of the total GNP in 1974. All of this wealth is in the hands of some twenty corporations with average assets of $9.1 billion each.[12]

Resource depletion and capital costs continue to be played off against each other in a game that cannot be won. As energy and other resources become more scarce and more expensive to convert into usable forms, more capital expenditure is required to do the job. At the same time, the increased costs associated with resource scarcity continue to depress return on investment or profit. Less return dampens the enthusiasm of those with power to invest in new capital, creating a capital shortage at the same time that increased resource scarcity and energy costs necessitate even greater capital outlays.

Between 1973 and 1985, according to the Chase Manhattan Bank, the energy companies would need to raise nearly 1 trillion dollars in capital in order to maintain and moderately expand their operations. Over half that capital has to be raised externally. (The energy companies now require greater capital infusions than any other single force in the marketplace.)[13] Those capital requirements cannot be met. Says James Neddham, president of the New York Stock Exchange: "We have become increasingly concerned about the supply and allocation of investment capital and our concerns have deepened with the realization that a capital shortage is no longer a threat for the future, but a fact of the present as inflationary pressures come to bear on capital markets."[14] The Exchange estimates that between 1975 and 1984 the overall capital requirements of the United States economy will be a whopping 4.7 trillion dollars—that's three times the capital outlay of the previous ten years (from 1965 to 1974). Actual savings, says the Exchange, will amount to only 4.05 trillion dollars during this period, leaving a capital gap of 650 billion dollars over the years just ahead.[15]

Even these figures are somewhat optimistic. They fail to take into consideration the "additional" capital outlays that will be needed by the energy companies and industry at large to cope with the mounting pollution crisis. While the government (namely the public through its tax dollars) will end up paying a great deal of the additional costs of commercially generated pollution—in effect subsidizing industry by absorbing this part of its production costs—the private sector will still be made to bear some of the burden. These additional capital outlay costs—which will continue to rise as the pollution crisis worsens—will exacerbate the inflation problem, creating smaller returns and further dampening new capital investments.

Despite the seemingly irresistible forces that are moving the United States economy to crisis, paralysis and decline, there are still a few scattered voices preaching old-fashioned Yankee ingenuity as the way out. While resources are limited, human inventiveness is not, argue the technocrats. Surely with the right combination of money, talent and willpower, new technologies can be developed and harnessed to arrest, or at least slow down, this declining growth trend. What they fail to realize is that technology is not autonomous. It exists in a symbiotic relationship with the nonrenewable and renewable resources on which it depends. As resources become scarce and less accessible to conversion to productive uses, more complex and expensive technologies have to be invented in order to squeeze productivity out of what remains.

Today, United States industry is placing less and less of its retained earnings into research and development, precisely because of the increased costs associated with new and more complex technologies. In the 1960s, research and development spending accounted for 7.9 percent of the GNP. In the 1970s, R&D expenditures dropped to 2.4 percent. The federal government is partially responsible for the drop. In 1965, we were spending 12.6 cents of every federal dollar on R&D. By 1975, that figure had dropped to 5.7 cents of every dollar. In industry, the drop has been even greater. Private sector R&D has nose-dived 29 percent since 1966. *Industry Week* reports:

> Industry, under pressure to maintain profits in the face of rising and new costs, has taken a harder look at Research and Development spending and demanded measurable results—quick results—thus taking money from longer range research.[16]

As a result, industry is spending more of its research and development funds on innovations that are incremental rather than revolutionary. "The digital watch, solid-state television and mini-calculators all represent advances, but basically perform the same function albeit more rapidly and conveniently than their predecessors."[17]

For the past thirty years, the American economy has been relying on technological advances in specific growth industries, most of which are now maturing and showing signs of leveling off in terms of growth. Wonder drugs, the computer industry, photocopying and television immediately come to mind. All of these growth industries have been heavily dependent on large amounts of energy and other nonrenewable resources. More important still, there appears to be nothing on the horizon that can begin to replace these older technologies. About the only major technological advances in recent years capable of reaching a consumer market potential of 100 percent are permanent press pants and pocket calculators.[18] It's not surprising that Dr. James L. Heskett, of the Harvard Business School, has remarked:

We have seen the topping out of technology. We won't have the technological advances we've had in the last twenty or thirty years.[19]

Everything we've been taught about technology tells us that it has no inherent limits. In fact it does. Limits are imposed by the scarce resources it feeds upon; limits are imposed by the cost of the marketplace; and limits are imposed by science itself. "A technology can not be indefinitely improved without encountering either thermodynamic limits or limits of scale beyond which further improvement is of no practical interest," comments environmentalist William Ophuls.[20] Or to put it another way, once the initial scientific insights are made, and technological designs are established, each succeeding breakthrough is both less significant and more costly in relation to the benefit accrued because of the ironclad law of diminishing returns. For example, now that we have succeeded in transmitting messages almost as fast as the speed of light there is little more of a qualitative nature that can be done because the speed of light is a fixed barrier that cannot be crossed.

The cumulative effect of technology creates its own outer limits. As already mentioned, new technologies are generally more complex and more expensive than those they replace, require greater uses of nonrenewable and renewable resources and add to the cumulative pool of high-entropy pollutant waste. The increased use of scarce resources and the resultant waste accumulation make it necessary to find new, more complex and more expensive technologies in order to maintain economic growth—all of which further exacerbates the entire problem. The process becomes self-perpetuating, and the crisis more pronounced. Moreover, there is no way to break the cycle without radically shifting our world view away from continued economic growth and technological dependence.

Depleting resources, increased pollution, rising costs of production, spiraling inflation, low return on investments, escalating capital shortfalls and limits to technology all add up to one unmistakable reality. The Golden Days are over. United States productivity, which for the two decades following World War II led the world's economies, has now bottomed out. (Productivity is the net value of output after subtracting the inputs of labor costs, capital costs and resource costs.) In 1978, United States productivity showed virtually no increase at all.[21]

In a speech before the Joint Economic Committee of Con-

gress in November of 1976, Jay W. Forrester, director of the
Systems Dynamics Group at the Sloan School of Management
at MIT, succinctly capsuled the economic picture of the next
twenty-five years. Dr. Forrester talked of economic growth in
terms of a long-range life cycle. During the first part of that
cycle, roughly the past 300 years, "growth swept upward in
an ever steeper curve," said Forrester. The second part of the
economic cycle, the one the world is in now, is a transition
period, where "growth follows a straight line." Forrester argues
that the current transition phase of extremely low growth will
last only two to three decades and will be followed by a final
stage of virtual zero-growth economic equilibrium. Summing
up the current state of economic affairs Forrester comments:

> In this present transition interval, counterforces from na-
> ture rise until they become strong enough to suppress
> growth. By pushing for more growth, we are causing the
> counterforces to increase. The harder we push, the harder
> nature will resist. We can exhaust ourselves by pressing
> into the regions of rapidly rising real costs induced by
> our placing ever higher demands on the environment.
> Resistance is mounting in the form of energy and re-
> source shortages, declining food reserves, and rising pol-
> lution.[22]

Forrester's grim projection is echoed by most of the major
economic forecasting units in the country. Chase Econometrics
forecasts a significant slowdown in the growth rate of the country in the 1980s, as does the Wharton Econometric Forecasting
unit. The Wharton economists report that all of the factors
studied "point toward a future with lower growth and higher
inflation than that of the last two decades."[23] Finally, the pres-
tigious National Academy of Sciences Committee on Mineral
Resources and the Environment says:

> Growth in a material sense has long been such a bedrock
> of conventional economic wisdom that it may seem he-
> retical to suggest that it will be less valid in the future.
> But our study strongly suggests that, for purely physical
> reasons, at least the material consumption part of
> the economy will increasingly encounter limits to growth.[24]

CAPITALISM, ZERO GROWTH AND REDISTRIBUTION OF WEALTH

The end of the age of material expansion is upon us. The liberal ethos, a world view that has dominated the thinking of the industrialized nations for the past three centuries, is about to meet its final, climactic challenge, as new values begin to vie for public acceptance. The manner in which the United States and other industrialized nations choose to adjust to the new realities brought about by the coming age of scarcity will determine the parameters of the struggle that lies ahead.

Our capitalist economic system is, by its very nature, unequipped to meet the requirements of a nongrowth steady-state existence. Capitalism's essence is expansion: expansion of markets and expansion of profits. Without constant growth, the capitalist system would be unable to provide the surplus needed for new capital investment. Growth is the stimulus upon which our entire economic system is based. Growth under capitalism is essential to provide entrepreneurial incentives, employment opportunities, and expanded consumption.

Under the capitalist arrangement consideration for resource conservation, the rights of future generations or the costs associated with high-entropy pollution are secondary. By and large, these factors are viewed as external costs; if they are not ignored altogether, they are made the responsibility of the public and government.

The bottom line for United States corporations is profit. The objective is to exploit resources, labor and capital in the most effective way possible; in the short run, to maximize return on investment. For this reason, little self-policing effort is exerted on pollution control, because that means greater costs in production and consequently reduced profit margins. Similarly, up to now, resource husbandry has been virtually ignored by United States corporations. As long as nonrenewable (and renewable) resources remained relatively cheap in relation to other production costs—labor and capital—capitalist corporations had no choice but to exploit them without concern for the depletion because it served to boost returns on investments and the immediate profit picture of their respective enterprises.

The accumulation of unnecessary waste is an essential by-product of corporate growth. Because high turnover of goods increases profit and growth, a premium is placed on planned obsolescence. For example, 100 years ago a man would purchase one razor blade and use it (with periodic sharpening) for the rest of his life. Today, corporations sell him throwaway razor blades, which he uses up on the average of two a week. Over a life time he will use and discard 6,000 more blades than his grandfather did 100 years ago. That's 6,000 times more resources being used. Multiply that kind of planned waste by millions of American men, bearing in mind that throwaway razors are only one example that can be multiplied by thousands of other examples, and the scope of the waste problem begins to come into focus.

Nowhere is the problem of quick profits, unrestrained resource exploitation and planned waste more evident than in the automotive industry. Automobiles use up gigantic amounts of the earth's resources and are a major cause of air pollution. They are far less energy-efficient than mass transit. Yet, they have become central to the American economy because they fit the two major prerequisites of the capitalist system: high short-run profit and high product turnover. Today, one out of every six people in the United States has a job that is directly or indirectly dependent on automobile production.[25]

Up to now, there has been little public outcry over the exploitative and wasteful ways of the capitalist system. To a large extent, this is because the system's continued growth insured a greater amount of the spoils for everyone concerned. As long as the capitalist economic pie continued to expand, most everyone benefited to one degree or another—even if only marginally. Now that the pie is beginning to shrink, there is less material abundance to go around. As this economic contraction becomes more pronounced in the years ahead, there will be a fundamental change in the psychology of the American public. The once dominant liberal plea for greater participation in an expanding economic system will be replaced by cries for a more equitable redistribution of the remaining store of available wealth.

Economist Robert L. Heilbroner outlines the explosive realities of the redistribution issue. He points out that effective redistribution will entail much more than the dismantling of a handful of giant family fortunes. The real pressure from below, says Heilbroner, will be placed on redistribution of the wealth of the upper-middle class, who now account for only one-fifth of the population, but who consume over 40 percent of the nation's income.[26] The struggle for control over the nation's dwindling wealth will be between the working class and the poor on the one hand, and the upper-middle and upper classes on the other, and is likely to be more traumatic than anything previously experienced in United States history.

Even as this domestic battle begins to take shape, external pressures on the United States for redistribution of wealth will come from developing nations all over the world. The developing nations account for 70 percent of the world's population but only 11 percent of the world's total productive income.[27] By every standard of measurement, the gap in distribution of wealth between the United States (and other industrial nations) and the Third World is truly staggering. For example, in 1974 the per capita income of the United States averaged 6,600 dollars. In twenty-six Third World nations it averaged less than 300 dollars. In an additional twenty-eight nations, it was less than 750 dollars. Even though the world economy continues to grow (though at a declining rate), two-thirds of the world's population, according to the World Bank, experienced an annual per capita gain in income of less than one dollar over the past twenty years. The World Bank figures also show that nearly one out of every four people on the planet (1.2 billion) had incomes under 150 dollars per year, as of 1975.[28]

The figures for food distribution are equally dismal. One out of four people on the planet go to bed hungry every night. Meanwhile, American livestock are being fed more grain than is consumed by the entire 600 million population of India.[29]

The United States population is gobbling up the nonrenewable resources of the planet as fast as the renewable ones. The average United States consumer uses up 122 times more commercial energy than the average Nigerian.[30]

The basic amenities which most Americans take for granted for survival are almost nonexistent in many Third World countries. Two-thirds of the world's population live without minimum sewage and latrine systems. This lack of sanitation takes a gruesome toll on human life. Every single day 35,000 children die the world over, largely as a result of infection and disease spread by poor sanitation facilities.[31]

Many of these same Third World countries are the last remaining reservoirs for much of the world's diminishing resources, a fact that is now being politicized for the first time. As the industrial nations begin to experience critical shortages in nonrenewable and renewable resources, Third World countries are increasingly banding together into raw material cartels to exact higher prices. Following the lead of the OPEC nations, Third World cartels have been formed by the bauxite, copper and iron ore exporting nations, forcing world prices for these commodities up. Similar cartels are being formed for chrome, rubber, timber, lead and wool.[32] Says *Fortune* magazine, "[If the material exporters] succeed in this endeavor, the days of sustained improvement in living standards in the advanced industrial countries may well come to an end."[33]

Raw material cartels are the only effective tools the Third World has for forcing a redistribution of wealth from the have to the have-not nations. These cartels also represent a growing awareness by Third World countries that the "trickle down theory" of economic development, espoused by the industrial countries for so many years, has proven to be counterfeit. Even with all the tremendous economic growth of the developed nations since World War II, very little, if any, of the gains spilled over into meaningful economic development for the Third World. If anything, such expansion was possible largely by exploiting the cheap resources and labor of these countries. Now that world scarcity is a reality for everyone, the poorer nations are determined not to be taken advantage of any longer, especially when they hold the ultimate trump card—the remaining store of resources.[34]

Of course, demands for redistribution of wealth and the leverage of cartels does not in any way assure a greater redistribution of wealth within Third World countries. The sorry fact of the matter is that many of the poor nations that scream the loudest about redistributing the world's wealth have the poorest record of internal distribution on earth.

Unfortunately, much of the Third World is in a mad scramble to mimic the industrial development schemes of the world's superpowers—schemes which are responsible for the ecological and economic crisis. Their newfound wealth—resulting from cartel arrangements—is to be used for industrialization at the very time when the world's carrying capacity is being reached. The dire consequences of such action will be profound, not only in the nations that continue on this route, but on the world itself.

TWO PARADIGMS FOR THE FUTURE

It is obvious that the pressures and strains brought about by the transition from a growth to a nongrowth society are going to force significant changes in both the American way of life and the institutional arrangements that govern our economic and political structure.

A recent Harris Poll asked the American people which of two alternatives they would prefer: changing their lifestyle to consume fewer physical goods or risking continued inflation and unemployment because of raw material shortages. According to Harris, an overwhelming majority, 77 percent, favor a lifestyle change even though they realize that it would mean "cutting back on the amount we consume and waste and lowering the U.S. standard of living."[35] Whether, in fact, the great majority of the American people are willing to make the necessary sacrifices required to achieve a more equitable redistribution of wealth (both domestically and internationally) is, at the very least, problematic.

The American people have essentially two paradigms for the future from which to choose. Both are tailored to the strict requirements and limitations posed by a nongrowth steady-state environment. The first is the ideal steady state in which cooperation and sacrifice for mutual survival are the norm. The second is a kind of Hobbesian order, in which the "war of all against all" for the spoils of a contracting economic pie dominates the personal, economic and political life of the nation.[36]

When ecologists talk of the ideal steady state of the future, they presuppose a society in which the balance between the human demands placed on the environment and the ability of the environment to meet those demands without serious dislocation or destruction is established. A steady-state society, argue the environmentalists and a growing number of economists, should adhere as much as possible to the principles that guide natural ecosystems. All agree that population size must be stabilized. If population continues to increase while the economy is in a steady state, the result will be impoverishment and chaos. Emphasis should be placed on decentralized, self-sufficient communities. Nonrenewable resources should be conserved in favor of renewable sources of energy—primarily the sun. To help conserve the existing store of nonrenewable resources, production should rely on labor-intensive, as opposed to capital-intensive, methods. This should apply equally to the agricultural as well as the manufacturing and service sectors. While technology is not to be totally abandoned, it will, by necessity, have to play a reduced role in the steady-state society of the future. Technology will be geared to work as a servant rather than a master of the natural order and will be especially important as a tool for controlling and recycling wastes.

In the ideal steady state, enormous disparities in wealth will be greatly reduced. Redistribution, however essential, will comprise only half the solution. A steady-state society will require that each person live a much more frugal or spartan lifestyle. Consumption, rather than being an end of human existence, will revert to its original biological function. In the new society, the less production and consumption necessary to maintain a healthy, decent life the better.

Goals in life will shift from the material and physical to the spiritual and transcendent. The nature of work, as we understand it, will undergo a fundamental transformation. Human labor will no longer be considered as an exploitable factor in the production mix. Instead, work will be regarded as an important means of attaining purpose and direction in the world. Its material dimension, while still important, will not be the only measure of individual value.

The concept of private property will apply to consumer goods and services, but not land and other renewable and non-renewable resources. The long-accepted practice of private exploitation of "natural" property will be replaced with the notion of public stewardship for the common good. The orthodox interpretation of the liberal ethos, that the sum of each person's individual self-interest always serves the common good, will be regarded with suspicion or, more appropriately, outright derision. Individual rights will be protected, but they will no longer be the dominant reference point from which society is judged. Instead, public duty and responsibility will once again be the dominant social motif, as it has throughout most of history.

Ecologists generally divide into two schools of thought on the economic and political aspects of future government. The first might be considered Jeffersonian Democrats. They believe that government is best that governs least. They favor popular democracy over rule by the few and emphasize economic arrangements in which individuals exercise equal voice in affairs that affect life both in the workplace and in the community. Self-managed workers run enterprises and small democratically run city-states are the preferred economic and political forms.

Others are less sanguine about popular democracy. While they agree on the features of the steady state, they hold that the economic and ecological complexities of such a society preclude the average man and woman from the basic decision-making process. Intuition, they contend, is not sufficient to qualify most people to make judgments on the design, planning and execution of a steady-state environment. Likening the new world to a spaceship, they argue that in a closed-end system where one wrong move can spell disaster, a captain must be in charge. Otherwise, the ship might easily go down. Their thinking follows the Platonic tradition, namely that of benevolent and wise leaders guiding the affairs of a cultured and civilized state for the greater benefit of all of its constituents.

Finally, in the model steady state, science will no longer reign supreme as the arbiter of an absolute set of truths upon which all life is governed. The reductionist world view of science will be challenged. No longer will society hold that the whole equals the sum of its parts; that reality is only what can be quantified, observed and measured; that it is possible to understand the universal by first examining the particular. The new world view will place emphasis on a holistic approach to understanding. This holistic approach will correspond more with the realities of the natural ecosystems, where the whole is always greater than the sum of the parts, and where universals cannot possibly be understood by examining particulars in isolation. The holistic approach acknowledges that nothing in this world is autonomous; everything is united in a delicate web of intricate interrelationships that can only be truly examined as wholes in a complete, orderly functional system.

Just before his death the great world historian Arnold Toynbee provided an assessment of the likely course of future history in the United States and other industrial nations. Like most of the ecologists and economists, he foresaw a permanent state of seige for the developed nations as critical resource shortages and mounting pollution forced a wartime austerity on these once affluent lands. He was less optimistic, however, about the manner in which these new realities would be addressed. According to Toynbee:

> [In the] developed countries there will be a bitter struggle
> for the control of their diminished resources. This strug-
> gle will merely worsen a bad situation; it will somehow
> have to be stopped. If left unchecked, it would lead to
> anarchy and to a drastic reduction of the size of the
> population by civil war, famine and pestilence, the his-
> toric reducers of populations that have outgrown their
> means of subsistence. Consequently in all developed
> countries, a new way of life—a severely regimented
> way—will have to be imposed by a ruthless authoritarian
> government.[37]

The authoritarian steady-state paradigm that Toynbee reluctantly envisions would emphasize "holding on" to past standards of affluence at any cost. Within the United States the
upper-middle and wealthy classes, in consort with the giant
multinational corporations and government machinery, are likely
to attempt to impose rigid restrictions on basic rights and freedoms and ruthlessly suppress any attempt by the working and
poor segments of the population to secure a redistribution of
wealth.

If this paradigm dominates, more emphasis will be placed
on resource exploitation and technological development and
less on pollution controls, as those in power attempt to maintain
an existing standard of living in the face of national and world
economic loss.

In order to maintain the privilege of America's ruling classes,
it will be necessary to insure the mobility (and access to world
markets) of America's giant multinational corporations. These
transnational enterprises are the key lifeline for pumping the
wealth of the Third World into the American economic artery.
Keeping that lifeline open in the midst of rising Third World
movements for redistribution of wealth will mean even greater
reliance on the coercive power of United States military strength
across the globe. Increased military budgets will further exacerbate resource shortages and put additional strains on the
environment; all of which will further worsen the material condition of the poor and working people both in the United States
and abroad.

The increased tensions which result from a more militant
United States military machine are likely to result in a catas-
trophe for the planet. In twenty years, according to Admiral
Gene LaRocque of the Center for Defense Information, nearly

100 countries will have the nuclear bomb. Forced to the wall by a United States military policy designed to protect the exploitive interests of transnational corporations, while at the same time experiencing massive starvation, disease and death, the likelihood of a nuclear strike by one or more of these 100 countries is real. Such a limited nuclear strike could easily touch off worldwide nuclear holocaust. In the final analysis, the irony of this would provide interesting commentary, if only there was someone left to chronicle it. After all, the first dramatic realization of the concept of "physical limits" was experienced in 1945 when the United States dropped the first A-bomb on Hiroshima. With the dropping of the bomb, humanity had finally arrived at the ultimate power that Bacon, Smith and Locke urged so long ago; finally, man, himself, was the undisputed master of the world's ultimate destiny. Unfortunately, the age of material expansion and the liberal ethos which brought us to the A-bomb and has now driven us to the limit of the earth's carrying capacity, never provided more than a rationale and an effective set of mechanisms for creating disorder and destruction in the world. The liberal ethos is reminiscent of a famous one-liner uttered during the Vietnam War. A United States general, after looking over the total devastation of a so-called "friendly city" by United States war planes, remarked: "We had to destroy the city in order to save it. . . ."

THE EMERGING ORDER

You can't stop progress! This phrase is so much a part of our concept of modern life that it has taken on all the dimensions of a religious conviction. It serves, at once, both as an article of faith in the unlimited material possibilities open to humanity and as a warning that progress is greater than any mere mortal and, as such, is not amenable to substantial reservation, qualification or restriction. Progress has, indeed, become an autonomous force, rushing inextricably forward with neither a specific destination nor timetable. Human beings, at first willing passengers on the rails of progress, were excited by the great potential adventures that lay ahead; now they have become increasingly disillusioned with the journey and their experience. Afraid to jump off for fear of being abandoned to an uncertain fate, and equally afraid to continue on a journey they are convinced is moving toward some terrible crash, they remain frozen and immobilized, unable to act, preferring instead to place their destiny in the hands of forces beyond their reach and control.

This describes the mass psychology of a nation which no longer adheres uncritically to the principal assumptions of its own guiding ethos. Even as the American people continue to hold on to the notion of unstoppable progress, they find it impossible to escape from the fragmented remains of what used to be a seemingly invincible vision. We tell ourselves, it isn't happening, that what we are experiencing and feeling is not real, or is, perhaps, only a temporary condition. We can't possibly afford to think otherwise. Soedjatmoko, former Indonesian Ambassador to the United Nations, put it well when he said: "Once growth ceases to be our reason for being, then we have to ask basic questions about the purpose and meaning of life."[38]

The liberal ethos—the consensus that emerged from the Age of Reason, science, technology and progress—no longer adequately answers our most basic questions. Our expansionary value system no longer fits the reality of a physical world where absolute limits to growth demand a revolutionary accommodation in our world view.

Other great economic transformations in world history forced similar changes in humanity's outlook. But as Lester Brown points out, the agricultural revolution took place over thousands of years, while the industrial revolution took several hundred years. In contrast, the transformation to the postmodern era of the steady state will take place in just a few short decades, forcing a revoluionary change in myths, values, and governing arrangements in a time span roughly equal to that which separates parent and child.[39]

The metamorphosis in values and social behavior that this calls for is profound. No ordinary measures, no amount of patriotism, no legislative resolves, can hope to replace the expectations of the past 500 years overnight. What is called for is a qualitative leap from the end of one epoch into the beginning of another. Such leaps are rare in human history. They require an act of collective faith of Herculean proportions.

For a half a millennium, modern men and women have defined their existence along a horizontal plane. Each generation has striven more and more earnestly to find its fulfillment in increased material wealth through economic growth. This is the guiding ethos of our existence, as surely as theocentrism was for the Middle Ages.

Throughout the modern age, skeptics have claimed to understand the dilemma of the human race and have decried our being caught up in a frantic, but futile search for the promised heaven on earth. For a long time these critics could be ignored because there was always the hope that through a combination of hard work, ingenuity and sheer willpower, the earthly cornucopia could be realized. Now that hope is vanishing, as human society comes up against the fixed limits of the horizontal world.

As this crisis deepens, especially in the West, a growing number of historians, ecologists, economists and anthropologists ask: What will replace materialism? Most agree that regardless of how the transformation to the age of scarcity takes place, the focus of human existence will change from the horizontal plane of materialism to the vertical plane of spiritualism. Only a massive spiritual upheaval, they argue, can provide both the elements of a new world view and the faith and discipline needed to put it into practice.

Some commentators already see evidences of a new spiritual revival in the mounting interest in Eastern religions, the rise of "cults," and the growth of the human potential movement. While these are certainly manifestations of an increased disenchantment with the philosophy of the modern age, it is unlikely that these forces will play the dominant role in the emerging spiritual revolution.

America is a Christian nation, and it is within the Christian community that a renewed religious awakening will be most deeply felt. In fact, though it is difficult to imagine, what may well emerge in the years to come is nothing short of a second Protestant reformation, one that may have as powerful an effect on the world as the first. Already Protestant doctrine is being transformed by the epochal shifts occurring in the economic world. These changes in doctrine are, in turn, beginning to shape and define the specific direction of these economic forces.

It is important to bear in mind that the physical and spiritual planes of human life exist in a symbiotic relationship. Religious beliefs are constantly being integrated into the physical of human existence. Similarly, people's economic life is continually being defined by their religious convictions. As already noted, the first Protestant Reformation was a driving force behind the economic expansion of the West. Capitalist development, in turn, helped institutionalize the Protestant ethic as a world view. Together, Protestantism and the liberal economic philosophy of capitalism transformed the planet. Now, a new order is emerging from the realization that the world is moving from the age of growth to the age of scarcity. Whether the emerging order will more closely resemble the cooperative steady-state paradigm of the ecologists, or the Hobbesian paradigm of a war of all against all, will to a large extent depend on the kind of religious transformation that American Protestantism undergoes in the ensuing two decades.

Of two things we can be sure: a massive religious awakening is in the offing and the first rumblings of this change can already be heard.

THE RELIGIOUS RESPONSE

AMERICA'S NEW SPIRITUAL AWAKENING

"The cumulative evidence suggests that the late seventies could, in fact, mark the beginning of a religious revival in America."

This is the central finding of an extensive and detailed survey of religion in America conducted by George Gallup in 1977. Gallup based his conclusions on several key factors. First, the percentage of Americans who believe that religion is increasing its influence over American life has nearly tripled since 1970. Secondly, for the first time in over twenty years, church attendance has begun to show a marked increase. Today 42 percent of all adults in America attend religious services at least once a week. Third, there has been a sharp increase in the number of Americans who are engaging in more experiential religious encounters, as opposed to the rather detached and formal church experience that characterized the 1950s and 1960s.

The two overriding reasons for this renewed interest in religion according to Gallup are: "The general turning inward to seek refuge from everyday pressures," and "a search for non-material values in light of the fading American Dream."[1]

While Gallup's explanations are a bit superficial, they in no way undermine his basic findings. The fact is that there is a storm brewing of major proportions within American Christianity. If it continues to gain in density it could well burst with a force powerful enough to change the American climacteric for a century to come.

The eye of this spiritual storm is the Christian Evangelical Movement. There are currently around 45 million evangelical

Christians in the United States.[2] Evangelical comes from the Greek root *evangelion*, which means the good news. Evangelism is the active spreading of the good news, "that Jesus Christ came into the world to save sinners from the consequence of their sins, to make them whole, to reconcile them to God."[3] While there are many shades of evangelical doctrine, there are three generally accepted tenets that most evangelicals adhere to: First, "the complete reliability and formal authority of Scripture in matters of faith and practice"; second, "the necessity of a personal faith in Jesus Christ as Savior from sin and consequent commitment to Him as Lord"; and third, "the urgency of seeking actively the conversion of sinners to Christ."[4]

Underneath this rather broad outer garment is an inner set of specific beliefs that seem curiously at odds with contemporary secular culture. In this age of space travel and computer technology, the spirituality of evangelicals appears almost like an aberrant intrusion upon the modern age, a relic from a mystical bygone era that is tolerated in our midst, like a piece of ancient architecture that has withstood the assault of centuries past. But before the cosmopolitan mind dismisses such views as interesting anthropological diversions, it should be pointed out that 58 percent of all Americans say these beliefs are very important in their personal lives.[5]

The specific beliefs they refer to, all of which are firmly embedded within the evangelical tradition, include the following:

*71 percent of all Protestants believe that God really exists and they have no doubt about it.

*86 percent of all Protestants believe in the Trinity—the Father, Son and Holy Ghost.

*73 percent believe that Jesus is God.

*57 percent believe that the Virgin birth was "completely true."

*44 percent believe that Jesus will "definitely" return to earth and another 10 percent believe it is probable.

*Over half of all Protestants believe that the "miracles actually happened just as the Bible says they did."

*75 percent believe their souls "will live on after death."

*71 percent believe there is a heaven and over 54 percent believe there is a hell.

*Over 65 percent say that belief in Jesus Christ as Savior is "absolutely necessary for salvation."

*52 percent believe that "holding the Bible to be God's truth is absolutely necessary."[6]

Just as important as these statistical breakdowns is the fact that nearly one in every three Americans now claim to have "been born again," that is, to have undergone a profound personal experience which has led to a renewed commitment to Christ. Moreover, many are anxious to share their experience with others in the hope of spreading the "Good News" and saving souls for Christ. Today 47 percent of all Americans say they have evangelized or witnessed with friends, family relations, neighbors and even strangers.[7]

All of this may come as a shock to the liberal Eastern establishment. But, there has been, for quite a long time, two different Americans in America; this second American has not received much attention until recently. In fact, since the American press pounded out their last line of copy at the Dayton, Tennessee, Scopes trial in 1925, evangelical America has remained a virtual nonstory—with the exception of an occasional report on anticommunist Fundamentalist sects and coverage of a Billy Graham rally from time to time.

Evangelical America is the silent majority that Nixon and Agnew spoke to and for during the turbulent years of the 1960s. Now, with liberal philosophy in shambles, with the economy on the skids and with a Christian conservative in the Oval Office, this silent majority is beginning to find its own voice. And that voice is beginning to find a larger and more attentive audience as America takes its first tentative steps into the 1980s.

Already, the evangelical renaissance has eclipsed the once powerful liberal-oriented mainline denominations represented by the National Council of Churches. Dean Kelley, in his book *Why Conservative Churches Are Growing,* points out that in the 1960s, for the first time in American history, "Most of the major church groups [the mainline churches] stopped growing and began to shrink."[8] They include the United Methodist, the Episcopal church, the United Presbyterian Church of the United States and the United Church of Christ.[9] While these mainline, liberal-leaning churches are showing significant declines in membership, the evangelically oriented churches are "overflowing with vitality." Evangelical denominations showing major growth in the past decade include the Southern Baptist Convention, the Assemblies of God, the Church of God, and the Pentacostals.[10] In addition, nearly one-third of the membership in mainline church denominations of the NCC are evangelicals.[11]

There are countless explanations for this historic shift within the Christian community. The major reason, however, is the growing gap between the ministry's definition of the role of the church and the layperson's individual needs. Since World War II, mainline church professionals have put increasing stress on the church as a vehicle for social involvement. This orientation reached its high-water mark in the 1960s as church bureaucrats and ministers urged their congregations to actively support and work for broad social changes that were taking shape during the Kennedy years and later under Johnson's Great Society campaigns. Relations between middle-of-the-road or conservative congregations and activist ministers and church officials became more intense and finally exploded into open hostility and recrimination in the late 1960s as the Civil Rights and anti-War movements turned more militant, and as rioting in the cities and carnage in Vietnam invaded the inner sanctums of middle American life.

Church officials were accused by parishioners of ignoring their primary responsibility to attend to the personal spiritual needs of their congregations, preach the scriptures, and bring converts to Christ. Church members were castigated by their ministers for turning away from Christian concerns for the world and ignoring the cries of suffering humanity at their doorsteps. Both were, of course, partially justified in their claims. The upshot was loss of mainline church membership and, for many, a turn toward the evangelical churches to answer the personal need for spiritual guidance and/or spiritual refuge.

With the liberal ethos in decline, the evangelicals are finding an even more fertile environment than in the 1960s for their theological doctrine. The country is turning to evangelicalism at the very time that it is beginning to question many of the basic assumptions that have underscored the American age of economic expansion, assumptions concerning the central role of science, technology, material values and the Age of Reason. The complex interrelationship between the new evangelical awakening and the larger changes going on in American life is the omega point for an examination of how the country will ultimately deal with the end of the age of expansion and the beginning of the age of the steady state.

Before beginning to dissect the interrelationship, a comparison between the new evangelical phenomenon and the counterculture phenomenon of the 1960s might prove helpful.

The counterculture movement was doomed from the start. The determination to forge an alternative lifestyle for society was effectively blocked, not so much by brute force (although that certainly came into play) as by manipulation and absorption at the hands of Madison Avenue advertising and Los Angeles promotion techniques. Like a giant threshing machine, the corporate establishment carefully separated the ideological content of the movement from the forms it came in. The content, in turn, was discarded while the forms were packaged and sold in the open marketplace as part of the "now" generation.

To be sure, the mercurial nature of the counterculture movement contributed to its own demise—as did the harsh realities in the larger society that continued to bombard it from every side. It was hard to sustain flower power in the midst of militant black power, student power, police power and military power.

Most important, the Woodstock Nation was simply lacking in the essential ingredients necessary to create a truly alternative society. The counterculture did not control its own communications and never developed a meaningful infrastructure. As a result, there was always a great deal of talk about creating a sense of community, but the community never went much beyond pitched tents, makeshift campsites, good dope, electric rock and mellow memories. In the end, Madison Avenue dictated the styles and Los Angeles promoters created the structures.

The evangelical movement of the late 1970s is very different. While the corporate establishment is doing its utmost to defuse the movement and package its more salable features for public consumption, it's finding the task more difficult than that with the counterculture. To some extent this is because the evangelical movement, unlike the counterculture, controls its own communications. Its messages are less amenable to take-over and reinterpretation by the commercial media, simply because its own communications structure is formidable enough to withstand a frontal assault. Equally important, the evangelical phenomenon has not emerged in a vacuum. It is backed up by a historical tradition firmly embedded in the popular mind and an infrastructure that is strong enough to provide the beginnings of a sense of community. In fact, that infrastructure represents the "only" permanent set of institutions in this society that are viable enough to offer an alternative base from which to challenge the existing order. This is not to imply that such a challenge is forthcoming, only that it exists as a potential possibility.

That very possibility, however, is continually ignored by social scientists who prefer to view the Christian subculture as a permanent appendage to the status quo. As we will see, their memory is short. Twice before in American history it was the evangelical Christian communications system and infrastructure that served as the lightning rod for a fundamental challenge to the established authority. The first great evangelical awakening gave birth to the American Revolution. The second great evangelical revival spawned the abolitionist movement and helped trigger the Civil War.

The evangelical Christian communication system is more highly developed and effective today than at any time in American history. The same holds true for the evangelical infrastructure. Evangelicals are building their own Christian community with a zealous determination that is apt to make an "outsider" feel more than a bit apprehensive. That structure is likely to serve one of several functions in the 1980s. It could become a refuge or retreat for the white Protestant middle class as they experience a worsening series of economic convulsions. It is even possible that at some critical point, it could serve as a springboard for a full-scale fascist movement, encouraged and supported by the immense power of the capitalist state. Then again, it may, as was the case during America's two great spiritual awakenings of the past, serve as a base of operations for a challenge to the existing order or a catalyst for a revolutionary vision of society. Of course, it is possible that the evangelical communications network and infrastructure could eventually fragment into many disparate parts, or peter out altogether, as a result of internal splits and divisions combined with overwhelming influence exerted on it by the secular environment.

Of one thing there is little doubt, the evangelical community is amassing a base of potential power that dwarfs every other competing interest in American society today. A close look at the evangelical communications network and infrastructure should convince even the skeptic that it is now the single most important cultural force in American life.

Evangelical Communications System

In an advanced technological society, communications are the chief weapons of control. Since the moment the RCA dog, Nipper, first cocked his head into a Victrola, corporate America has exercised a virtual monopoly over the country's expanding mass communications arsenal. Now, for the first time, the major TV and radio networks and their commerical sponsors are being directly challenged by a powerful new communications force. Its programming philosophy is to spread the good word of Christ. Its sponsors are tens of millions of born-again Christians. Its market audience is the planet earth. Its advertising goal is to bring three billion human beings to Christ between now and the millenium in the year A.D. 2000.[12]

Today, 1300 radio stations—one out of every seven in America—is Christian owned and operated. Every seven days a new Christian-owned radio station is established.[13] Together, these stations reach a listening audience of 150 million people. At the same time, Christian broadcasters are adding one new owned and operated television station to their arsenal every thirty days:[14] presently these stations claim a viewing audience of thirteen million households, or nearly 20 percent of the entire United States viewing public. In fiscal 1970, Christian TV programs purchased a whopping half-billion dollars worth of commercial airtime, much of it prime time, to spread their message. Evangelical Christian religious shows like Rex Hubbard's "Cathedral of Tomorrow" and "Oral Roberts and You" are now watched by as many viewers as the "Merv Griffin Show" and other popular commercial talk-show programs. All indications are that such programming will continue to grow even more significantly over the next ten years.

Backed up by the most sophisticated communications hardware that money can buy, evangelicals are now threatening the long-standing hegemony over the airwaves previously enjoyed by CBS, NBC and ABC. With earth-satellite stations across the world, two Christian television networks are already beaming live programs to every major market twenty-four hours per day.[15] All of this is just for openers, boasts Jim Bakker, head of PTL Television Network. PTL stands both for "People That Love" and "Praise The Lord."[16] The network was started just four years ago. In that short time span, its anchor program, the "PTL Club," has become, "the most viewed daily television program in the world." With 179 TV affiliates (ABC has 191) PTL is now the fourth largest purchaser of airtime in the United States. The "PTL Club" provides a talk-show format, featuring well-known celebrities from the evangelical world, politics, business, sports, and so forth. To qualify as a guest, however, one has to have had a "born-again" experience and be willing to share it, on camera, with PTL's twenty-million Christian viewers throughout the nation and the world.[17]

Recently the PTL network installed its first fully operated satellite hookup for live coverage to every continent. At the dedication ceremonies, Mr. Bakker proclaimed that "this [satellite hookup] is one of the most historic developments in the entire church history to fulfill the great commission of Christ to go in to all the World and preach the Gospel to every creature." "We have begun a broadcast," said Bakker, "that will not stop 'til Jesus comes."[18]

From its broadcast center in Charlotte, North Carolina, a staff of over 550 employees,[19] using nearly two million dollars of the most advanced TV equipment available, prepare a range of daily programming while simultaneously serving the one-half million PTL "members" whose yearly contributions of twenty-five million dollars keep the whole operation afloat.[20]

A rival network, the Christian Broadcasting Network (CBN), with headquarters in Virginia Beach, Virginia, is headed up by its founder Pat Robertson. Like the "PTL Club," CBN has its own anchor program called the "700 Club." The format is virtually identical to Bakker's. CBN has also installed world-wide satellite communications, boasts a staff of 700 and brings in its twenty-two million dollars a year operating budget in contributions from 500,000 members around the country.[21]

Both the "PTL Club" and CBN's "700 Club" have pioneered the concept of "two-way television." During the show viewers are urged to call in and discuss their personal and spiritual problems with some of the 7,000 trained volunteers staffing some sixty regional telephone centers strategically placed across the country.[22] The "700 Club" alone received over 1.25 million calls last year.[23] The "PTL Club" received approximately the same number.

. . . The studio lights darken, the camera scans the audience as heads are lowered in prayer . . . looking into camera left, the Reverend James Bakker, attired in an egg-blue suit, standing against a blue-velvet background, begins quietly:

There is a prostate gland condition that God is healing right now . . . there is a spinal condition, perhaps a missing disc that is being restored . . . someone to my left has a kidney ailment . . . there are growths and in the name of Jesus those growths are gone . . . you will not need surgery . . . there is something that goes into the marrow of the bone, maybe it's leukemia . . . the Lord is healing it.[24]

A toll-free telephone number is flashed on and off the TV screen. The telephone banks begin to light up as thousands of callers from across the country dial in. The operators have a computer form in front of them listing ailments in alphabetical order, starting with arthritis. Other boxes list major emotional and spiritual problem areas.[25]

Back in the studio, Bakker urges his home audience to join in *now:*

Today his spirit is saying you will accept Jesus in your heart . . . You say to me, "Jim, some other day." You've said that so many days. Don't turn off the TV. Don't say, "I can't make a decision." Pray with me. Call one of our counselors at 704–555–6000. Say "I pray with Jim and I have given my heart to Jesus."[26]

From the audience, soft cries of "Thank you, Jesus" and "Praise the Lord" are barely audible underneath the organ music. Back in the counseling center, a staff member has just finished an emotional conversation with a lady caller.

Phew! She was in bad shape. She's divorced and depressed and misses her husband very much. She had her toes cut off and they were sewn back on and she's in pain . . . I said she should focus her eyes on Jesus. She said she was. I said she should focus more. She said every time she picked up the Bible she couldn't concentrate on it. So I gave her some verses. [She pointed to a printed blue card all the counselors had before them, on which inspirational Bible verses were grouped by subject.] I gave her some from "Depression," "Divorce" and "Fear."[27]

Both Bakker and Robertson are Charismatic evangelicals. The gift of spiritual healing plays a major role in their broadcast ministries. Says Robertson, "We get about 25,000 reports a year from people who are healed. . . . All we can say is that if they are all wrong, there are an awful lot of liars out there."[28]

The philosophy of both networks is summed up by Bakker. "I believe that Christian television will be the tool that ushers in the triumphant return of Jesus Christ."[29]

To insure that there will be a steady supply of well-trained Christian reporters, technicians and programming experts available between now and then, both CBN and PTL have just completed multimillion-dollar communications schools. They are being flooded with applications from every state.[30]

Because they realize that in order for Christian TV networks to succeed they will have to compete with the commercial networks in providing a varied schedule of programming, both PTL and CBN are expanding their repertoire of shows to include sports coverage, sitcoms, variety shows and soap operas. Yes, even Christian soap operas.

> Why has John lost interest in being a daily Bible reader? Will Marsha meet her visitation quota this month? And what will happen when Pastor Perkins discovers his choir director is a Moonie?[31]

CBN announced that it would inaugurate a fourth television news network to compete with Cronkite, Chancellor and Reynolds in the fall of 1978. Headed by former *New York Times* editor, Robert Slosser, and a projected staff of 200 correspondents from all over the world, Robertson says he expects to capture 10 percent of the evening news audience. That means one out of every ten Americans receiving their total news information each night from an evangelical-owned news network.[32] Slosser says of the new thirty-minute global TV news show:

> The Christian journalist should bring God back into consideration, and, in fact, give Him number one spot. I believe with all my heart that Jesus Christ is the light of the world and we should be able to view the world through that light.[33]

Robertson's determination to build a fourth news network is reflective of the interest he shares with many other evangelical leaders who are anxious to present a Christian perspective as an alternative to what they regard as a strictly secular, humanist perspective on the events of the day appearing in the commercial media. Robertson's own approach to politics and world events is eclectic and hard to categorize. For example, discussing the concept of political legitimacy, Robertson remarked that:

> God wants stability. It's better to have a stable government under a crook than turmoil under a honest man.

Robertson says that if people do not agree with their political leaders they should vote them out of office. Of course, as one reporter noted, he doesn't say what his viewers in Brazil and the Philippines should do, since both countries are run by military dictatorships. On the other hand, Robertson has gone much farther than the other electronic evangelists in advancing the issue of economic justice. In a recent edition of his newsletter to supporters, he called for a jubilee year, the cancellation of debts between rich and poor nations, and a greater concern for redistribution of resources between all people. His television broadcasts have occasionally highlighted the problems of world hunger and he has many times expressed concern over the need for all Christians to serve as stewards, protecting God's creation and sharing God's resources equitably.

While Robertson has not involved himself in the political fray to the extent of Jerry Falwell he has made clear his belief that more evangelical Christians need to be involved in electoral politics. "The thing to do," says Robertson, "is to locate born-again Christians, and when you find them, put them in office."[35]

While PTL and CBN are receiving the most attention by media observers, they have by no means cornered the Christian TV market. Others like Jerry Falwell, Oral Roberts, Billy Graham, Rex Hubbard and Robert Schuller oversee massive multimillion-dollar TV and radio operations which match CBN and PTL in both audience and income generated.

In addition, thousands of neighborhood Christian churches are beginning to turn to television as a primary medium to reach into their communities. Local churches are actively involved in a crusade to capture local cable TV outlets. With twelve million homes already served by 3400 cable systems, the outcome of these evangelical efforts to dominate cable programming is of growing importance.³⁶ When two California broadcast consultants filed a petition to the FCC in 1975 to limit the use of noncommercial TV frequencies by religious groups, the government agency was besieged by a record number of letters from evangelical Christians opposed to the suit. The petition argued that such noncommercial frequencies were meant to be used for educational and religious programming of a broad denominational nature, but that the evangelicals were taking to the airwaves with a one-sided religious viewpoint that is "narrow, prejudiced, blind and stultifying."³⁷

Local evangelical Christians appear undaunted by the charges. Warning the faithful that the devil already "has quite a few stations" in his camp, believers are encouraged "not to surrender the airwaves to Satan."³⁸

All Christian programming, whether it originates from the slick studios of CBN in Virginia Beach or from local church basements, is mainly viewer and listener sponsored. That's not to suggest that the evangelicals haven't picked up a few pointers from Madison Avenue. On the contrary. As advertising consultant Bob Bloom observed: "We are trying to sell a product, and that product is Jesus Christ." Bloom's high-powered Texas advertising agency was commissioned by the Baptist General Convention of Texas a few years ago to spread the "Good News" of Jesus Christ to every man, woman and child in the state through a saturation TV, radio and print media advertising campaign. After their market research showed them that the number one problem troubling Texans was "hopelessness," the Bloom agency set about developing a series of slick thirty-second ads featuring well-known sports and entertainment personalities telling of how Christ changed their lives from ones of despair to hope. Over 4,000 local churches tied in with the media campaign in an effort to evangelize new recruits into their denominations. For example, in Paris, Texas, the local church hosted what it referred to as "A Double Miracle Day" to double church attendance. The day's events featured revivals led by "an assistant Dallas Cowboy coach, a millionaire interior designer, Miss Teen-Age America and the Yo-Yo champion of the World."³⁹ Texas is known for doing things up in a big way. Still this use of mass-media advertising is bush league compared to the recent "I found it" campaign conducted throughout the country:

Ad Voice: I found it... and you can find it too.

Ad Voice: You've heard it on radio. You've seen it on TV, on billboards. So, what does it mean?

Ad Voice: Is it a new bank?

Ad Voice: I think it's one of them fried chicken places.

Ad Voice: Beats me. It's a movie, right?

Ad Voice: Sorry, so far you're not even close. But don't worry. When you find it, you'll know it.

Announcer: For your free book call 555–1710.

When people called into local phone banks in cities all over America, they found that "it" was the "Good News" of Jesus Christ as Savior, and the free book they received outlined how they, in turn, could be saved.[40]

This multimillion-dollar advertising campaign is only a warm-up for what lies ahead. A consortium of major American business leaders, led by Nelson Hunt, of the Hunt Oil Company, and Wallace Johnson, founder of Holiday Inn, has joined with Bill Bright of Campus Crusade for Christ in announcing a one-billion-dollar mass-media advertising campaign to evangelize every man, woman and child on earth, at least once, in preparation for the millenium. That's right. One billion dollars. The first one hundred million dollars is already in hand. This campaign will mark the largest "single" budget ever amassed for electronic (and print) advertising, thus dramatically eclipsing anything previously done by any of the major corporate advertisers.[41]

Network executives at ABC, NBC and CBS and their friends a few blocks away on Madison Avenue are beginning to sit up and take notice of this new evangelical communications phenomenon. Even as they try to find ways to undercut its challenge to their dominance of the American airwaves, the commercial publishing industry finds itself facing a similar challenge. A few years ago not many editors on publishers row would have even recognized imprints like Moody, Revell, Zondervan, Eerdmans, Word and Logos International. Today those imprints are threatening to match, dollar for dollar, the sales figures of some of the commerical publishing houses. The Christian book publishing market has grown signifcantly every single year since 1969. In fiscal 1977 its 2,300 member bookstores experienced a 19.3 percent increase in gross sales over the previous twelve months.[42] Says Charles Shanks, general director of a thirteen-store chain in Pennsylvania: "There was a time when the religious bookstore business was limited to the active, involved churchgoer. But now the general public is interested in religious books." [43] Indeed, they are. So much so that total religious book sales in 1976 were nearly one billion dollars, which amounted to one-third of the gross sales of the entire commercial book market. Although *The New York Times* best-seller list has long refused to acknowledge the Christian book market, it is a fact that the number one best-seller of 1976 was not Woodward and Bernstein's *The Final Days*, but Billy Graham's *Angels*. And in 1975, it wasn't *Looking for Mr. Goodbar* or *Bermuda Triangle,* but Marabel Morgan's *Total Woman* which topped the charts. [44]

Even the music industry has been invaded by the evangelical movement. Christian recording artists like Anita Bryant, Dave Stookey, Carol Laurence, Johnny Cash and Debbie Boone, whose Christian song, "You Light Up My Life," was the top record of 1977, are in growing demand. As a result, Christian recording companies are growing by leaps and bounds. [45]

The evangelical challenge to the commercial publishing and recording industries, though formidable, is still secondary in importance to its newly developed relationship with the television medium. The potentially historic impact of this relationship can only be appreciated by comparing it with the advent of print just prior to the Reformation.

The Gutenberg printing press made printed material available to the masses for the first time in the early sixteenth century. By 1500, according to the *Encyclopedia Britannica:*

> more than 1700 presses in almost 300 towns had produced one or more books. It is estimated that almost 40,000 editions were published during the fifteenth century, comprising somewhere between 15,000,000 and 20,000,000 volumes . . . mainly liturgical, theological and legal works . . . [46]

Before the invention of the printing press, the written word was preserved largely through the efforts of monks who were subject to the Catholic Church. This gave the Church a virtual monopoly over reading and manuscript duplication and assured their authority over the interpretation of Christian doctrine as well. The printing press changed all of that overnight. By making the Bible readily available to everyone, Gutenberg helped set the conditions for the Reformation's challenge to the authority of the Church. Luther and Calvin's emphasis on the need for each sinner to read the Bible and serve as his own priestly interpreter of God's revealed truths could not have happened without the revolution in communications brought about by the print medium.[47]

Now six centuries later, the print medium is being eclipsed by a new medium—television. In just thirty years, electronic communication has changed the entire way people conceptualize the world around them. In the process, it is dramatically changing the way people perceive Christian faith and doctrine. A revolution in Christianity is beginning to unfold, and it owes much of its impetus to television, just as the Reformation owed much of its impetus to print. The movement from print to TV has transformed the human mind. The sensual and experiential mode of instant television communications has replaced the objective and analytical mode of reflective print communications. Time and distance have been overtaken by spontaneity and immediacy.[48] The individual no longer thinks as much as he acts. He no longer ponders as much as he experiences. This new conceptual mode will transform much of Christian doctrine between now and the turn of the century. The Charismatic phenomenon represents the first significant step in that transformation process. (See Chapter 10.)

Of course, it's not the intention of TV evangelicals to revolutionize Christian theology. If they thought there was a chance of that happening, they probably would not be rushing in where Reformation angels would, no doubt, fear to tread. Instead, today's TV evangelical pioneers still believe they can use the electronic medium to spread a doctrine born and weaned in the old print medium. Along the way, they are finding out, however, that certain innovative approaches and appeals work better on TV than others in winning over their audiences to Christ. It is this innovative trial and error process that is unconsciously helping to shape the components of a new theological perspective. While evangelicals continue to exploit the TV medium to influence their public, they have not yet fully realized how much the medium, in turn, is influencing their own personal shifts in theological emphasis and interpretation.

In the meantime, an article in the evangelical publication, *Christianity Today*, entitled "Moving Upon the Media," perhaps best sums up the current thinking on the need to expand Christian efforts in the electronic arena.

They [evangelicals] should be infiltrating the field of communications, taking over posts of leadership, moving up and moving in . . . God has no desire to turn over the communications system to the prince of the power of the air . . . God did commit to "us" the saving message of the Gospel. We are servants of truth . . . commissioned to carry the divine treasure. We are told not to throw this treasure to the swine, we are told to offer it to men—through the media.[49]

INFRASTRUCTURE
"BUILDING A TOTAL CHRISTIAN COMMUNITY"

Evangelical Christians are much more likely to focus their social life around church related programs and activities than other Christians. A survey done by sociologists Glock and Stark found that among evangelicals, over half of their close friends are likely to belong to the same congregation, whereas among liberal churchgoers, such as Presbyterians and Congregationalists, few or none of their close friends are likely to be members of their local church.[50]

The evangelical church, then, is much more than a place of worship. It also serves as a community for its members. In the past eight or nine years the community aspect of evangelical involvement has mushroomed. So much so that critics now worry out loud that the so-called "Christian Community" might begin to pose a serious threat to the notion of religious tolerance in America. Others, more favorably disposed, see this trend toward the development of a "total Christian lifestyle" as a precursor to a possible assault on the materialist oriented secular culture.

Evangelicals now talk enthusiastically about the development of a "total church living complex." Typical of this new approach is Faith City, a Baptist church complex under construction in Tampa, Florida. When completed, Faith City will contain a senior citizens home, an orphanage, a college campus, a ranch for boys, a church and a Sunday School, a bus garage, a lake and parks. Other evangelical churches are planning to set up Christian banks, Christian cafeterias, Christian medical offices, Christian motels, and even Christian beauty shops "where women can get their hair curled to the glory of God."

This is all part of a new concept, the "Christian shopping center." Piggybacking off the success of commercial shopping centers, many evangelicals believe that a central church complex surrounded by a mall featuring "specialty" services can provide for the "total" needs of the evangelical Christian, and thus keep the church at the center of the believer's daily life.[51]

In fact, it's not just the daily life of their members they are concerned with. It's also their night life. In the past few years Christian nightclubs have been popping up all over the country. Most of the clubs prohibit dancing, and none serve alcoholic beverages. The Daisy in Beverly Hills, California, is typical. Ironically, in the early 1960s the Daisy was the home of the most fashionable discotheque in the country. Its founder said that the disco's success was largely attributable to the fact that celebrities needed someplace "evil" to go. Its Christian replacement, however, is better known for its wholesome grape juice cocktails and the sound of gospel groups with names like the "Spiritual Essence." A born-again Christian can now travel to many of America's major cities and find himself a cozy Christian supper club or night spot to unwind in.[52] With names like Little Eden and Lighthouse, the clubs, by and large, seem to be thriving. Says the assistant manager of Heralds Christian Supper Club in Minneapolis, "The club seats 250, and we're packed every weekend."[53] Still, the competition is skeptical. David Aronsohn, owner of the Blue Ox, a singles bar a few blocks away from Heralds Christian Supper Club, says: "Booze is the answer. Nobody else has done it without booze." Mr. Vogel, the forty-one-year-old owner of Heralds, says he's placing his faith in Jesus instead:

> I believe that if God leads you to do something, he will
> see you through. My only sustaining power is that faith.
> Without it, I probably would be a nervous wreck.[54]

God might well be rooting for Mr. Vogel, but just to insure that his prayers are answered, he can always advertise in the Minneapolis St. Paul "Christian Business Directory." The directory is one of several hundred in cities across the country that contain the names of businesses whose owners have signed an oath that they are born-again Christians. According to the

Christian Yellow Pages, one of the two nationally franchised directory organizations, this one located in Modesto, California (the other is called the Christian Business Directory, with national headquarters in San Diego),[55] to qualify as a "born-again" Christian, a businessman must have "accepted the fact that Jesus came to this earth—died on the cross of Calvary to pay for our sins—was resurrected—and lives now in the heart of those who believe."[56]

In return for signing such an oath, a Christian business owner not only is "allowed" to purchase ad space in the Christian Yellow Pages, but he is also given what amounts to a Christian version of the Good Housekeeping Seal of Approval. That is, for the millions of evangelical Christians around the country who receive a free copy of the local Christian Yellow Pages through their churches, the fact that a "born-again" business owner is listed means he can be trusted and that it's God's will that they take their business to him over non-born-again merchants.[57] Needless to say, not everyone is happy with this new expression of Christian brotherly love. The Anti-Defamation League of B'nai B'rith, a Jewish organization, has joined with Catholic codefendants in filing several lawsuits in California against both the Christian Yellow Pages and the Christian Business Directory, charging them with violations of the state's antidiscrimination laws regarding business practices. "It's an insidious evil," says David A. Lehrer, legal counsel for the ADL.[58] W. R. Thompson, national director of the Christian Yellow Pages, disagrees. Says Thompson:

> We don't feel we discriminate against anybody.... We'd like everybody to be a born again Christian ... the fact is that the bias of the Christian Yellow Pages is not *against* any one person, but rather *for* born again Christians.[59]

According to legal authorities the outcome of the pending suits is unpredictable because of lack of precedent.[60]

Christian Yellow Pages, while controversial, only begins to scratch the surface of evangelical business-oriented activities. For example, there are organizations like World Vision International that, among other things, specialize in "Christian Management Techniques" and conduct training seminars for Christian businessmen across the country. Then too, in case Christian management techniques come up short, there are always Christian

Industrial Chaplains, a new breed of clergy hired by United States corporations to counsel (and evangelize) employees right on the shop floor. The Reverend Wilbur T. Hendrix, an industrial chaplain for a large textile company, is often seen talking with workers on the line or counseling individuals in small corporate conference rooms. Says Hendrix, "I needed to get to people who might not be touched otherwise." According to *New York Times* reporter, Michael Jensen, however, corporate motives for hiring industrial chaplains are often less than charitable: "They often reason," says Jensen, "that a happy well-adjusted worker is likely to be a productive worker—and a productive worker can help produce a healthy bottom-line profit."[61]

For Christian businessmen, there are two national associations with over 500 active chapters in almost as many American cities. The Christian Businessmen's Committee USA and the Full Gospel Businessmen's Fellowship hold prayer meetings, invite speakers on various topics, publish newsletters and engage in a number of other business-related activities.

While the men are kept busy with these and other worldly matters, the women have their own evangelical associations. The Christian Women's Clubs, whose national headquarters are in Kansas City, are mostly oriented toward the social needs and concerns of suburban middle-class housewives. Fashion shows, cooking instruction, entertainment and outside speakers are standard fare.

To make sure that when Christian women turn the other cheek they will radiate the appropriate Christian beauty, there are the Patricia French Christian Charm Schools and Patricia French Cosmetics. The schools cater to "Christian women of all ages who desire to improve their poise, voice, diction, personality, social graces and appearance." Patricia French Cosmetics, in turn, are made "especially for Christian women."[62]

For families in need of counseling, there are now Christian alternatives to the traditional secular therapies. The Bill Gothard's Institute in Basic Youth Conflicts is perhaps the best known. The Gothard Clinics, which are held all over the country, rely on Biblical text (with psychology as a secondary source) in attempting to deal with the entire range of problems that beset parents and children.[63]

According to the statistical abstract of the United States, "More American people attend church in an average week than attend all professional baseball, basketball and football games combined during an average year." *Christianity Today* magazine reports that, while all sporting events combined drew only about 5.5 million spectators per week, nearly eighty-five million attend church each week.[64] But, just to make sure that "no bases go untouched," evangelicals have even organized Athletes for Christ, a collection of professional celebrities and amateurs who bear witness and win souls, sometimes at halftime rap sessions, during sporting events. The best known groups are Athletes in Action and the Fellowship of Christian Athletes. The FCA's stated purpose is "to confront athletes and coaches—and through them the youth of the nation—with the challenge and adventure of following Christ." Many professional Christian athletes relate personal stories to their audiences that are similar to the testament of Greg Brezina, the Atlanta Falcon's linebacker. "Now that I'm right with God, I can accept myself," says Brezina. "It makes me able to stand here today and say 'I love you' to a black man, where two years ago I couldn't have done that."[65]

In June of 1972, Dallas Cowboy quarterback, Roger Staubach, told over 80,000 fans crammed into the stands of the Cotton Bowl in Dallas that: "The goal line we must get across is our salvation . . . God has given us a good field position." The fans broke out in wild applause and began a spontaneous chant that reverberated back and forth across the field:

> Two bits, four bits, six bits, a dollar.
> All for Jesus, stand up and holler![66]

The fans were not there for a football game. They were part of Explo 72, the International Student Congress on Evangelism. The massive student conclave, which Billy Graham likened to a Religious Woodstock, was sponsored by Campus Crusade for Christ, one of several evangelical organizations whose goal is to develop a sense of "Christian Community" on the college campuses. The Crusade is the largest of these campus operations, boasting a budget in excess of twelve million dollars, a staff of over 3,000 and chapters on 450 campuses. Founded back in 1951 by Bill Bright, the Crusade no longer restricts its domestic programs exclusively to the university. Aside from its student programs, the Crusade trains over 100,000 adults in its special lay institutes on evangelism each year, and it also has active missions in fifty countries throughout the world. Still, its primary focus remains the university. Its goal, says

Bill Bright, rather unabashedly, is spiritual revolution before the year A.D. 2000.

> As the head of a large international movement, I am involved with thousands of others in a conspiracy to overthrow the world. Each year we train tens of thousands of college ... students from more than half the major countries of the world in the art of revolution, and daily these revolutionaries are at work around the globe, spreading our philosophy and strengthening and broadening our influence.[67]

While the Campus Crusade for Christ is considered conservative and aggressive in its evangelism, the Inter Varsity Christian Fellowship, the oldest of the campus evangelical organizations, is a bit more moderate and low key. Founded back in 1941, the IVCF now has active chapters on over 800 college campuses. Members of local IVCF groups meet in weekly Bible study, prayer and discussion sessions. In marked contrast to the Christian Crusade, some IVCF chapters tend to emphasize issues of social concern—though, even here, the emphasis is slight and extremely moderate.[68]

Evangelical groups exist on just about every college campus in the country today. They are, for the most part, small and generally attract little active support from the larger student bodies. The important thing to note, however, is that these groups are often the only nonacademic related action groups that exist at many schools. Like the SDS groups of a decade ago, their zealous commitment to doctrine makes them a potential lightning rod for galvanizing broader student support around specific issues or controversies that might suddenly arise on campus. In fact, the emotional response to student evangelical appeals is not unlike the response generated by the new left proselytizing in the 1960s. Take, for example, Asbury College in Wilmore, Kentucky. Several years ago, the school was forced to cancel classes and shut down its normal activities for over a week—not because of student protests but because of a spontaneous outpouring of evangelical fervor by hundreds of students.

The revival began unexpectedly during a regularly scheduled morning chapel period. A professor of religion asked if there were any students "with hungry hearts who would like to come and accept Christ as your personal Savior." Students started pouring forward; the floodgates, once opened, could not be reshut. For days students amassed in the auditorium, coming forward one at a time to tell their own story, to bear witness and to accept Christ before the assemblage. There was nonstop singing and praying for days on end. Word spread to neighboring towns and schools. Busloads of Christians began to arrive and join in the revival. A local minister later remarked,

> I have never seen such an awesome demonstration of the supernatural power of the Holy Spirit. . . . My faith is just leaping out. . . . Why not let God start it all over the country.[69]

On the high school level, organizations like Youth for Christ and Young Life minister to teenagers through a range of afterschool programs and activities. Youth for Christ, whose national offices are in Wheaton, Illinois, has a full time staff of 800 and is active in over 1,250 United States high schools. Young Life was founded back in 1941. There are currently over 67,000 high school students actively involved in Young Life clubs. Their programs are overseen by a staff of 425 full time employees with an annual budget of fifteen million dollars. Young Life's objective is to "come together for fun, fellowship, singing and a talk by the leader in comfortable everyday language about Jesus Christ and his reality in today's struggles."[70]

All of the above programs, activities and organizations are attempting to build what evangelicals hope will be an alternative Christian community within the larger secular culture. Nowhere is that task taken more seriously than in the Christian school movement. In recent years, a bold new frontal attack on the American public education system has begun to emerge, and it is as significant as the evangelical challenge to the commercial mass media. If it succeeds, the evangelical community will have drastically altered the entire educational framework of American society. The impact on the country would be profound.

THE CHRISTIAN SCHOOL MOVEMENT

There are no locks on the lockers at Norfolk Christian High School. There is, however, a sign over one of the entrances that reads, "This is my Father's World." "This is a quiet place," said John Fink, one of the students. That quiet often turns to a still hush as students pause for prayer before classes begin. Norfolk Christian is an orderly, serious place. Everyone goes about their business with a sense of calm. If one were to categorize the atmosphere of Norfolk Christian in one word, the word that would come first to mind is respectful. That, of course, is exactly what the school's administrator and parents expect. Their expectations come directly from Proverbs 1:7: "The fear of the Lord is the beginning of knowledge."[71]

Norfolk Christian High School is part of a revolution going on in elementary and secondary education in the United States; a revolution of such magnitude that even its few close observers are reluctant to make more than a few tentative predictions as to the effect it will have on American society over the next half-century.

In the 1950s, 91 percent of all children in America attended tax-supported public schools. Today, only 74 percent of the nation's children are still enrolled in public schools. The rest are in private schools. Even more important, the fastest growing segment of private school enrollment is among evangelical Christians.[72] There are now well over one million schoolchildren attending over 5,000 Christian (evangelical) elementary and high schools. *Two new Christian schools are being established every twenty-four hours.*[73] "In the past ten years our Christian School Movement has more than tripled," says Reverend Arno Weniger, exeuctive vice president of the American Association of Christian Schools.[74] The growth in Christian schools is truly one of the most significant cultural phenomena of the decade. By and large the students come from lower-middle-class families whose incomes lie in the ten thousand to fifteen thousand dollar range. Despite the often heard criticism that Christian school growth has been motivated by racial prejudice, the reality is just the opposite. Less than 5 percent of these private schools are segregationist oriented.[75] The overwhelming majority are deeply committed to fostering integration between the races. Why the extraordinary growth, then? According to Weniger of the AACS, it's a direct result of "an increasing dissatisfaction with the public schools and what they're producing."[76] *Christianity Today* magazine is a bit more specific. It says that evangelical Christian parents are turning to the Christian school movement because of:

a desire for biblical education for their children; . . . a
desire for quality education . . . that is thought to be synonymous with discipline; . . . a desire to escape the violence and tension in public schools; . . . and a desire to
promote a deep-seated patriotic conservatism, which fundamentalists charge is absent in public schools.[77]

What makes the Christian school movement so utterly mind-
boggling is that it has begun to seriously undercut a century-
long trend in popular education in America. Before the Civil
War, most popular education was firmly imbedded in an evangelical Christian framework. With the rise of industrial capitalism and the emergence of the modern era, education became
increasingly secularized and institutionalized in the public
arena. For the past half-century, our public education philosophy has rested on a set of principles that include: professional control over school administration, curriculum and
teaching procedures; a secular humanist approach to learning;
and the ultimate primacy of scientific truth. The Christian
school movement has turned this educational philosophy out,
in favor of an older, Christian-based philosophical approach
to education.

To begin with, according to the National Union of Christian
Schools, one of four national associations coordinating Christian school development, the parents (not the professional
teacher, the state or even the church) are the ones responsible
for control over their children's education. This responsibility,
they argue, is clearly prescribed in the scriptures.[78]

And thou shall teach them diligently unto thy children,
and shall talk of them when thou sittest in thine house,
and when thou walkest by the way . . . Deut. 6:6–7

The key to parental responsibility, argue the evangelicals,
is to make sure that the "Bible is the basis upon which the
school's philosophy is founded." What is difficult for outsiders
to fully comprehend is that in a Christian school, the Biblical
view of the world and each person's role in it is the *only*
perspective by which all subjects are taught. Writing in *Christian Teacher* magazine, Dr. Robert Siemens sums up the philosophy behind Christian school education.

In the Christian school we place ourselves under the
authority of the Word of God. What the Bible says is

the standard for faith and practice. Reason and professional responsibility are not abandoned, but simply take their proper places under the authority of Scripture. Because the Bible is authoritative, its interpretation of fact or life is the interpretation placed upon all subject matter teaching in the school and becomes the standard for all relationships within the school.[79]

In practice, this means that over a million schoolchildren in America today are receiving a completely different interpretation of the basis of knowledge, truth and reality than their counterparts in public schools. For example, in social studies, Christian curriculum stresses that original sin is the basis of all human behavior in the physical world. Classroom instruction emphasizes that God is the "Creator, Preserver, Redeemer and Ruler of all People."[80] Likewise, all evaluations and judgments concerning economic, social, cultural and political issues are to be made from a Christian perspective, not a humanist one. In natural science, the creation story in Genesis and not evolutionary theory is the basis for scientific inquiry. The creation theory is central to evangelical educational doctrine. It posits that all life comes from God, and is, therefore, accountable to God. There is no room in Christian education for alternative theories that stress a nonprovidential view of the origins of life.[81] Still, it should be made clear that Christian schools are not in any way antiscience. On the contrary. Their concern, however, is that science be approached not as a set of ultimate autonomous truths, but as a "process" of discovering partial truths whose origins are always traceable to God's ultimate truths.[82]

No one really knows if or when the Christian school movement will begin to show signs of slowing down. In the meantime, its phenomenal growth is already serving as a testimonial to both the seriousness of the Christian revival taking place and the determination of evangelicals to forge an alternative Christian community within the country.

While the Christian school movement is flourishing, evangelical colleges and seminaries are also experiencing new growth. At hundreds of Christian colleges across the country, curriculum is being upgraded and facilities improved and expanded as the evangelical awakening begins to draw students away from more traditional secular education.

Evangelical seminaries are turning out a new generation of

informed and sophisticated theologians who, in turn, are beginning to give shape and definition to the broader revival taking place.

The faculty at these schools are churning out a spate of new theological tracts and writings, much of which is just now beginning to seep down into local church congregations. Like the evangelical movement itself, the new theological perspectives are diverse. While schools of thought are developing, no clear-cut theological pattern has yet become dominant.

In fact, one of the signs of the new vitality within evangelical higher education is the competitiveness and theological diversity being exhibited. Evangelical colleges and seminaries now run the entire ideological gamut from bedrock Fundamentalist orientation at places like Bob Jones University in Greenville, South Carolina, and Dallas Theological Seminary, in Texas, to the more progressively inclined schools like Fuller Seminary in Pasadena, California, or North Park Seminary in Chicago.

For tens of millions of evangelical Christians, the notion of a Christian reality and an alternative Christian community is no longer just Sunday morning church rhetoric. Christians can now spend an entire day within an evangelical context, even as they continue to function in the broader secular culture.

In the morning, husband and wife wake up to an evangelical service on their local Christian owned and operated radio station. The husband leaves for work where he will start off his day at a businessman's prayer breakfast. The evangelical wife bustles the children off to their Christian Day School. At mid-morning she relaxes in front of the TV set and turns on her favorite Christian soap opera. Later in the afternoon, while the Christian husband is attending a Christian business seminar, and the children are engaged in an after-school Christian sports program, the Christian wife is doing her daily shopping at a Christian store, recommended in her Christian Business Directory. In the evening the Christian family watches the Christian World News on TV and then settles down for dinner. After dinner, the children begin their Christian school assignments. A Christian baby-sitter arrives—she is part of a baby-sitter pool from the local church. After changing into their evening clothes, the Christian wife applies a touch of Christian makeup, and then they're off to a Christian nightclub for some socializing with Christian friends from the local church. They return home later in the evening and catch the last half hour of the "700 Club," the evangelical Johnny Carson Show. The Christian wife ends her day reading a chapter or two from Marabel Morgan's best-selling Christian book, *The Total Woman*. Meanwhile her husband leafs through a copy of *Inspiration* magazine, the evangelical *Newsweek*, before they both retire for the evening.

There is no doubt that the mushrooming growth in evangelical believers, evangelical communications and evangelical infrastructures is the most significant cultural phenomenon in American life today. Whether the new evangelical revival will reshape the American climacteric, or rather be reshaped and absorbed by the secular culture, depends upon a number of key factors. The most important of these will be the manner in which the evangelical community addresses the monumental issues presented by the transformation of the present expansionary economic order to a steady-state mode.

America's long evangelical tradition provides the framework for the kinds of response that are likely to emerge from the Christian community.

EVANGELICALISM AND AMERICA: THE FIRST TWO CENTURIES

It's a safe bet that 99 out of 100 evangelical Christians, and an equal number of nonevangelicals, have no idea whatsoever of the role evangelicalism has played in American history. An urbane New York liberal is likely to associate evangelicalism with a hot summer evening in the Houston Astrodome, with tens of thousands of beautifully scrubbed Donny and Marie Osmond lookalikes smiling blissfully as the electronic scoreboard flashes "Jesus Loves You" in bright red and yellow lights into the evening sky. Or, they might think of the move *Marjoe*, with slick fly-by-night rip-off artists fleecing small-town crowds with their exhortations to accept Christ and pass the contributions up front. For many evangelicals, evangelicalism is more often a call to good manners, clean sex, tidy homes, unswerving respect for political authority and a belief in a kind of free enterprise system that has never existed outside of their own imaginations.

Both groups would probably be shocked if they were told that evangelicalism helped spawn the early resistance to the crown, the overthrow of the monarchy and the American Revolution. It was also instrumental in defining the constitutional form of American government, was the primary catalyst in the abolitionist movement that led to the Civil War, was the chief force in the movement for popular education, and was a central element in the early feminist movement of the mid-nineteenth century.

In short, evangelicalism was a driving force in virtually all of the major social reform movements of the eighteenth and nineteenth centuries in America (with the exception of the labor movement). The fact that its legacy has been obscured, and in many instances virtually obliterated from much of the historical record, is a testimonial to the increased secularization of American society in the twentieth century as well as the retreat of modern evangelism from its own radical past.

Yet, a knowledge of evangelism and the central role it has played throughout American history is absolutely essential to understanding the American character. America was, in its early years, a Reformation culture. While the liberal ethos was present even in the early days of the young republic, its appeal was largely confined to the intellectual, and to a lesser extent, political elite. If there was a commonly accepted ideology at all during the first two centuries of this country's existence, it was the evangelical doctrine of the Puritans, and later the Presbyterians, Methodists and Baptists.

The liberal ethos remained in the background until after the Civil War, allowing Calvinist theology to shape the foundation of the American character structure. This was in sharp contrast to England where the liberal ethos emerged out of, and finally eclipsed, Christian Reformation thinking nearly seventy years earlier. This time lag between the Old and New World can be traced to the differences in industrial development between the two countries. England was already well along in industrial development by the early 1800s, when America was still a sparsely settled agricultural society. The liberal ethos, as already pointed out, was the ideal value system for the era of capitalist expansion.

By the time the United States began to industrialize in the last quarter of the nineteenth century a great deal of its unique cultural style had already been filled in by evangelical theology. When the liberal ethos finally triumphed over its Christian Reformation roots in the United States, as it had earlier in England, the victory was only a partial one. While the liberal ethos has dominated the life of the country since the Scopes monkey trial of the 1920s, it has reigned precariously. Its hegemony has always been tempered by the Christian evangelical bedrock upon which it is built.

America, then, is made up of two cultures which exist in a carefully structured relationship to one another. The Reformation culture of John Calvin remains the basis of the American experience. Its bastardized successor, the liberal ethos, remains superimposed on top, but it is continually influenced by the subtle shifts and quiet rumblings of its earlier foundation. Only by understanding evangelicism's history and present state in America is it possible to assess the likely fate of its liberal superstructure and anticipate the kind of ideology that may take its place in the years ahead.

From a religious perspective American history has gone through two distinct periods. The first, extending from the early days of the Puritans to the outbreak of the Civil War, was characterized by a reliance on the Old Testament. America was, to its early settlers, a cross between the new Garden of Eden and the promised land. The American people combined the virtues of Adam and Eve before the Fall with the hunger for freedom from bondage that marked the Israelites' exodus from Egypt 3000 years earlier. The terrible divisions, hatreds and suffering of the Civil War, says historian Richard Pierard, added "the theme of death, sacrifice and rebirth to the official religion."[1] The New Testament theology quickly moved to the front, and the Old Testament receded slowly into the background, as America turned the corner into the twentieth century.

"In the beginning all the world was America," observed John Locke.[2] Certainly the discovery of America easily conjured up visions of the Garden of Eden, virginal and untouched by the centuries of corruption heaped upon corruption that plagued "civilized" Europe. The newness of America brought forth a flood of optimistic expectation among European scholars and philosophers. Imagine, if you will, what it must have been like, all of a sudden, to discover an entire new continent, a continent that fit the description from Genesis of the Garden itself, complete with an abundant supply of nonfallen Adams and Eves, the American Indians. Of course, the idealistic description of the American Indian was quickly replaced with the Hobbesian notion of the universal savagery in nature—a description that better suited the expansionary design of the new European settlers as they attempted to justify their annihilation of the natives. But still the notion of Genesis, of beginnings, of unbridled optimism and unlimited possibilities, remained very much a part of the American character well into the first half of our present century. Along with it, Americans have retained an almost fanatic obsession with youth itself, unlike any other people on earth. The young are our Adams and Eves, as uncorrupted as our country was once uncorrupted, and a beacon of light and hope for all of us and for the world as well.

While Genesis imagery was an important backdrop of early colonial life, it was Exodus that supplied the main theme.

The Americans were the Israelites who had escaped from the bondage and tyranny of Europe to the promised land. Just before the Puritans stepped upon Plymouth Rock in 1630, their spiritual leader, John Winthrop, preached a sermon that Moses himself might have delivered before the Jews went forward into the land of Canaan.

> We shall find that the God of Israel is among us, when ten of us shall be able to resist a thousand of our enemies, when He shall make us a prayse and glory that men shall say of succeeding plantacions; the Lord made it like that of New England: for we must consider that we shall be as a city upon a hill, the eyes of all people are upon us . . .[3]

The concept of chosen people has gone through many interpretations since Winthrop first addressed his tiny flock aboard ship. In the nineteenth century it was conveniently converted into the concept of Manifest Destiny to justify imperialist expansion, first against Mexico and later against Spain in the Spanish-American War.[4] In the second half of the twentieth century, the final remnants of the original concept were torn to shreds, as America found itself in the position of tyrannical Egypt, fighting against the just liberation of a tiny nation halfway around the world in Southeast Asia.

There is, however, another aspect to the idea of America as a chosen people that still remains central to our concept of society. That is the notion of "Covenant." Winthrop, in his sermon aboard ship, reminded the faithful of the concept of covenant in Leviticus, where God says to his chosen people, the Israelites:

> I am the Lord your God who brought you forth out of the Land of Egypt, that you should not be their slaves; . . . If you walk in my statutes and observe my commandments, then I will give you your rains in their season, and the

land shall yield its increase, and the trees shall yield their
fruit... and I will give peace to the land... and I will
have regard for you and will confirm my covenant with
you... but if you will not harken to me, and will not do
all these commandments... but break my covenant... I
will appoint over you sudden terror.

Winthrop, in like manner, proclaimed a similar covenant
for the "new" chosen people of America:

Thus stands the cause between God and us. Wee are
entered into covenant with Him for this worke... Now
if the Lord shall please to heare us, and bring us in peace
to the place wee desire, then hathe He ratified this covenant... but if wee shall neglect the observation of these
Articles... and... shall fall to embrace this present world
and prosecute our carnal intentions seeking great things
for ourselves and our posterity, the Lord will surely break
out in wrath against us, be revenged of such a perjured
people and make us knowe the price of the breach of
such a covenant.[5]

From the very beginning, the American political framework
was based on the concept of the Judeo-Christian covenant.
Samuel Eliot Morison, the great American historian, put the
concept in focus. To Americans, said Morison, covenant has
always meant: "God, I've done my part, now you do yours."[6]
For the Puritans, covenant meant a dual obligation for people: first, the obligation each individual had to serve God; and
second, the obligation that the total community shared together
in serving each other and God. Thus the covenant depended
upon both the internal piety of the individual and the external
responsibility to the collective community. Neither was seen
as separate or apart. For the early Puritans there was no difference between individualism and communalism. Each was
indispensable to the other, and only by working together could
God's glory be served.[7]
Robert Bellah, the distinguished sociologist, notes that
America has gone through two great covenant experiences in
its short history; it now faces a still-to-be-defined third, and
possibly decisive one. In both cases the covenant experiences
were preceded and catalyzed by evangelical revival movements. The first such movement was the great awakening, a

series of evangelical revivals in the 1730s, 1740s and 1750s which spawned the American Revolution and the covenant of the Constitution. A second series of revivals in the 1800s ignited the abolitionist movement and led to the Civil War and the covenant ending slavery (the thirteenth and fourteenth amendments to the Constitution).[8] The third in this series of revivals is just now beginning to emerge. While its specific targets are still undefined, it is, at base, a reaction to the degradation of the human spirit and the destruction of the physical and material world at the hands of modern science, technology and capitalism. It remains to be seen whether this latest series of revivals will lead to a major social upheaval and the reformulation of an American covenant.

Bellah draws a parallel between Christian conversion and covenant and the secular concept of liberation and revolution that is useful if we are to begin to understand the role of evangelicalism in America's past and present. According to Bellah:

> Revolution, like conversion, is an act of liberation, a leaving of old structures, a movement away from constraint. Both revolution and conversion open up the deepest levels of the psyche, touch the springs of our deepest hopes and fears. If these acts of liberation did not contain elements of antinomianism and anarchism they would not be genuine, for the old authority must be radically broken before the new order can be born. But unless the free act of liberation moves rapidly toward an act of institution or constitution, an act not throwing off the past but of establishing the future, then even the liberation itself turns into its opposite. Conversion that does not move toward covenant becomes a new hardness of heart. Revolution that does not move toward constitution quickly becomes a new despotism . . .[9]

Very few Americans realize that in this country it was evangelical revival movements that served as the liberating or revolutionary force in our two greatest internal upheavals. Both times, these revival movements led to covenant in the form of constitutional change. Today, as we enter what appears to be a third series of revivals, the vision of covenant has not yet taken shape. The danger, if such a covenant fails to manifest itself, will be severe. The liberating fervor, unleashed and undefined, will of necessity turn either to nihilism or to an even stronger, if not more ingenuous, glorification of the very institutions, conditions and values that are the cause of the evangelical rebellion.

THE GREAT AWAKENING

A Dutch reform minister in a tiny congregation in the Raritan Valley in New Jersey can be credited with starting the first great awakening. Theodore J. Frelinghuysen, "the beginner of the great work," was sent to America in 1719 by the Dutch Reform Church. Finding the local congregation imbued with orthodox practice but totally lacking in meaningful Christian faith, Frelinghuysen began to evangelize the sinners. By the year 1726, his revivalism had begun to spread to other Dutch Reform communities. That same year, a young Presbyterian minister, Gilbert Tennent, who had been sent to nearby New Brunswick, to preach, met Frelinghuysen. Tennent was impressed with what was transpiring in the Dutch Reform congregation. So much so, that he began to evangelize almost immediately among the Presbyterians. Like Frelinghuysen, Tennent was distraught by the lack of inner faith among his parishioners. The zeal of the early church believers had long since worn off. Each succeeding generation had become more comfortable with formal ritual and less with personal faith. Tennent preached for a new "conviction." His fire and brimstone evangelism caught on. By 1729 Presbyterian congregations as far north as Staten Island were feeling the effect of his revivals. By the late 1730s revivals had spread throughout the region.

Then in 1734 revival broke out in New England from the pulpit of Jonathan Edwards. Unlike Tennent and Frelinghuysen, Edwards was very much a part of the inner circle of the New England church establishment. Educated at Yale and respected as one of the brilliant theological minds of the day, Edwards use of revivalist evangelicism unsettled some of the established ministry of the region. His success, however, turned others to the task.

While all three of these efforts spawned regional revivals in the 1720s and 1730s, it wasn't until the arrival of George Whitefield in Philadelphia in 1739 that a truly national revival emerged. At the age of twenty-four, Whitefield became the first of several major evangelical figures who were to greatly influence American life in the next 200 years.

Whitefield traveled throughout the colonies, his reputation preceding him as larger and larger audiences began to come and hear his evangelical sermons. It was said that his gift of oratory was so great that "by merely pronouncing the word Mesopotamia" he could bring tears to the eyes of his listeners. By 1770, at the time of his death, Whitefield had, according to historian Winthrop Hudson, done "as much to shape the future of American religious life as anyone else."[10]

Revivals were not always welcomed by church leaders and local ministers. To a large extent the evangelical preachers were repudiating the sterile orthodoxy of the established churches. As George Whitefield remarked, "the reason why congregations have been so dead is because dead men preach to them."[11] Comments like this were not appreciated. Even more frightening to the professional ministry was the emphasis the revivals placed on "inward" experience over church doctrine. Uneducated lay persons were encouraged to participate, even preach the Word of God to their fellow sinners. This had the effect of undermining the authority of the established clergy. Historian Richard Hofstadter describes the deep schism that developed between the old guard and the new evangelical preachers:

> To the exponent of a religion of the book, for whom a correct reading of the Bible was a vital concern, this was the ultimate heresy: that one who was possessed of the Spirit could, without study and without learning, interpret the Word of God effectively enough to be an agent of the salvation of others. And here we have the nub of the difference between the awakeners and the spokesmen of establishments. Whether it was more important to get a historically correct and rational understanding of the Book—and hence the Word of God—or to work up a proper emotion, a proper sense of inner conviction and of relation to God.[12]

Hofstadter, mind you, has his doubts about the efficacy of the evangelical phenomenon. In his seminal work, *Anti-Intellectualism in American Life*, he argues that revivalism, by unleashing strong anarchistic feelings among the masses, has often led to hysterical outbreaks of anti-intellectualism in this country. This was certainly true during the 1920s and again in the early 1950s, when evangelicalism joined forces with ultra-right-wing groups in a crusade against the "egghead" intelligentsia who were suspected of being soft on, or in collusion with, communism in America.

Still, even Hofstadter acknowledges what Robert Bellah and others have observed about the evangelical phenomenon. Namely, that *its very emotional appeal against established authority, be it religious or secular, has been the primary "liberating" force that has periodically renewed the democratic impulse in American political life.*[13]

The first great awakening set the tone for the American Revolution just two decades later by helping to unify the previously isolated and disparate colonies and by encouraging the democratic spirit. The great awakening, says Winthrop Hudson, was great because it was general. "People everywhere were caught up in the movement, and its influence was spread by innumerable local pastors, passing itinerants and lay exhorters. No one could escape the excitement or avoid the necessity to declare himself as friend or foe."[14] The awakening crossed colonial boundaries, and at a time when the thirteen colonies were constantly bickering over economic and political matters, it provided a common ideological focus between the people themselves. In a very fundamental way, it was the first national movement to forge a sense of ideological unity among the various colonial people. The term American, as opposed to Virginian or Pennsylvanian, began to take on meaning.

The evangelical emphasis on the doctrine that *all* are sinners, that salvation is every person's individual responsibility and that anyone can preach the Word of God opened the floodgates for popular democracy. The revivalist attack on church authority brought democracy to church life in colonial America. According to historian William Sweet, one of the main effects of the first great revival was the development of popular participation in church affairs. The Baptists early on adopted a democratic form of church governance, with emphasis on decentralized local church control over church affairs, which remains essentially intact among the Southern Baptist congregations today. The Methodists, says Sweet, "though highly centralized and authoritarian, nevertheless gave full rights of self-expression to every member, women as well as men."

The Presbyterians, though nominally affiliated with the Church of Scotland, were in practice also a self-governing body, says Sweet.[15]

The democratic impulse first unleashed during the great spiritual awakening of the 1730s and 1740s eventually found its way into the political life of the colonies as relations with the monarchy continued to deteriorate.

On January 30, 1750, Jonathan Mayhew took to his pulpit in Massachusetts. He had been ordered to make a speech on the anniversary of the execution of King Charles, a day that was supposed to be given over to public repentance for the slaying of the former ruler. Instead, he turned the occasion and his sermon into a discourse on the duty of all committed Christians to resist corrupt, tyrannical leaders. With this sermon, the great revival took an unalterable turn toward politics and from there to open rebellion and finally to revolution itself. Mayhew's words speak eloquently of the effect that the evangelical revivals were to have on the birth of the first popular democratic republic in modern history.

> Rulers have no authority from God to do mischief. They are not God's ordinances or God's ministers in any other sense than as it is by his permission and providence that they are exhalted to rule . . . and as magistry duly exercised and authority rightfully applied in the enacting and executing of good laws . . . must be supposed to be agreeable to the will of the beneficient authority and Supreme Lord of the Universe whose Kingdom ruleth over all. . . . It is blasphemy to call tyrants and oppressors God's ministers. They are more properly "the messengers of Satan to buffet us." No rulers are properly God's ministers but such as are just, ruling in the fear of God. When once magistrates act contrary to their office and the end of their institutions—when they rob and ruin the public instead of being guardians of its peace and welfare—they immediately cease to be the ordinance of God and no more deserve that glorious character than common pirates and highway men. . . . It is our duty to obey our King for this reason; that he rules for the public welfare. It follows that when he turns tyrant . . . we are bound to throw off our alliegance to him and to resist . . .[16]

EVANGELICALISM: THE FULCRUM OF
AMERICAN POLITICAL IDEOLOGY

Pollsters and political pundits are busy conjecturing over the possible political direction of the new evangelical phenomenon in the 1980s. Their machinations will mean very little unless they first develop a firm understanding of the close relationship that has always existed between American evangelical theology and popular political ideology.

Political thought in this country has historically been divided along conservative versus liberal lines.

It is important to bear in mind that, within the American experience, both conservative and liberal political beliefs are children of a common parent, the liberal ethos. Each accepts the notion that individual self-interest and unlimited material growth are the sine qua non of human social existence. Both place their total faith in science, technology and capitalism as the ruling deities of the modern world.

Conservative and liberal politicians are constantly attempting to seduce the evangelical part of the American character to their respective secular planes. To be sure, for conservative or liberal, the process is unconscious, but at the same time the pursuit remains relentless.

Like the evangelical Christians, political conservatives start with the notion that all people are evil. But the similarity begins and ends there. The conservatives take their inspiration from the philosophy of Hobbes. While Hobbes agrees with the evangelical Christians on the nature of human beings, he does not, in turn, believe in a covenant with God. For Hobbes, the natural state of war between all people cannot be escaped by faith, salvation or covenant in Christ. Instead, Hobbes takes a purely secular and utilitarian attitude toward evil. In order to lessen the natural fear and suffering that human beings experience in nature, Hobbes says they join together in a social order. Rules, which clearly limit natural aggression and evil instincts, are established and commonly adhered to. In return for giving up some natural freedom, people secure a modicum of security over their own person. The bottom line for Hobbes is not salvation and covenant, but brutish self-interest. Evil is not overcome, but merely regulated for the good (or bad) of all.

Political liberals, on the other hand, believe in a covenant with God (or at least a secular version of it), but not in original sin. Their philosophical basis is to be found in the ideas of the eighteenth-century Enlightenment, and especially in the ideas of the Deists. The Deists first emerged in seventeenth-century England. They were intent on finding a theological basis for overcoming the many schisms that existed within the Christian family. Heavily influenced by the Age of Reason, they attempted to posit a series of axioms to which all Christians could adhere. According to Winthrop Hudson, the five essentials of their rationalizing dogma were: "the affirmation that God exists; that He is to be worshipped; that the practice of virtue is the true worship of God; that man must repent of wrongdoing and that there are future rewards and punishments." To the chagrin of the evangelical Christians, however, the Deists make no reference to man's "sinful nature and consequent need for redemption or of any necessary dependence upon Biblical revelation."[17]

Jefferson, Franklin and many of the intellectual lights of the American Revolution fancied themselves as Deists. Many of them were enamored with the Roman concept of "public virtue," which amounted to little more than a secular version of the Christian concept of covenant. The rational religion of the Deists was, from the beginning and continues to be in a more secular form today, a minority-held view—but one that has, nonetheless, exerted great influence on the affairs of the culture. As with Jefferson, Madison and America's other early intellectual leaders, the various shades of Deist doctrine have been particularly attractive to the intellectual and cultural elites of the country up to the present time.

For the evangelical, both doctrines hold out a seductive lure. On the one hand, political conservatives share the conviction that human beings are naturally evil, but they don't believe in a saving God or humanity's covenant with him. On the other hand, while political liberals start with the concept that human beings are basically good, not evil, they join ranks with the evangelicals in believing in the concept of God (or in its most secular form, a Messianic age) and people's need for covenant.

In times of rising expectations, of growth and expansion, the political liberals have definitely had the edge in winning the support of most "Christian" Americans. In good times, the concept of evil recedes and the notion of shared covenant and human progress dominates. In contracting periods of economic

stagnation or political and social instability, the political conservatives are usually blessed with a more approving "Christian" audience. The notion that human beings are naturally evil
appears all too real in a society wrenched by the throes of lost
expectations, cynicism and doubt.

Then, there are those rare moments in American history,
where evangelical Christianity takes to the fore on its own
volition with its own unique mission, uninfluenced by either
the liberal or conservative political attitudes of the liberal ethos.
In these rare moments, evangelicalism sets the agenda for politics, and both conservative and liberal political ideology adjust
accordingly. This was the case during the great awakening
before the Revolution and again during the second great revival
preceding the Civil War. In both instances, evangelicalism
became the vanguard for social change, precisely because it
was able to combine liberation with a vision of a new covenant.
It spoke to people's desire to overcome evil; it converted people
to Christ; and it demanded a commitment of them to fight for
and establish a new covenant with both God and their fellow
human beings. In so doing, it put the *totality* of its doctrine
into practice, leaving little room for seduction by either wing
of the liberal ethos. Of course, these moments were few and
short-lived. The remainder of the American historical experience is a record of both the liberal and conservative political
wings of the liberal ethos, picking at and using the evangelical
foundation for their particular ends.

THE SECOND GREAT REVIVAL

The Red and Gasper rivers wind their way through a small
section of Logan County on the Tennessee border. This des-
olate, Godforsaken area was a little hellhole in the year 1800.
Nicknamed "Rogues Harbor" because it was often used as a
sanctuary for outlaws and runaway slaves, an inhabitant described the territory as follows:

> There was not a newspaper printed south of the Green
> River, no mill short of forty miles, and no schools worth
> the name. We killed our meat out of the woods, wild;
> and beat our meal . . . as for coffee, I am not sure that I
> ever smelled it for ten years.[18]

In the hot steamy summer of 1800, God paid a visit to the Red and Gasper rivers territory. Shortly thereafter, the second great series of revivals shook America. By the time they had subsided, the western migration was won over to Baptist and Methodist evangelical affiliation; the abolitionist and feminist movements became an American obsession as Christian colleges began to dot the geography of the expanding continent; and the individual spirit of Calvinism combined with the Puritan concept of covenent in the formation of a nationwide network of voluntary benevolent associations—a new kind of institutional model which was virtually unique to America.

Two Presbyterian ministers, William Hodges and John Rankin, presided over the four-day camp meeting on the Red River in June of 1800. On the fourth day one John McGee rose to plead with his neighbors "to let the Lord Omnipotent reign in their hearts." McGee, recalling that moment, said:

> I turned to go back and was near falling [but] the power of God was strong upon me. I turned again, and losing sight of fear of man, I went through the house shouting and exhorting with all possible ecstasy and energy.

By the time McGee had reached the backside of the room. pandemonium had broken out. People were screaming, tears flowed and all "crying out what shall we do to be saved?"

The news of what had taken place spread quickly through the backwoods. The next month another camp meeting with similar results took place on the Gasper River. Then a series of camp meetings began to take shape almost spontaneously. By the following summer, nearly 25,000 people jammed onto Cane Ridge in Bourbon County for a massive revival.[19] The camp meetings became a central part of the early nineteenth-century revivals, especially in the outlying western provinces.

By the early 1800s the westward expansion had turned into a near stampede, as tens of thousands walked their way across the Appalachians into Ohio, Tennessee, Kentucky, Indiana, Missouri, and southwest into Mississippi and Alabama. Very few had taken the Bible along with them. The revivalist preachers were determined to amend the situation.

These new western settlements were primitive. Homesteads were isolated from one another. There were no schools, and generally no civil authority. Life was harsh and exacting; the normal civilities characteristic of New England society were absent. In this milieu, the Christian call to conversion, peni-

tence and convenant needed to be as tough and uncompromising
as the people and conditions themselves. As a consequence,
the revivals of this era were much more heated than their predecessors in the 1740s and 1750s.

There was more raw emotional release, greater frenzy, and
a more intense communal outpouring at these spiritual gath-
erings, since life was often short, and there was precious little
time to spend examining the doctrinal side of theology. Repentance and conversion were swift and cathartic. Still, the
camp meetings served their purpose. Evangelical revivals spread
to the West, and then back to the East and North as well. In
1800 only about one in fifteen Americans was a church member. By 1850, one out of every seven belonged to a church.[20]

Most of the new church membership accrued to the evangelical Methodists and Baptists. Each was ideally suited in
temperament and doctrine to take advantage of the westward
migration.

The Methodists, from the start, put great emphasis on the itin-
erant minister. The lone preacher, armed with only a Bible, a
horse and a mission, seeking out sinners one by one in the backwoods of frontier America, became synonymous with the Methodists. Such preachers were known as "circuit riders." Often
during terrible rainstorms it was said: "There's nobody out to-
night but crows and Methodist preachers." It was this kind of
fierce dedication that turned American Methodism from a small
sect of 3,000 in 1775, to the largest Protestant denomination eighty
years later, with over a million-and-a-half members.[21]

The Baptists, because of their long history of local church
autonomy, and their emphasis on lay people preaching the
Gospel, were also able to take advantage of the unstructured
nature of the American frontier. As Richard Hofstadter points
out, a Baptist preacher "might be a farmer who worked on his
land or a carpenter who worked at his bench like any other
layman, and who left his work for Sunday or weekday sermons
or for baptisms and funerals."[22]

Decentralized authority, undereducated ministers, democratic control over local church policies, an emphasis on emotion over reason and personal salvation over correct doctrine
were all central features of the western revivals. As communities began to grow out of temporary settlements and life
became less brutish and more "civilized," these essential aspects of Baptist and Methodist evangelism began to fade, but

never completely. Both church denominations have still retained enough of these original qualities to be able to at least
claim some affinity with their early roots.

The final surge of America's second great revival broke
out in New York state and spread throughout the Eastern and
Northern states during the 1830s and early 1840s. Its lightning
rod was a young lawyer, turned Presbyterian preacher, Charles
Finney. It's ironic that so few Americans today have any knowledge of this man, who, more than any other single individual
of the nineteenth century, was responsible for sparking the
abolitionist and feminist drives, the demand for increased education and the development of voluntary associations in the
United States.

Finney's conversion from law to the ministry took place
late one night in his law office in Adams, New York.

> The Holy Spirit descended upon me in a manner that
> seemed to go through me body and soul . . . I wept aloud
> with joy and love; and I do not know but I should say,
> I literally bellowed out the unutterable gushings of my
> heart.

The next day when a local deacon called upon Finney to
remind him of a case he was to try in court that morning, he
is said to have remarked, "Deacon, I have a retainer from the
Lord Jesus Christ to plead his cause, and I cannot plead yours."[23]

After finishing his theological studies, Finney began to move
through midstate New York preaching the word of God to the
sinners in hamlets like Rome, Utica and Boonville. By 1828
he was already gaining national attention for his evangelicalism
when he began moving into the larger cities of Philadelphia,
Wilmington and New York.

Finney was an imposing figure. His preaching was dignified
and more in the style of a laywer arguing his case in court,
but it transformed audiences everywhere. Says Finney of the
impact of one of his revivals: "The congregation began to fall
from their seats in every direction and cried for mercy . . . Nearly
the whole congregation were either on their knees or pros-
trate."[24]

In 1837, a severe economic depression swept the country.
Finney warned that the economic collapse was God's judgment
for man's "sinful acquisition of goods." The judgment theme
struck home for millions of anxious Americans. Along with it,

however, Finney preached a form of Christian perfectionism. He argued that through conversion and sanctification human beings could *"approach"* perfection in this world.[25] Finney vehemently opposed the traditional Calvinist doctrine of pre-election (as did the Wesleyan Methodists and Baptists), arguing that it created an "aristocracy of the elect." Finney argued that all could be saved and that it was solely the responsibility of each individual to decide for himself whether to accept Christ and salvation or be damned forever. This kind of egalitarianism fit the mood of the country during the days of Jacksonian democracy and the glorification of popular participation in government.

Finney admonished his audiences that conversion and perfectionism were not won easily. Since selfishness was, for Finney, the basis of sin, it stood to reason that benevolence and good works were the basis of perfectionism. Finney's doctrine of perfectionism, though rigorously challenged by much of the old-guard Presbyterian leadership, changed the shape and character of pre–Civil War America. Benevolent societies sprang up everywhere to help the downtrodden and dispossessed, especially in the cities. More important, his perfectionist preaching converted an entire generation of new evangelical reform leaders, who put theory to practice in spearheading the antislavery and feminist movements of the 1840s and 1850s.[26]

Even the church proper was to come under Finney's watchful and mostly disapproving eye. Finney argued that the perfectionist doctrine was to be applied by the church as well as by the individual.

Now the great business of the church is to reform the world—to put away every kind of sin. The Church of Christ was originally organized to be a body of reformers. The very profession of Christianity implies the profession and virtually an oath to do all that can be done for the universal reformation of the world. The Christian church was designed to make aggressive movements in every direction—to lift up her voice and put forth her energies against inequity in high and low places—to reform individuals, communities and governments and never rest until the kingdom and the greatness of the kingdom under the whole heaven shall be given to the people of the

on, or interest in the country. The notion o
s received its primary thrust in the secon
e nineteenth century. At first, local churche
concept of voluntary associations for joir
. Later, societies were formed by evangelica
form humanitarian functions. By the Civil Wa
he volunteer association had broken out fror
ines of the church and had entered the secula
or force in the social and cultural life of th
nost voluntary organizations today retain a kin
-goodism" philosophy, their early evangelica
a very specific theological rationale behind them
entioned, Charles Finney and others popularize
f "Disinterested Benevolence" during the secor
aking off from the perfectionist theme, it was fe
God's glory could best be achieved by living a li
sted benevolence." Toward this end, voluntary o
nd benevolent societies provided a structure throug
ork together to foster the interests of everyone

saints of the most High God—until every form of inequity shall be driven from the earth.[27]

EVANGELICALISM AND THE ABOLITIONIST AND FEMINIST MOVEMENTS

When one thinks of the abolitionist movement, the name
of William Lloyd Garrison comes to mind, and when one
thinks of popular support for the movement, the Unitarians
and Congregationalists are the first to be identified with the
cause. While Garrison was certainly a towering figure in the
abolitionist struggle, and the urbane Unitarians and Congregationalists of Boston were certainly involved as well, the
simple fact is that the evangelical Methodists and Baptists
and their denominational preachers like Theodore Weld and
Orange Scott were the central driving force in the abolitionist
drama. For example, at the 1835 Anti-Slavery Society convention, two-thirds of the delegates were ministers and two-
thirds of them were either Baptists or Methodists.[28] According
to historian William Sweet:

'Too much credit, or discredit, for the abolition movement
has been given to conspicuous Unitarian leaders such as
Theodore Parker, whereas it would have amounted to
little if there had not been a large following in the rural
towns and countryside where the revivalistic churches
had their greatest strength.[29]

Perhaps the greatest evangelical preacher and abolitionist of
the period was Theodore Weld. A onetime assistant to Charles
Finney, the *Dictionary of American Biography* describes Weld
as "the greatest of the abolitionists . . . [and] one of the greatest
figures of his time." A relentless campaigner for the antislavery
cause, Weld traveled the country preaching the Word of God
and freedom for blacks to Christian audiences.[30]

As early as the 1780s the Presbyterians, Baptists and Methodists took official stands against the practice of slavery in
America. In fact, all of the major revivalist groups in the South-

ern colonies developed antislavery views by the end of the War for Independence.[31]

In 1807 antislavery Baptists in Kentucky formed a "Friends of Humanity" association. Membership was based on sharing antislavery views. Similar Baptist associations were formed in Illinois and Missouri.[32]

Many Methodist ministers were firmly dedicated to preaching the antislavery cause. Divisions in the church over the question of support or opposition to slavery eventually ended up in schism and separation, as Orange Scott led the antislavery forces into a new church formation—the Wesleyan Methodist Connection of America.[33]

It should be realized that the motivations of the evangelicals in regard to the question of slavery were theological and doctrinal. The issue was not simply a moral one. At the heart of the matter was the Word of God. The evangelicals looked to the Bible and found that Paul was clear on the question of slavery. "There shall be neither Jews nor Greeks, there is neither bonded nor free, there is neither male nor female, for ye are all one in Christ Jesus."

Blacks, like all other men and women, were made in God's image, argued the evangelicals. Like their white brothers and sisters, they too were equally sinful in the eyes of God and therefore equally in need of being saved in order to do God's glory on earth. Slavery, then, was blasphemy and had to be struck down with all the righteous indignation committed Christians could bring to bear.

It was probably only logical to assume that the evangelical views on slavery would find their way to the issue of equal rights for women as well. According to historian Donald Dayton, Charles Finney's revivals had more to do with generating the nineteenth-century feminist movement than any other single factor. One of Finney's "new measures" in his revivals was the encouragement of women to come forward and speak and pray in public along with the men. Oberlin College, which was formed by evangelicals (Finney was, for a brief time, the president of the college) was the first coeducational college to confer degrees on women. Many of the early graduates of the evangelical college went on to become leaders in the feminist cause, including Lucy Stone.[34]

The Grimké sisters, well known to modern-day feminists as leaders of the early women's rights struggle, were also deeply tied in with the evangelical revivals of the pre–Civil War period.

Evangelicalism

Angelina Grimké
protégé). Using t
just cause, the Gr
to Galatians 3:28:
are all one in Chri
which appeared to ju
remarked: "I must en
of some passages by

By the 1860s Wesl
into the clergy. Even
sponsible for the foundi
Seminary, one of the le
tions on the East Coast,
rapher, a feminist as well
younger Gordon, his father
enfranchisement and their e
cial privilege enjoyed by me

The Salvation Army was
ence in catalyzing the femini:
founder, Catherine Booth, argu
of women in the ministry. Wor
were afforded equal status alon

140

every cause, fixat
volunteer societie
revival wave in t
began to use the
ecumenical task
groupings to pe
the concept of
the narrow con
realm as a ma
nation. While
of secular "do
prototypes had
As already m
the doctrine o
awakening. T
that serving (
of "disintere
ganizations a
which to w
society.[39]

EDUCATION AND THE VO

While the major contribution of
this country was the abolitionist driv
feminist movement), there were two
a lasting impact on nineteenth-century
The first was in the field of education
of the voluntary association in the Uni

Before 1830, the two major evangel
tists and Methodists, had no significant r
in this country. As a result of the second g
their relationship to education radically ch
and the Civil War the Methodists establi
leges and the Baptists twenty-one. Virtuall
formed west of the Alleghenies were of re

The United States, unlike any other cou
is unique in its encouragement of and participa
societies. There appears to be some kind of

7

MODERN EVANGELICAL HISTORY

POST–CIVIL WAR

In 1840, at the height of the second great awakening, America was still largely the kind of agrarian society Jefferson and the architects of the Revolution had known when they fashioned the founding documents of the country. By 1875, in the span of just thirty-five years, the country had metamorphosed into an industrialized, urbanized power, with all of the attendant problems that go along with it. The rather homogeneous Anglo-Saxon population of the first half of the century was being literally overrun by hordes of eastern and southern European immigrants, many of them Catholic, and unsympathetic to evangelical appeals.

In the Northeast and Midwest, millions of farmers were selling off their livestock, packing up their bags and heading into the sprawling cities of Cleveland, Pittsburgh, Philadelphia, New York and Boston. America was becoming truly citified. At the same time, the new urban proletariat of the postwar industrial boom brought with it labor strikes, slum conditions and a plethora of new demands and needs, which the country was largely unprepared to grapple with.

Along with increased immigration, industrialization and urbanization came a steady assault of new ideas, theories and concepts, each born of a scientific age that was transforming America into the first gadgetized society on the planet. Of these new ideas, one was to deliver a crushing blow to evangelicalism as a dominant force in American life. Darwin's theory of biological evolution had a devastating impact on reformationist theology, mainly because people bought into it so readily. Buying into it meant rejecting the Genesis account in the Bible, the very Word of God. The willing, almost enthusiastic acceptance of Darwin's theories by the public was as much a reflection of their conversion to science as the new and ultimate truth, as it was to Darwin's particular theories.

As if all of this wasn't enough to contend with, several new academic disciplines made their debuts, most important of these, sociology and psychology. A new breed of intellectuals began to feverishly pick away at the seeming incongruities and contradictions in the Bible. For example, how could Noah have filled his little Ark with two of every species when there were well over two million species inhabiting the planet at the time. It would have been much too cramped. "Higher criticism" of the Bible, as it was called, took on God's word with a vengeance and, frankly, God came out looking a little less than "all knowing" in the process.

Finally Freud came along and said that religious experience was, simply speaking, the result of a host of "animal" anxiety patterns associated with a combination of complexes, neuroses and other internal struggles and turmoils, all to be found in the average "normal" individual.

The pre–Civil War evangelism of circuit riders and benevolent societies was suddenly thrust into the historical archives. Meanwhile, the abolitionist issue, which was such a central theme of the second great awakening, had been, at least, partially resolved with emancipation and passage of the thirteenth and fourteenth amendments.

Then, there was the effect of the war itself on the psyche of the nation. The carnage and hatred unleashed by the five years of fratricidal warfare left a deep scar on the American character. Gone was the innocence and naive optimism that de Tocqueville and other European observers had so often taken note of in the young America. For the first time, a sense of pathos crept into American life. With it came the first acknowledgment of lost youth and a new feeling that perhaps we were no longer the chosen people of Winthrop's vision. The Old Testament liturgy, which had played such a dominant role in American life from its very beginning, was being eclipsed for the first time by the imagery of crucifixion, death and resurrection of the New Testament.

The shift in view over the meaning of the millennial reign among evangelical Christians signaled another crucial turning point in the role of Christianity in American life.

Millennialism refers to the Book of Revelation in the Bible and the question of when and under what conditions the Savior will come back to earth to establish, once and forever, the perfect kingdom of God. Before the Civil War, the evangelical movement was firmly ensconced in the postmillennial vision. After the Civil War the premillennial view took over.

The postmillennial view of Charles Finney and the evangelical reformers of the first half of the century was a reflection of the optimism of the era and the notion that Americans had truly become God's chosen people. According to the postmillennial view, Christ would return in judgment after a peaceful millennial reign of 1000 years. In this view, the role of the church and all good Christians was to prepare for the ushering in of the millennium by "perfecting" the state of society. Social reform, then, was an essential aspect of postmillennial eschatology.[1]

While the evil nature of people was always to be reckoned with in postmillennial doctrine, it became an obsessive concern of the premillennial eschatology after the war. It was not terribly difficult to understand why. As Americans looked on the suffering and despair wrought by their own actions and relived over and over again the painful memories of neighbor fighting against neighbor and relatives taking up arms against their own kin, the notion of people's fallen nature began to take on an importance that Americans had never before experienced. The premillennialists' view stressed humanity's fall and its depraved nature. They believed that evil was spreading its influence over the secular world and that it would continue on its path until the final days when all the world would destroy itself (Armageddon) in one final explosive holocaust to be followed by the return of Christ and the establishment of the "perfect" kingdom of God. According to this very pessimistic view of the future, only those select few who had been converted to Christ would be saved in the final moments before the holocaust and be physically taken up into heaven by Christ himself.[2] The premillennialists had little hope for this world. Their anticipation of the approach of the final days and Christ's return led to withdrawal (for the most part) from attempts to improve or reform society—after all, why try if it's all going to blow up at any moment.[3] More importantly, they had little faith or optimism in people's own ability to improve their lot in this lifetime. For the premillennialist, the chosen people of the Old Testament had been replaced by the individual sinners of the New Testament. There was no place for covenant among the premillennialists, since collective action to advance social betterment only acted as a roadblock to the approach of Armageddon and Christ's return to earth. In other words, the worse things got, the quicker the end would come and the sooner Christ would return to begin the world anew.[4]

Thus, while the postmillennialists were concerned with saving souls in order to perfect society and prepare for the millennium period, the premillennialists were merely interested in saving souls to spare as many as possible from the imminent and total destruction that was about to take place. For those who had already experienced a taste of what the holocaust might be like during the War Between the States, the premillennial message of the new evangelism was appealing. This psychological appeal was especially seductive in the South, where the destruction of the war and Sherman's bloody march to the sea was still a recurring nightmare.

The premillennial message also spoke to those who were losing their homes and their former way of life to the onslaught of the industrial machine. The small farmers, displaced from the land and facing a bewildering and unsure future in the vast new city slums, were particularly amenable to premillennial eschatology. Massive industrialization and urbanization created a tremendous body of isolated, disenfranchised and confused laborers, men with little hope who were mercilessly exploited by the new forces of capitalism. It's no wonder, then, that premillennialism, with its emphasis on rampant evil and hope only in individual salvation, presented a more compelling theology for those who no longer believed they were a part of the chosen people.

Mainstream evangelicalism made a historic turn away from covenant and social reform after the Civil War. The New Testament emphasis on individual salvation, premillennialism and withdrawal from social reform was best reflected in the ministry of Dwight D. Moody, the greatest revivalist of the period and the first of the modern big-city evangelists.

Moody was a successful shoe salesman until 1860, when he decided to go into Christian mission work. For the next thirteen years he was active in the YMCA. Then, in 1873, while in England on an assignment for the YMCA, he was invited to conduct a series of local evangelical meetings. He was an overnight success, and for the next two years he kept his British audiences spellbound, if not always faithful to the Word itself. Returning to the States in 1875 (his fame in England had already long since preceded him), the way was quickly paved for his coronation as the king of evangelicalism in post–Civil War America.[5]

Moody was never ordained a minister, but this seems to have been no great obstacle in his successful efforts to bring the new infidels of the nation's great cities to God's kingdom. Moody fit the style of the new industrialized era. It is said that he not only looked and dressed like a businessman, but preached like one as well. In fact, his entire evangelical organization became the model of modern business practices normally associated with successful twentieth-century evangelism. Moody combined the showmanship of P. T. Barnum with the calculating financial acumen of Andrew Carnegie. Advance men, publicity agents, advertising campaigns, guaranteed gates, were all part of the accouterments of the new big-city revivalism. And it worked. True to modern accounting procedures, his organization kept strict records of cost effectiveness in the field; 2,500 saved in Chicago, 3,500 saved in New York City, and so forth. This "conversion" body count provided a sort of sales performance record from which to judge the effectiveness of the amount of investment put out. Moody even brought his sales and marketing techniques directly into his sermons:

> Who'll take Christ now? That's all you want. With Christ you have eternal life and everything else you need. Without Him you must perish. He offers Himself to you. Who'll take Him?[6]

Moody preached a conservative evangelism. No social reformer like Finney and evangelists of the pre–Civil War period, he emphasized the premillennial view.

> I have heard of reform, reform, until I am tired and sick of the whole thing. It is regeneration by the power of the Holy Ghost that we need.

It's no wonder that Moody became a favorite of the captains of industry, who were as tired and sick of the word reform as he was. Moody made his big leap to fame on the coattails of the great depression of 1873. He preached personal repentance and salvation as the cure for the ills besetting the American economy. The business titans liked what they heard. Worried over growing labor unrest, strikes and talk of socialism, America's new capitalist ruling class found in Moody a man whom they could trust. A man who preferred saving souls over saving society. They were only too eager to assist his efforts and God's glory with financial underwriting of his great revival campaigns (and this was before it was tax deductible). In Chicago, Cyrus McCormick and George Armour pitched in with funds and, of course, "moral support." In Philadelphia, it was John Wanamaker, the department store king. In New York the welcoming committee was led by Cornelius Vanderbilt and J. P. Morgan. Moody responded to these acts of Christian charity in kind. In Chicago, for example, he said to McCormick and Armour and their friends:

> I say to the rich men of Chicago, their money will not be worth much if communism and infidelity sweep the land... There can be no better investment for the capitalists of Chicago than to put the saving salt of the Gospel into these dark homes and desperate centers.[7]

Moody was the first of the modern-day evangelists to preach the "Gospel of Wealth." His answer to the economic depression of the 1870s was salvation in Christ, not unions, not redistribution of wealth and certainly not godless communism. God always provided for those who accept him in their hearts, reasoned Moody.

> It is a wonderful fact that men and women saved by the blood of Jesus rarely remain subjects of charity, but rise at once to comfort and respectability... I never saw the man who put Christ first in his life that wasn't successful.[8]

This theme, first expounded by Moody, was to be recycled over and over again by popular evangelists up to the present day. According to the "Gospel of Wealth," as articulated by its most vociferous advocate, Andrew Carnegie, "civilization" depends on a triple law made up of the sacredness of private property, open competition and the unrestrained accumulation of wealth.[9] This is God's law, pure and simple, and anything that undermines it is the work of the devil. Correspondingly, those who live in strict adherence to the three principles of God's economic law can't help but prosper. For Carnegie, capitalism was not a system of rules devised by people, but a natural process willed to humanity by God Almighty. It follows that those who become successful in the commercial world are obviously the most God-fearing Christians. Correspondingly, anyone who is poor and destitute is obviously not as deserving, and is certainly less than Christian in his spiritual conduct.

While part of the evangelical movement in America moved into premillennial eschatology and the preaching of the gospel of wealth, another group began to work out a very different approach. These evangelists were less willing to give up the social reform tradition of pre–Civil War evangelicalism. Yet, they became painfully aware of how inadequate the concept of "disinterested benevolence" and "voluntary action" was amidst the ravages of the industrial era. Individual acts of charity could do little or nothing to alleviate the class conditions of millions of American laborers.

The panic of 1873, the violence of the early struggles between working people and the new capitalist class, the growing disparity in wealth between the elite and the masses, the squalid conditions of the urban ghettos all heightened these evangelical reformers' sense of concern for the plight of society. By the last decade of the century, a new approach to social reform was being advanced by this group of evangelical Christians; it was called the "social gospel."[10]

Contemporary historians and sociologists often make the mistake of contending that the social-gospel movement, which later turned entire denominations toward modernism and secular liberalism during the twentieth century, was somehow the stepchild of the earlier "rationalist" religious groups, the Unitarians and the Congregationalists. This was only partially true. Some of the impetus behind the social-gospel movement came from evangelists within the reform tradition of the Finneyites and postmillennialists of the early part of the century.[11]

The social gospelists, says William Sweet, insisted that:

You cannot make a better world by "snatching brands from the burning," by proceeding with the conversion

of people one by one. They insisted that the church must
deal with society as a whole, with basic causes for sinful
living.[12]

Those causes were, of course, institutional, which meant
that capitalism itself had to be taken on. This by no means
suggests that the social gospelists were socialists, although
some eventually turned in that direction. More often than not
they took a more moderate approach to institutional change,
challenging the worst excesses of capitalist exploitation and
advocating legislation to protect working people and mitigate
the suffering of the poor.[13]

Theirs was the familiar patchwork or Band-Aid approach to
institutional change, which would become synonymous with
the term liberalism after 1932.

At the same time, the social gospelists were in a desperate
search for a new theological rationale which would allow them
to adjust to the ideas of Darwinism, Freud and the "higher
criticism" leveled at the Bible by modern scholars. They found
it in the works of theologians like Horace Bushnell. Bushnell
said that there was really no discrepancy between scientific
observation and reason on the one hand, and Christian faith on
the other. Bushnell argued that when the heart tells a Christian
one thing and the mind another, it is not a contradiction at all,
because as Pascal once said, "The heart has its reasons which
reason does not know." This provided a rationale for the Christian believer to continue in his faith while accepting the truths
of a secular world. For the new liberal theology, knowing God
was a self-authenticating personal experience which required
no scientific proof. The experience of the heart was the only
truth necessary and the only truth possible. Thus, it was possible
to entertain all scientific and secular ideas, but they were ultimately to be placed under the watchful judgment of the ultimate authority, the Lord, as witnessed and experienced through
the heart of each believer.[14]

The different paths taken by postwar evangelists soon developed into a full-scale schism in American Christianity and
finally led to separation during the Fundamentalist-modernist
battle of the 1920s. The advocates of the personal gospel and
the gospel of wealth put their stress on individual salvation to
the virtual exclusion of covenant and social reform. In so doing,
they became aligned with the elite classes and became staunch
supporters of the capitalist establishment. The advocates of

covenant and reform, the social gospelists, stressed institutional change to better the human condition. In the process, they became increasingly secular in their approach, style and values and lost touch with the spiritual needs of the individual sinner in search of personal salvation.[15]

FUNDAMENTALISTS VS. MODERNISTS

Darwin's theory of evolution turned out to be the greatest little invention of the twentieth century. It became the undisputed philosophical premise for the emerging modernist society.

Before World War I, people were satisfied with a little more than a chicken in every pot. After World War I, the cry was for a Ford motorcar (or even two) in every garage. Ours was to be the century of growth, of mobility, of expansion. We adjusted rather well to the new pace, all things considered. Overnight, Americans became obsessed with the concept of new, better and more. Telephones, refrigerators and radios were all for the taking; that is, with the help of a little installment credit. It was the new paradise. The consumer kingdom replaced the kingdom of God, and advertising helped cushion the turmoil of transition by reminding everyone that values are really styles. And, since styles change every season, woe to those who find themselves out of tune, out of touch and out of the running. Jefferson once said, "Nothing is unchangeable except the inherent rights of man."[16] Madison Avenue quickly changed rights into wants, and announced that everything was, in fact, exchangeable—unless, that is, they were temporarily out of stock.

Darwin saved the day for a new, motorized America; in return, he received not so much as a dime in compensation. What he provided, however, was worth its weight in gold. Darwin clothed the new modern man and woman with a philosophical garment that was tailor-made for the occasion. He said that the biology of life was fluid, mobile, forever changing, growing and expanding. Nothing was fixed. There were no absolutes in nature, no fixed points of reference from which to make black and white judgments. Everything indeed was relative and relational. *Voila!* Right or wrong, it was an idea whose time had come. It was indeed a perfect rationale for the expanding material culture of the turn of the century. But Darwin's theory was not accepted carte blanche. It still had to overcome a final and climactic test of strength. As it turned out, Darwin's theory was more than sufficient for the task.

The decisive battle began on July 10, 1925, in Dayton, Tennessee. At issue was the question of whether a high school biology teacher named John T. Scopes could continue to lecture on the theory of evolution in the classroom. Sometime earlier, the Tennessee legislature had passed a law prohibiting the teaching of "any theory that denies the story of the divine creation of man as taught in the Bible and to teach instead that man had descended from a lower order of animals."[17] Scopes was on trial for violating the state statute.

The entire nation watched intently as the new order faced off in deadly combat with the old in the town of Dayton. The question was both theological and cultural. On the religious side, it was the question of the inerrancy of the Bible and the Word of God vs. modern science. On the cultural side, it was small-town America, with its traditional values of home, family, and strict sexual mores, against big-city America, with its fast, mobile lifestyles, easy virtue and cosmopolitan tastes.

The nineteenth century was meeting the twentieth century head-on, and the evangelicals, once the vanguard of the social reform movements, now found themselves boxed in as the defenders of outworn ideas and values.

Clarence Darrow, the brilliant East Coast trial lawyer, led the defense team. William Jennings Bryan, the tireless populist campaigner and champion of agrarian and small-town America, led the prosecution team. By the time it was over, Bryan and his evangelical supporters had been thoroughly humiliated by Darrow's brilliant defense of Darwin's theory. The national press and the American people passed their judgment as well. Science was now supreme. The Bible (the Word of God) would simply have to make the necessary adjustments.

Much of the American religious community had already begun to make such an adjustment. The social gospel advocates of the late nineteenth century were slowly "evolving" into the modernists of the early twentieth century.

Shailer Mathews, dean of the Chicago Divinity School, wrote an essay in 1924 entitled, "The Faith of Modernism." It provided a good capsule definition of the new liberal theology.

The use of the methods of modern science to find, state and use the permanent and central values of inherited orthodoxy in meeting the needs of a modern world.... The modernist movement is a phase of the scientific struggle for freedom in thought and belief.... Modernists are Christians who accept the results of scientific research as data with which to think religiously.... Modernists are Christians who adopt the methods of historical and literary science in the study of the Bible and religion.... The modernist Christian believes that Christian religion will help meet social as well as individual needs...[18]

A more popular description of a modernist, and perhaps more to the point, is to be found in a novel of the period by Luther Little entitled, *Manse Dwellers.*

Jesus was born of a human father and mother. He was divine only as are other men. He was the greatest of prophets and ethical teachers...He is himself not the object of religious trust and worship. His recorded miracles are mainly myth and fiction, the imaginings of fond disciples...there was no real resurrection and ascension. There was, doubtless, belief in the resurrection, but it was based in manifestations like those of modern spiritualism. They are simply psychic phenomenon of the subjective kind...Christ's present influence is like that of many great men who have lived.... The New Testament records themselves are conglomerates of a little truth and a great deal of fiction drawn from the surrounding ethnic religions or the imaginations of the writers themselves.[19]

By the end of World War I the traditional evangelical churches were split on the question of liberalism and modernity. The more conservative churches, determined to force a showdown, began to marshal their strength under the loose banner of Fundamentalism. The name is derived from a series of ten small books edited in 1910 by two "scholars" of the Moody Bible Institute entitled, *Fundamentals: A Testimony to the Truth.* The volumes were sent free to every minister in the country. They were meant to be a litmus test of evangelical faith. Their five main principles of faith were: "1) the verbal inspiration of the

Bible, 2) the virgin birth of Christ, 3) His substitutionary atonement, 4) His bodily resurrection and 5) His imminent and visible second coming."[20]

For the Fundamentalist, the question clearly boiled down to acceptance or nonacceptance of the principle of Bible inerrancy and the Word of God. On this question, the Fundamentalists argued there was no room for compromise. The gauntlet was down. The Fundamentalists were led by two forces. One was spearheaded by a small cadre of Biblical scholars clustered around J. Gresham Machen and the Princeton Theological Seminary.[21] Their approach was scholarly. The other force, "the Dispensationalists," proved to be much more prone to emotional excesses in the ensuing battle. For them, any deviation from orthodoxy, no matter how slight, was the work of Satan and to be resisted.[22]

The Fundamentalists attempted to seize control of the major Christian denominations but were soundly defeated by a coalition of moderate and liberal forces. By the 1925 Scopes trial, according to historian Winthrop Hudson, "the obscurantism, violent language and smear tactics of the more vociferous Fundamentalists had so alienated public opinion generally that there was little prospect that the Fundamentalists would gain control of any major Protestant denomination."[23]

EVANGELICALISM AND THE GREAT DEPRESSION OF THE 1930s

Four years after Clarence Darrow routed the Fundamentalists at Dayton, Tennessee, the American economy collapsed. Many expected that the Depression would bring a resurgence of "old time" religion as millions of desperate Americans looked back to the Bible and God for some surefire answers and, of course, salvation. It never happened. There was no great revival like the two that shook this country in the 1740s and again in the 1840s. Many sociologists of a later period credit this to the increasing secularization of society which, they argued, had all but eliminated the last remaining vestiges of religious revivalism in the American soul.[24] This postmortem on revivalism, of course, turned out to be premature as the evangelical awakening of the past decade has demonstrated.

Why, then, was there no great awakening? On a more superficial level, it would be easy to place the blame on the Christian churches themselves. The liberals, lacking a firm theological base of their own and existing more or less as an appendage to the secular order, exhibited throughout the Depression little more than a "knee-jerk" reaction to the larger economic and political forces unfolding around them. The Fundamentalists, discredited and ridiculed by the media and most of the general public, and plagued by internal divisions and quarrels, continued to withdraw from involvement in the critical affairs of the day. Their concerns over evolution and other points of theological doctrine were of little meaning to millions of Americans standing in the breadlines.

These explanations aside, there is a more substantial reason for the religious quietism of the period. In the previous two great awakenings, evangelical fervor found its expression amidst an immediate background of depression and hard times. Still, in both of the former instances, the revivalist upsurge was also taking place during a major shift from one economic epoch to another. In the 1740s, the colonies were beginning the process of economic separation from the British Empire, which required the wholesale development of a new set of economic relationships, arrangements and understandings. The great awakening provided the *liberating energy* needed to challenge the old economic order. It also provided a covenant vision which was essential to the establishment of a new set of economic and political arrangements.

The second great revival in the 1830s and 1840s was similar. While it is true that Finney and his cohorts were able to seize on the immediacy of the 1837 depression to spread their evangelical appeals, it was the larger economic backdrop that turned this series of revivals into a national political movement to restructure the country. In the 1840s, America was experiencing its second major economic shift. The agrarian society of the new republic was giving way to the emerging industrial era. The concept of agrarian democracy and of decentralized political and economic control lodged in the separate states did not fit the prerequisites of an industrial order. Capitalist expansion required national decisions governing international import and export regulations; centralized authority over questions regarding rail transportation, interstate commerce, coordination of production and markets; and a host of other items that go along with the transformation from an agrarian to an industrial economy.

The second great awakening, with its emphasis on ending slavery, provided the necessary lightning rod for the destruction of the old order based on state autonomy and a plantation economy. It was the liberating force that led to the Civil War. It also provided the theological doctrine of "perfectionism" which was later transformed into the vision of a secular covenant ideally suited for the expansionary ethos of post–Civil War capitalist development.

The Depression of the 1930s more closely resembles the situation surrounding Dwight Moody's rise to fame in the bad years of the 1870s. In both instances, the economic downturns were unrelated to any major economic shift. The Depression years under Franklin D. Roosevelt did not lead to a fundamental shift in our economic arrangements. We nose-dived into the Depression with the same economic order with which we stumbled out in 1945. The modus operandi of the economic system continued to be based on technological efficiency, profit and expansion, and all of the other essential hallmarks of an industrial order. To be sure, the introduction of Keynesian economics and New Deal government intervention into the private sphere were new ingredients, but both were regarded, and rightfully so, as simply "recharging" agents for the existing economic system. There was still no change in the basic economic mode itself. Industrial capitalism, though with a face-lift, continued as the prevailing ethos.

During the Depression years, "serious" questioning of the economic order was not at issue in the popular mind. Though the Communist party made some inroads within the labor movement and various socialist ideologies enjoyed a modicum of attention and interest, most Americans retained their faith in the system, especially in the conceptual framework that underlay it. For most people, scientific truth reigned supreme, and if there were institutional problems that needed to be ironed out, then new techniques and technologies would be found to make the proper adjustments. In this context, F. D. R. won over the American people precisely because he was the tinkerer, the adjuster, the technique manipulator par excellence. The New Deal administration constantly presented the impression that they were hard at work, fine-tuning the economic and political gears, and assured the public that it was just a matter of time until they came up with the ideal combination to put the giant economic machine back in tip-top working order.

If loss of faith occurred during those years, it was with individual leadership rather than the economic order itself. As a result, the conditions that were manifest at the time of the first two great awakenings simply were nonexistent during the Depression years. For this reason, there was no great revival fervor, no *liberating force* to challenge the existing economic order and no reformulated doctrine to justify the establishment and consolidation of a new economic vision and covenant.

Against this reality, the liberal church community continued to provide a somewhat innocuous presence during the Depression years. If anything, their new role seemed more suited to the function of chaplain rather than prophet.

Meanwhile, the remnants of the Fundamentalists withdrew further into sectarian squabbles and internecine warfare to the point where they were regarded largely as a fringe sect of little consequence to the national life. Fortunately for them, they hit on a new target during the late 1930s which was to "resurrect" their fortunes for a brief period during post–World War II America. The target was communism. It supplied for the Fundamentalists all of the necessary ingredients for a return to their former glory. With evolution no longer a source of contention for most Americans, the Fundamentalists seized on communism as an ideal substitute—one that could insure an emotional response among the people. Communism soon became the catchall (as evolution had been earlier) for everything evil in America. Communism was seen as the devil's plot to bring atheism, sexual licentiousness and totalitarian collectivism to the country. Its proselytizers and fellow travelers, argued the Fundamentalists, were the same intellectual and professional elite with their ideas about evolution, psychology and "higher criticism," who had sought to disparage and undermine the Word of God and Biblical truth at the turn of the century. By the late 1940s, the Fundamentalists' forces were riding full-gait once again, this time atop a new steed. With their fanatical anticommunist crusade, the Fundamentalists became deeply and inextricably immeshed with the ultra-right-wing forces and establishment business interests, a relationship that continues to exist, though less pronounced, to this day.

THE EMERGENCE OF THE NEOEVANGELICALS

Many orthodox evangelicals were uncomfortable with the obscurantism, separatism and fanatic anti-intellectualism of the hard-core Fundamentalists. When the hard-liners formed the militantly separatist American Council of Christian Churches in 1941,[25] the less extreme evangelicals were caught in a bind. On the one hand, they were doctrinally closer to the Fundamentalists than to the liberals. On the other, they were strategically opposed to the separatist approach of their own colleagues. With nowhere to go, they decided to establish their own organization. The National Association of Evangelicals was formed in 1942. While its leaders made it clear from the start that they were as opposed as the Fundamentalists to the current liberal apotheosis within the Christian denominations, they made it equally clear that they were determined to draw a strategic wall between themselves and the Fundamentalists.[26] The NAE forces, led by Harold Ockenga, also let it be known that they were open to dialogue and, on occasion, cooperation with other schools of thought; were prepared to develop a rigorous academic defense of their theological position; and were more concerned with converting the culture as opposed to simply withdrawing from it.[27] The NAE represents many denominations including the Baptist General Conference, Conservative Congregational Christian Conference, Evangelical Free Church of America, the Christian and Missionary Alliance and the Free Methodist Church. According to religious historian Richard Quebedeaux, the NAE also takes in much of the "membership" within the Southern Baptist Convention, the Lutheran Church and Missouri Synod, as well as representatives of individual churches from the Presbyterians of the United States, the United Methodist Church and the American Baptist Church.[28]

In the summer of 1947, the NAE took a new turn with the publication of a controversial book entitled, *The Uneasy Conscience of Modern Fundamentalism* by Carl Henry. Henry's book argued for a return to the commitment to social concern that had characterized the evangelism of the early years of American development.

> There is a growing awareness in fundamentalist circles that, despite the orthodox insistence upon revelation and

redemption, evangelical Christianity has become increasingly inarticulate about the social reference of the Gospel . . . Though the modern crisis is not basically political, economic or social—fundamentally it is religious—yet evangelicalism must be armed to declare the implications of its proposed religious solution for the politico-economic and sociological context of modern life.[29]

The NAE began to give lip service to the notion of social concern, if not social reform itself. With the emergence of *Christianity Today* in the 1950s, under the editorship of Carl Henry, an attempt was made to hammer out a theology of relevance on the major issues confronting contemporary American society. Twenty-five years later, however, the NAE leadership candidly admitted in their own magazine *(Christianity Today)* that they had failed in their mission.

Evangelicals have failed to articulate, except in broad generalities, the positive requirements of a Christian civilization. Here, perhaps lies our greatest failure. So often we have concentrated one-sidedly on purely spiritual activities and have left social problems, politics and education and other important areas to their own fate. . . . Often we think only in terms of personal witness, of winning individual persons to Christ, and neglect the many burning social problems of our time and the broad and difficult questions of culture in general.[30]

While the neoevangelicals failed as social theorists, they did succeed in restoring evangelicalism to the national life of the country. Their success is attributable, in a large part, to their chief popularizer and evangelist extraordinaire, Billy Graham.

Graham began his evangelical ministry in 1945 with Youth for Christ. He didn't attract much attention, however, until the fall of 1949, where in Los Angeles he decided to borrow a few chapters and verses from the Fundamentalist repertoire. Conjuring up visions of Armageddon, Graham warned against the worldwide menace of communism, which he claimed was already at work, endeavoring to weaken the defense of the nation from within. For an encore, he went after deficit spending, labor unions, pinkos and perverts in high office, and by the time he was through pointing his finger to the audience and then to the heavens above, America had found itself a new inspirational leader.[31] With the help of millionaire media mogul, William Randolph Hearst, Graham received guaranteed national media attention everywhere he went.[32] Of course, along with national visibility and success came a certain degree of respectability; hobnobbing with important members of America's crème de la crème had its effect in smoothing the rough edges off Graham's excessive rhetoric and belligerent, almost Fundamentalist style. Under the influence of Ockenga and the NAE group, Graham became more ecumenical in his organizing approach and less political in his sermons (though he retained some of the anticommunist rhetoric). The result was an evangelist for all people and for all seasons—moderately conservative, moderately Charismatic and moderately cooperative, Graham was more than a proper match for the moderate culture of the fifties.

Graham, more than any other single force, was responsible for preparing the groundwork for the acceptance of neoevangelicalism. In fairness to Graham, his political and social views have changed somewhat over the years, as changes have occurred in the broader culture. Still, no one dare accuse Graham of being a prophet or a man ahead of his time—he was not a trailblazer in the Civil Rights movement, although he insisted on integrated rallies and belatedly threw his support to the struggle for black rights in the political arena. He never took a stand on the war in Vietnam, although he finally remarked that it had been a tragic mistake to have become involved there in the first place.[33] In short, Graham's success was due not to his forward thinking, but to his uncanny ability to accurately reflect the mood and attitude of Middle America. He was like a direct mirror to society. If ever there was a bellwether of American public opinion, Graham could certainly vie for the honors along with Gallup, Harris and Roper.

The great success of Graham, the NAE and related organizations in preparing the country for a new evangelical awakening has also been their undoing. Like Moses, who led his people to the promised land but was never to step foot in it himself, the neoevangelicals face a similar fate today. A new generation of evangelical leadership has emerged, weaned on the theories and assumptions of elder statesmen like Carl Henry and Graham, but no longer willing to entertain mere talk of social concern and involvement. For these new evangelicals, many of whom experienced the social upheavels of the 1960s, the time for talk is over. The pressing business now, they contend, is to put theory to practice, and shape a new theological doctrine and covenant that can speak to the changing needs of American society over the next quarter-century.

8

TODAY'S CHARISMATICS AND EVANGELICALS: A TWO-PART THEOLOGICAL MOVEMENT

The evangelical awakening is moving in two distinct but related directions. The Charismatics are providing the kind of *liberating energy* that is essential for any full-scale assault on the authority of the existing economic (and political) order. Their success in marshaling all forms of communications— both mass and interpersonal—attests to their potential power as a mobilizing medium for a new movement. The evangelicals, on the other hand, are beginning to provide the philosophical components that are vital in developing a reformulated theological doctrine for a new order and a new covenant. Their success in building an educational infrastructure and an organizational base for social action will be crucial in determining whether they will be able to sustain a mass movement for fundamental change.

If the Charismatic and the evangelical movements come together and effectively unite a liberating energy with a new covenant vision, America could experience a third great awakening. For these reasons, it is important to look in detail, at both the theology underlying these spiritual forces and the economic, political and cultural context in which that theology will find expression.

THE EVANGELICAL THEOLOGY

There are, of course, many differences of opinion within contemporary evangelism over what constitutes "correct" theological doctrine. The neoevangelicals like Carl Henry and Billy Graham, for example, will often differ with the more radical evangelicals on specific theological questions. There are also differences of opinion on which aspects of doctrine should receive the most attention. Despite the differences there are some broad areas of agreement within the evangelical community concerning theology—these common denominators provide a reasonably coherent theological foundation for current evangelical thought. (Note: Fundamentalists' views are not considered part of the "evangelical" theology.)

BIBLICAL AUTHORITY

The trend among the more progressive evangelicals is to accept the authority of the Bible as the Word of God, but reject the notion of scriptural inerrancy. The stress is now laid on the inspired word as opposed to the written word. In other words, unlike the old-school Fundamentalists, many of today's evangelicals no longer believe in the so-called "dictation" theory; i.e., that the Biblical writers and apostles merely wrote down, verbatim, God's word on all matters. There is now a growing agreement (at least among the newer evangelical leaders) that the actual written words by the apostles and writers were influenced by the historical and cultural environment in which they lived. So, while there may be inconsistencies and even errors in some of the passages as a result of the "human" translation of God's word, the overall message and truths are themselves the inspired word of God and therefore infallible. For many evangelicals today, "authoritative" has replaced inerrant in their view of the scriptures. It is also important to note that many evangelicals are putting more emphasis on the Holy Spirit as a means of assisting the individual in illuminating God's word in the Bible. Even though God's word is not always immediately self-evident from a reading of the text, the true meaning can, nonetheless, become evident under the guidance of the Holy Spirit.[1] This new emphasis on the Holy Spirit and revealed truths is a key theological link between the new evangelicals and the Charismatics.

THE SOVEREIGNTY OF GOD

The evangelicals believe in an infinite personal God. Although they believe he is transcendent, they do not consider him to be inaccessible or disinterested in the affairs of the world. While God is not bound to this world, he does choose to interact with it through the indwelling spirit of the Holy Ghost. In this sense, God is intimately concerned with our daily lives; he is a personal God, but he also retains his transcendent Spirit. Therefore, God is neither the vague and abstract impersonal absolute of the Deists and rationalists, nor is he like the kind of finite gods of the Greeks that are always on hand at the beck and call of human beings. He is, at the same time, the infinite God that transcends all history and the personal God who interacts in history.[2]

SIN AND EVIL

The evangelical believes that all people, without exception, are sinners. While man's and woman's created nature is good, it has been corrupted by the Fall (in the Garden of Eden). To the evangelical, sin is essentially the pride of hubris, the belief that human beings can reshape themselves and the world in their own image and do a better job in the process than God did. This view of human nature is radically at odds with the Enlightenment or liberal view that people are born into the world basically good, although they may, in fact, then be corrupted by an evil environment. With the liberal view, the focus becomes one of changing the evil aspects of the environment in the belief that, in so doing, the natural goodness of human beings will be allowed to come from under and flourish. The evangelical would assert that not only are evil and sin an inherent part of every person's life from the beginning, but that it is also impossible to completely expurgate that evil or the temptation to do evil in this world by simply changing the world around us.[3]

CONVERSION, SALVATION AND GRACE

Human beings cannot be saved by their own good works or intentions. To believe so is to continue to embrace that basic hubris or pride which is the essential element of sin itself. Each person, according to the evangelicals, can only be saved by God's grace. Only when the individual finally gives up any further pretensions of his own independent omnipotence and immortality and places himself totally and without qualification in God's hands, will he be saved from his sins by God's grace.[4] Here the question of a person's free will becomes important. A person cannot be saved by his own actions. Good works (as Calvin argued) will not assure a person a place in God's kingdom. Only God can pardon us for our evil ways and reserve us a place in heaven. Therefore, as long as a person refuses to confess his depravity and helplessness, he will continue in bondage, although he may well labor under the illusion that he is, in fact, free. Personal freedom, for the evangelical, means "liberation" from the evil ways of this world by confession, God's grace and salvation. Only a liberated person, one who has put his complete and total faith in Christ, can really be free in the sense of being able to work alongside God, in covenant, to advance the glory of his kingdom.

Needless to say, today's evangelicals believe that all sinners can be saved, that God's grace is potentially available to everyone. Most evangelicals no longer believe that part of the old Calvinist doctrine that asserts that individuals are either elected or damned at birth.

SUBSTITUTIONARY ATONEMENT AND HOLINESS

According to the Bible, a person is not only pardoned of his sins by God's grace, but also cleansed of those sins as well. But this cleansing process entails a cooperative effort. The individual must continually renew and purify himself throughout his life. This is part of the process of serving the glory of God.[5]

Just as Christ suffered and died on the cross as "substitutionary atonement" for humanity's sins, so too must every Christian suffer in a life of true discipleship for Christ.[6] According to evangelical doctrine, leading a life of personal holiness in Christ is a way of bearing witness to Christ's own suffering for all of us. While it is impossible to ever reach holy perfection in this world, the effort itself can help prepare an imperfect beginning for the eventual return of God's glorious kingdom.[7] The question of exactly what constitutes a life of holiness has created long and bitter schisms within Christianity. Some of the hard-core Fundamentalists believe that personal holiness can only be maintained by complete separation from the secular world. For them, God's world and this world are two different and mutually exclusive planes. As long as a person continues to take part in this world, the world of "the flesh," of depravity and of sin, he will be unable to cleanse himself of the evil and the temptations around him. Therefore, the only answer for these believers is a life of total separation (a subcultural monasticism) from the affairs of the secular culture. Contact of any kind, they argue, can only tarnish.[8]

The newer evangelicals perceive holiness in a different light. Like the pre–Civil War evangelicals, they draw a distinction between God's world and this one, but they are quick to point out that Christ did not ignore this world while he was here. On the contrary, he continually confronted the evils of society head-on with the good news of the kingdom of God. Like Christ, they argue, a true life of holiness means continually confronting the evils of this world while at the same time attempting to take part in the kingdom of God. The life of every Christian, they argue, should be committed to bringing the world to Christ, not turning one's back on it in a life of monastic quietude.[9]

WITNESS AND SERVICE

From the evangelical notion of personal holiness flows the idea of witness. When Christ proclaimed the kingdom of God, they contend, he did not mean it to be some far-off abstraction. When people take on a life in Christ, they are already a part of God's kingdom. Although that kingdom cannot possibly reach its total fulfillment and perfection until Christ's return to earth, it still exists, in part, in the obedient service of God's faithful on earth. Just as God made the blind see and the lame walk as "signs" of the greatness of the kingdom of God, so too must every Christian lead a life in service to his fellow human beings, as a continuing sign of the presence and glory of God's future kingdom. A Christian's unselfish service and devotion, his attempt to witness, even imperfectly, God's future kingdom on earth, is part of God's "Good News." Of course, the question of what exactly constitutes bearing witness and doing service is what divides many of the older neoevangelicals from their younger counterparts. [10]

WEALTH AND POWERS

While the establishment evangelicals have repeatedly given lip service to the concept of bearing witness and doing service, they have, as was already mentioned, done little to hammer out a coherent doctrine of how that service should be performed. The newer, more progressive evangelicals have moved into this theological vacuum with a passion. Groups like the radical evangelical Sojourners have begun to articulate the beginnings of a theology of service that is at least gaining an attentive audience within broader evangelical circles.

These evangelicals have formed their assumption about the nature of proper service from what the Bible has to say about two related concerns, economics and the "powers and principalities."

Jim Wallis, one of the country's leading young evangelical writers and a member of Sojourners, contends that questions concerning wealth, poverty and economic justice take up more space in the Bible than probably any other item. On the question of economics, says Wallis, the scriptures "are not neutral." Wallis points out that on economic issues:

> The Bible is clearly and emphatically on the side of the poor, the exploited and the victimized. Nowhere in the Scripture are the rights of the rich proclaimed... Throughout Scripture, however, the rights of the poor are proclaimed.... The rich are instructed to serve the poor and relinquish their wealth and power for the sake of the poor. [11]

The new evangelicals argue that just as Christ, in his own life, set an example by championing the rights of the poor against the established order, service in Christ today necessitates a similar type of commitment.

"To live in radical obedience to Jesus Christ," exhorts Wallis, "means to be identified with the poor and the oppressed."[12] This analysis, in itself, is not all that earth shattering. Evangelicals of the early nineteenth century shared a similar view. What is different and unique about the contemporary analysis of service is the approach being advocated to "championing" the rights of the poor. The Finneyites of the last century believed in service almost exclusively in individual terms. The concept of "disinterested benevolence" often conjured up the image of individual Christians committing individual acts of charity for the downtrodden. In contrast, today's young evangelicals are concentrating both on individual acts of charity and on broader institutional change. They recognize that poverty is more than an individual affair, that it is a direct manifestation of prevailing institutional arrangements which concentrate wealth and power and perpetuate a system of economic injustice. Unlike traditional secular liberals, however, these evangelicals take their inspiration, not from some vague humanist notion of doing good, but directly from the Bible. The Bible talks about the "powers." These are the structures God created to bring order and regularity into people's secular life. They include the entire fabric of economic, political and cultural rules, laws and institutional arrangements of society. These powers, like human beings, were originally created by God and were good. But, just as people rebelled, so did the powers. Like people, they began to claim absolute power and dominion for themselves. It is these powers that humankind has turned into idols and through which it remains in continued bondage. Even as the powers are fallen, it is clear that people cannot live without them. But neither can they live with them.

According to the young evangelicals, the dual relationship that exists between the fallen powers and fallen humanity is the source of the evil which enslaves us all, and which creates injustice and perpetuates poverty. The powers manifest themselves in a thousand different ways, from institutional discrimination against certain types of people because of their race or ethnic background, to tax loopholes in the laws which favor the super-rich and penalize the middle class. The answer to the problem of the powers, contend evangelicals like the Sojourners, is to be found on the cross and in the resurrection. Jesus' crucifixion was a victory against the powers. "He [Christ] disarmed the principalities and made a public example of them, triumphing over them in Him" (Col. 2:13–15). By refusing to acknowledge the powers' hold over him, Christ broke their hold over a suffering humanity as well. As a result, every Christian has a similar responsibility to do as Christ did, to refuse to acknowledge the powers' hold on individuals or humanity. Taming the powers and continually subjecting them to a higher truth, the Word of God, is the embodiment of service that the Bible speaks to and that Christ died for and triumphed over on the cross.[13]

The new evangelicals, then, take a dual approach to sin. Unlike the liberals, they do not see human beings as basically good but merely forced to live in an evil world. This line of thinking leads only to continued attempts at changing the institutions, leaving the individual untouched. Nor do they share the very limited perspective of some of the older evangelicals that sin is purely a personal matter, unrelated to the institutional arrangements of the larger society. For the new evangelicals, sin is inherent to both the individual and the institutions. Both are fallen, both need to be changed. Only then will the faithful Christian be performing his true service to God and bearing witness to the future coming of the kingdom.

THE ROLE OF THE CHURCH

The new evangelicals are opposed to the kind of secular liberalism that overran the institutional churches in the 1960s, and that still exerts a dominant presence. They believe that the commitment to broad social and economic change led the churches to abandon their role as spiritual guides for the individual sinner in need of salvation. On the other hand, they are also opposed to those mainline evangelical churches that concentrate exclusively on questions of individual salvation, while abandoning any social commitment in the larger society. Commensurate with their view of service, these new evangelicals see the church as God's community in this world. Its function is, first and foremost, to bring people to Christ and to salvation. In order to fulfill God's commission, however, they assert that the church, as a community of Christians, must also play a role of service and bear witness. It must challenge economic, social and political injustice and offer Christian al-

ternatives for people's lives. Many of the elder statesmen of
evangelicalism would agree with this definition of the function
of the church, though disagreeing both on the nature of church
involvement as well as the particular issues which should be
addressed. Some see the church taking on a more passive tu-
torial role, advising its congregations on the relationships between Christian values and contemporary social ills, but not
advocating particular positions and certainly not becoming "actively" involved as a corporate body. On the other end of the
spectrum are those, like the Sojourners, who see the church as
an active participant, a corporate body exercising its responsibility to bear witness and perform service. For them, the
failure to take a stand on important issues is either a cop-out,
at best, or tantamount to a stand in favor of the status quo, at
worst.

THE CHARISMATIC THEOLOGY

The Kansas City football stadium had never sported an event
quite so unusual. Tens of thousands of Bible-carrying, hymn-
singing Christians of all shades and denominations squeezed
into the stands, the bleachers and overflowed onto the playing
field on July 21, 1977, for what turned out to be the first annual
Superbowl of the burgeoning new Charismatic movement. They
were Catholic, Baptist, Presbyterian, Episcopalian and Methodist, all praising the Lord and embracing each other in brotherly love. Even for a casual observer of Christian religious
history, such a moment of ecumenical bliss certainly gave the
impression that a miracle had, indeed, taken place. While it
was not a single miracle that brought these Christian believers
together in Kansas City, it certainly is fair to say that thousands
of individual miracles did. These people call themselves Charismatics, and they are the fastest growing evangelical renewal
movement in America today.[14]

Their name comes from the Greek word, charis, meaning
grace. The Charismatics believe they are empowered by the
Holy Spirit to do certain "supernatural" acts, like speaking in
tongues, faith healing and uttering prophesies. While the roots
of the present Charismatic movement can be traced to the Pentecostal Holiness churches that sprang up at the turn of the
century, in many ways, the current phenomenon is quite unique.

Unlike the pentecostal movement, which flourished among the small-town and urban poor, the Charismatic movement is decidedly middle class, and even suburban in orientation. It has also attracted a heavy Catholic following. It is estimated that the traditional Pentecostal churches have a membership of nearly four million. The Charismatic movement, in the space of just a few years, is already estimated to have over thirteen million adherents.[15]

The Charismatic movement started back in the early 1950s with the formation of the Full Gospel Businessman's Fellowship in Los Angeles. Now boasting a membership of over 100,000, the group has been instrumental in spreading the Charismatic message and legitimizing its appeal for middle-class America.[16]

In 1959, Dennis Bennet, an Episcopalian minister at St. Mark's Church in Van Nuys, California, received what Charismatics call "the Baptism of the Holy Spirit." Within the next several months, eight more ministers and over a hundred lay people were similarly baptized.[17] Overnight, word of this new religious experience spread throughout California and the West Coast. The Charismatic movement was off and running. Seven years later at Duquesne University in Pittsburgh, four Catholics were baptized with the Holy Spirit, thus setting off the Catholic stage of the modern Charismatic revival.[18] There are now nearly a million Catholics baptized with the Holy Spirit, and the movement itself has become the most significant development in Catholicism in this century.[19]

One of the most remarkable characteristics of the Charismatic movement is its ecumenicism. No other religious movement in history has ever been able to bring together Catholics and Protestants (not to mention Protestants and Protestants) into such close spiritual fellowship. The "Baptism of the Holy Spirit" has provided a common experience which has crossed all doctrinal lines, tearing down in its path long-held religious superstitions, prejudices and defenses. In this sense, the Charismatic movement has already shown itself to be a "potentially" powerful force in the renewal of Christian faith and the reformulation of Christian doctrine. A knowledge of its underlying theology is important in understanding both its current success and its probable future impact on American culture.

Although Charismatics are evangelical, they differ in one major respect from mainline Protestant evangelicalism. Charismatics believe that the Word of God speaks authoritatively

to Christian believers not only through the written word of the
Bible, but also through the continuing indwelling of the Holy
Spirit. The revealed Word of God, then, is potentially available
to all who have received what the Charismatics call the second
Baptism of the Holy Spirit. Passages in the Book of Acts
provide the basis for the movement. According to the scriptures, on the first Pentecost Sunday, the twelve apostles heard
a sound:

> like the rush of a mighty wind and it filled the house
> where they were sitting—and there appeared to them
> tongues as of fire, distributed and resting on each one
> of them. And they were filled with the Holy Spirit and
> began to speak in other tongues, as the Spirit gave them
> utterance.

The gift of tongues is one of nine special gifts mentioned
in the scriptures which are considered to be direct communications from the Holy Spirit to the individual. Being blessed
with one or more of these spiritual gifts means that the Holy
Spirit has entered an individual life and is communicating God's
revealed truths to him. Unlike some of the more traditional
evangelicals, the Charismatics do not put as much stress on
the abstract doctrines of the Bible. While they accept the Bible
as the authoritative Word of God, they believe that the revealed
word, as communicated to the apostles and Biblical writers, is
also potentially available to people throughout history who have
received the Baptism of the Holy Spirit and the special gifts
that manifest God's personal presence. Many of the younger
evangelicals share the Charismatics' belief that God speaks just
as authoritatively through the Holy Spirit as the written word
of the scriptures. This new emphasis on ongoing Divine revelation and outward observable manifestations of the presence
of the Holy Spirit has brought together Christians who otherwise might never have come together because of a long history
of doctrinal differences regarding interpretation and meaning
of the scriptures.

The Charismatic experience is one of the heart. It is a deeply
subjective emotional encounter with God. It does not rely on
the kind of rational scholasticism that is a central feature of
more orthodox Christian belief.

The Charismatics' emphasis on continual revelation (the
kind that is potentially available to every person) makes Chris-

tian faith much more vibrant, immediate and real for its adherents. Instead of relying solely on the revealed Word of God as written down nearly 2000 years ago for a people of an ancient culture, the Charismatics can feel that their lives and their history are just as important to God today. The special gifts are a physical manifestation that God is still personally interacting in history, as forcefully and powerfully as he did when Paul and the apostles were writing the scriptures. Through the indwelling Spirit and the special gifts for communicating the revealed word, the Charismatics have found a personal living God who cares, is present today and provides essential truths to live by.

In an age where institutional "authority" and "expertise" reign supreme, the Charismatic movement has reintroduced the concept of *personal* authority in a powerful, if not roundabout, way. Because they believe that the ultimate authority, God, can potentially speak through every person, the Charismatics tend to place less reliance on institutional authorities, at least within the church. As a result, there is more of a spirit of shared authority than might otherwise exist in a traditional church setting. Still, there is a tendency to "idolize" certain Charismatic superstars made popular through the mass media.

Up to now, the Charismatic movement has been characterized by a lack of structure. Its fluidity and spontaneity have been largely responsible for its remarkable success. Most Charismatics are content with coming together for spiritual renewal and then returning to their own denominations and congregations to spread the "Good News." While there are a few visible national leaders within the Charismatic movement, most of the leadership is localized. If anything, the Charismatics show a distinct lack of interest in developing national structures and centralized authority. In many ways their theology is anti-institutional. It is much more communal and experiential. Developing rigid authority and doctrine would, say many Charismatics, destroy the very heart of the movement and undermine the basic vitality and significance of the religious experience.

One of the major criticisms leveled at the Charismatic movement is its lack of social concern and its unwillingness to reject those parts of the popular culture that are inimical to a life of holiness and service. In fact, among Charismatics, there is often a tendency to glorify the secular culture. Many Charismatics seem to relish the fact that famous TV and movie personalities, and even some powerful politicians (and former politicians), are among the faithful and take every occasion to parade these converts before the public altar.[20] While most Charismatics are worldly in outlook, they show little enthusiasm for taking on the "powers and principalities" and championing the cause of the disenfranchised in society. Many are moderate to conservative in their political views or totally apolitical. There is, however, evidence that this situation is changing. Both conservative and liberal political influences are beginning to work on the Charismatic community, each tugging it in their own direction.

Many observers make the mistake, however, of looking at the political or nonpolitical involvement of the Charismatics in traditional terms. In fact, the Charismatic movement is probably the single most political movement in America today—not in the everyday sense of advancing particular issues and concerns—but in a much deeper more profound sense. Though largely unconscious of its own incredible politicization, the Charismatic movement is a barometer of deep changes in the American psyche that are threatening to topple the existing economic order, and along with it, many of the values that have enjoyed an absolute sovereignty over the individual and collective affairs of the nation.

The Charismatic movement, for all its ecumenicism, has met its share of criticism within the Christian community. The Lutheran Church's Missouri Synod, for example, has condemned its emphasis on "personal experience over the authority of the Bible."[21] The Charismatics have also been accused of anti-intellectualism and elitism. The emphasis on special gifts and revealed truth, sometimes over scripture, and the subjective emotional appeal of the Charismatic experience is leading to anti-intellectualism within the movement, its critics charge. At the same time, Charismatics are often accused of flaunting their "personal gifts" and exhibiting a kind of holier-than-thou elitist attitude—a posture that invites animosity and division within church congregations, and even within Christian families.[22]

THE PROTESTANT ETHIC AND ECONOMIC CHANGE

The new economic epoch we are moving into is still largely undefined. Yet, there is no doubt that it will bring with it a new or at least redefined value system that will serve to reinforce the essential features of a contracting economy.

Much of what's going on within the new evangelical-Charismatic movements can be seen as a reaction to the powerful economic readjustments that are taking place. Still, it is foolish to cling to the limited and exclusive notion that economic history alone determines the makeup of humanity. It is also true that people make their own economic history. Consequently, just as the current economic changes are influencing the spiritual awakening, it is equally the case that the religious revival is, in turn, influencing the economic situation. Both exist in a symbiotic relationship to each other; for human beings have always lived in two worlds simultaneously: the material world of the flesh and the supernatural world of the spirit. The continued tension and changing relationship between these two planes of human existence is what history has been all about from the beginning. It's also what history is all about today, as the changing economic forces meet head-on with America's spiritual awakening.

With this perspective in mind, it's essential to trace the specific changes that have been occurring in the modes of production and consumption; the effect these changes are having on the individual, the family and the culture; and the relationships between all of these factors and the evangelical-Charismatic phenomena.

If one were to draw a portrait of Reformation theology and its secular offspring, the liberal ethos, three characteristics would dominate the canvas: hard work, frugality, and individual self-reliance. The modern age of materialism was built around an attitude that favored production over consumption and the interests of the individual over the needs of the collective.

It is interesting to note that when we think of materialism today, we are likely to think immediately of consumption. Yet, during most of the modern era, materialism was associated more with production. Reformation theology has, since the beginning, emphasized the work ethic, not the consumption ethic. The Protestant emphasis on work for work's sake and frugality over licentiousness provided the perfect theological rationale for the liberal ethos and the age of growth.

Until very recently, almost every schoolchild in America was carefully weaned on two axioms which are at the core of the Protestant work ethic, to wit: "Idle hands are the devil's workshop" and "A penny saved is a penny earned." These sayings have become so engrained in the popular mind that they have become almost second nature to us. For a long time they served as a kind of internalized self-regulating mechanism. That is, whenever we entertained the prospect of either slacking off or indulging our immediate whims, our Protestant conscience would remind us of our primary duty and steer us back onto the one true path to salvation: the path of hard work and frugality.

While hard work and frugality have always been considered the prime virtues of the modern age, the notion of self-reliance has always been afforded the highest esteem. To the Reformation mind, self-reliance was the necessary condition for salvation. In the final analysis, each person must stand alone before his God, according to Calvinist doctrine. This idea is essential to Protestantism. After all, it was the Reformation theologians who replaced the priesthood of the Church with the idea of the universal priesthood of all believers. The individual Christian who, for nearly a thousand years had depended on "the Church" for help in securing his own salvation, was suddenly left to his own devices in the aftermath of the Reformation. As a result, it wasn't long before the new Protestant person was living by a creed that has survived virtually intact until the present day. The notion that "God helps those who help themselves," has been the undisputed foundation of the Protestant ethic for nearly five hundred years. It has defined the day to day behavior of over twenty-five generations of European and American Christians.

Self-reliance and salvation, then, are inseparable in Reformation theology. Of course, this duality in no way precludes the concept of shared covenant with one's fellow human beings. It does mean, however, that covenant is entered into by individuals, each retaining his own self-worth and autonomy and each ultimately responsible for his own personal salvation. According to this view of covenant, there is never a unique collective will of the whole, but only a collection of individual wills pursuing a common objective.

In its secular form, this conception of covenant has led to the liberal belief that each person's individual self-interest, when added to all others', always advances the good of the whole society. From this point of view, the free market economic system and the liberal form of government are both tangible reflections of this guiding assumption.

Today, the virtues of work for work's sake, frugality and self-reliance—the behavioral principles of the Reformation age and the liberal ethos—are falling victim to a new economic reality: a reality highlighted by a basic change in the mode of production, a shift to a service economy and an increasing emphasis on consumption over production. These broad economic changes are beginning to undercut the Protestant ethic, which has for so long provided the theological justification for the age of growth. In so doing, they are creating a theological vacuum which grows larger by the day. Before examining how that vacuum is being filled, a closer look at each of these three major economic changes is in order.

THE CHANGING PRODUCTION MODE

> So God created man in his own image; in the image of
> God He created him; male and female He created them.
> Genesis 1:2

Not so long ago an article appeared in the *British Journal of Psychiatry* entitled, "Theory of the Human Operator in Control Systems." It described the modern industrial-era person in quite different terms from those used in Genesis.

Man may be regarded as a chain consisting of the following items: (1) sensory devices, (2) a computing system which responds . . . on the basis of previous experience . . . (3) an amplifying system—the motor nerve endings and muscles . . . (4) mechanical linkages . . . whereby the muscular work produces externally visable effects.[1]

Nowhere is there mention of man and woman, the human being, complete with a soul and transcendent spirit. These characteristics are immeasurable; they can neither be observed nor quantified. As a result, they play no functional role in the day-to-day performance of the modern person within the production process. Human beings, who were originally made in God's image, have been virtually replaced by a person fashioned in the image of the machine. Eight hours a day, five days a week, year in and year out, the average person of the industrial age functions as an extension of the machine process. This is the overwhelming reality for modern men and women. Yet, a casual glance through Christian literature of the past quarter-century demonstrates an almost total lack of discussion, commentary or understanding of this central feature of modern existence.

All of us are constantly bombarded with buzz words like alienation and depersonalization. We know there is a reality to such phrases because each of us feels them on a very personal level. Yet, we find it nearly impossible to define their source in any concrete way. The clergy tell us that we are alienated from our government, our culture, our family, ourselves and our God. All of which is true. But nowhere do they mention as a possible source of our alienation the one place where we spend most of our active day, the workplace. Never is there the slightest suggestion that the production process of modern capitalism might, in some way, be the cause of much of the fragmentation of the human character and the destruction of the human soul and spirit.

Every year pollsters like Gallup and Harris ask who has had the greatest influence on American life in this century. The poll results have never included the name of Frederick Taylor. Yet Taylor has more intimately affected the day-to-day behavior and activity of more Americans in the past half-century than any other single "soul." It is Taylor's principles of work that have led directly to the reshaping of human beings in the machine image. It's strange, indeed, that the evangelical Christian community, which is often so preoccupied with people's fallen nature and the evil influences around them, has never, even once, mentioned the individual most responsible for severing twentieth-century human beings from their own free will and casting them adrift from God's image.

Frederick Taylor is the father of modern "scientific management." His philosophy and approach to work have shaped every aspect of the modern production process. Scientific management is, according to economic historian Harry Braverman, "the analyses of work into its simplest elements and the systematic improvement of the worker's performance of each of these elements." Its objective is to improve the productive efficiency of labor and thereby increase output. Says Braverman, "[scientific management] may well be the most powerful as well as the most lasting contribution America has made to western thought since the Federalist Papers."[2] If one judges history solely by the material growth of a nation, Braverman is justified in his claim. Even if one judges history more broadly, in terms of the changing relationship of people to their environment, there is still no doubt that scientific management has made its mark on today's world.

The basic philosophical principle behind scientific management is control—control over the work process and the worker himself. Control, for Taylor, was much more than a simple matter of supervision. Under supervisory control, management acts principally as a combination referee, cheerleader and occasional disciplinarian. While the workers are told broadly what to do and how to do it, a great deal of "discretionary" control over the details of getting the job done are left to the workers themselves. Taylor argued that such a system did not produce "a fair day's work." Actually, the phrase is a bit of a misnomer. For Taylor, a fair day's work meant producing the optimum possible under ideal conditions.[3] When left to their own devices Taylor observed that the workers' natural instinct was to produce only what was necessary to reproduce their own labor. Workers would see no distinct advantage to working at top speed all the time, first, because the increments in pay for each successive level of speedup become smaller and smaller and therefore less an incentive, and secondly, because they don't believe the extra energy expended is worth it in terms of their other unmet psychological and social needs.

In a natural environment, the normal inclination is to put out approximately the amount of work energy necessary to

reasonably provide for one's basic needs. This natural inclination carries over into the workplace as well. Peer group
pressure militates against 100 percent optimum output without
relaxation or reprieve. Normal social interaction alone takes
attention away from total concentration on the machine or the
work process being attended. As long as the workers retain
any control at all over their immediate work environment, contended Taylor, they would not give 100 percent to the process
itself. The answer, argued Taylor, was simple and direct. All
control over every single aspect of the work process—down
to the tiniest detail—must be removed from the workers and
placed in the hands of management. They, in turn, must sys-
tematize all available knowledge of how the work process is
performed, design an optimum plan for how the work is to be
executed, then instruct the workers in every detail of their performance, leaving no decisions, regardless of how small they may
appear, to the workers themselves. Taylor reasoned that, as
long as workers were allowed to think for themselves, they
would think about avoiding work, at least part of the time.
". . . if the worker's execution is guided by their own conception, it is not possible . . . to enforce upon them either the methodical efficiency or the working pace desired by capital."[4]
The key principle of scientific management, then, is separation
of thought from action, of conception from performance. The
management becomes the mind and the workers the body.

   Lest Taylor be unjustly accused of exhibiting extreme malice
toward assembly-line workers, it should be made perfectly clear
that the principles of scientific management have been applied
across the board, in both the shop and the front office, manufacturing and service industries, in blue-collar as well as white-
collar employment. Just as each minute task on the assembly
line is timed and prescribed, the same scientifically designed
control procedures are applied in office work. Secretaries and
clerks perform simple, repetitive tasks, all tightly prescribed
and timed in advance, to assure maximum performance and
output. Taylor succeeded in domesticating the work force by
reducing human labor to the objective role of a nonthinking
but responsive piece of hardware.

   Work, which for thousands of years involved the individual
laborer in a process of both thinking and doing, had been
eliminated for the first time. Braverman sums up this epochal
shift in people's relationship to their own labor in his landmark
work, *Labor and Monopoly Capital:*

Thus, after a million years of labor, during which human beings created not only a complex social culture but in a very real sense created themselves as well, the very cultural-biological trait upon which this entire evolution is founded has been brought, within the last 200 years, to a crisis. . . . The unity of thought and action, conception and execution, hand and mind, which capitalism threatened from the beginning, is now attacked by a systematic dissolution employing all the resources of science and the various engineering disciplines based upon it. The subjective factor of the labor process is removed to a place among its inanimate objective factors.[5]

In short, the worker as human being, complete with mind and body, is transformed into the worker as nonthinking machine, all thanks to Frederick Taylor and the principles of scientific management. As for the management side of the equation, the total number of "technical engineers, chemists, scientists, architects, draftsmen, designers and technicians represented not much more than 3 percent of the total labor force in 1970,"[6] according to Braverman. This is the new elite, the alphas of the Brave New World of industrial society—a small coterie of professionally skilled technicians who regulate the activity, the behavior and the lives of nearly eighty million American workers each day.

Taylor's "machine man" is quite different from the men and women that have been carefully sculpted in God's own image. Severed from their own minds, the new men and women of the machine age lacked the independent free will that is essential to securing their own salvation. With the rise of mass production and scientific management the virtue of self-reliance, that had been so pivotal to Reformation doctrine, suffered its first crushing blow.

More than anything else, scientific management was a statement of society's loss of faith in people's independent free will. Taylor argued that a person without a free will is potentially more productive than one with a free will. So while Protestant theologians have long considered increased productivity and free will as indispensable in securing salvation, Taylor demonstrated that, in the final analysis, one must choose between the two. In the end modern industrial society chose production over salvation and the "machine man" over the person of independent free will.

Taylor, then, helped secularize Calvin's doctrine of un-ceasing work and specialized callings. While Calvin used the scriptures as his inspiration, Taylor relied on the truths of science and technology. Calvin designed his doctrine to better serve the glory of God. Taylor designed his doctrine to better serve the new gods of the industrial age, the capitalist owners.

THE SHIFT TO A SERVICE ECONOMY

A hundred years ago, the United States made a dramatic shift from an agricultural to a manufacturing-based economy. Today a second shift, just as dramatic, is taking place. The economy is now moving from a manufacturing base to a service base. In 1900, according to economic historian Daniel Bell, only 30 percent of all workers were involved in the service sector. This sector includes personal services, like retail stores and barbershops; business services, like banking and insurance; and government services, like health, education and scientific research. Just before Pearl Harbor, the service sector employed about the same number of workers as the manufacturing sector. By 1960, however, the service sector had increased to nearly 60 percent of the entire labor force. By 1980, the number of service-related jobs will likely top 70 percent. As Bell points out, the United States is now the first nation "in which the service sector accounts for more than half the total employment and more than half the GNP."[7]

The fastest growing part of the service economy since World War II has been the public sector: health, education, welfare and other government services. In 1929 only 6.6 percent of the labor force worked for local, state or federal government. Today, twelve million workers, or 16 percent of the labor force, are employed by various government agencies.[8] The public sector is being increasingly relied upon to provide goods and services that cannot be purchased adequately in the market-place. The American people are beginning to demand more and more public expenditures for health care, pollution and environmental control, transportation, police and fire protection, utilities and education.

With the shift to a service economy and greater government involvement in the economic sphere, the nature of economic decision-making is also beginning to change. Up until recently, the marketplace and, more specifically, the owners of production, made most of the major decisions regarding the production and distribution of goods and services. Now, with the public-service sector becoming increasingly important, economic decisions are beginning to move out of the marketplace and into the political arena. While the private-sector financial community continues to hold its control over the economy, it is becoming increasingly difficult. Wall Street hegemony is now being challenged by the emergence of many competing groups, all with their own demands. Behind these demands are both tax dollars, which have become so indispensable in the economic decision-making of the postindustrial service economy, and increasingly, pension-fund dollars—the newest form of capital ownership. Pension capital is the workers' money. It has also emerged as the largest pool of private capital in the world. Pension funds already own 20 to 25 percent of the equity in the New York and American stock exchanges, and in ten years they will provide over one-half of all the new external equity financing in the private sector. Up to now, the private financial community has had virtual carte blanche control over these funds. It appears likely, however, that American workers, through their unions and local and state governments, will begin to demand a role in how their pension monies are used, just as they are demanding a greater role in how their tax dollars are being spent. All of this suggests that there will be increasing strains in American society in the 1980s as the public (and private) service sector continues to be politicized and as individuals and groups escalate their demands for control over the economic system.

With each major shift in the economy—from agriculture to manufacturing and from manufacturing to service—the "self-reliant" individual that Reformation theologians and liberal philosophers extolled has retreated further into the background. The Calvinist individual, and later his bourgeois stepchild, were made for the early states of capitalist development, when there were still frontiers to conquer and vast entrepreneurial adventures to seize upon. In fact, when we think of the Protestant ethic, the image that first comes to mind is the small independent farmer eking out an existence in the wilderness and the independent tradesman building up a thriving business from scratch.

Today's economic reality is far removed from these early images. Yet, we continue to adhere to a set of theological principles that were designed for an era now long past. As a result, the everyday world we live in continues to thwart our belief system, our faith and our world view. How could it be otherwise? The history of the modern era has been one of increasing complexity. At each stage of the economic process, the individual has been forced to give up a greater portion of his self-sufficiency in return for the increased productivity and growth that comes with concentration of economic power. The shift from an agricultural to a manufacturing economy and from a manufacturing to a service economy has increased the dependency of every individual on the larger economic order.

Still, Reformation theology continues to see each man and woman as an autonomous force in the world, seeking their own salvation alone and in solitude. The tacit assumption has always been that since faith is an individual concern, economics should be, too. As mentioned earlier the secular version of this assumption has been the liberal philosophical concept that everyone's individual self-interest, if left unfettered, will advance the common good.

As long as we continued to live in a world of abundant resources and material growth, it was still possible to maintain the belief in the notion of individualism in both its theological and economic dimensions. Now, the economics of a contracting high-entropy society are forcing us to abandon our earlier philosophical and theological constructs.

Today, many basic economic needs can no longer be met in the open marketplace by the free exchange of goods and services between individual buyers and sellers. Now that the economic pie has begun to shrink, as a result of the exhaustion of the earth's nonrenewable resources, a lifeboat mentality has begun to set in. Many basic economic decisions now have to be made collectively. In a "lifeboat" economy, where there is a dwindling amount of available resources to go around, it is simply untenable to adhere to the philosophy that "God helps those who help themselves." With the emerging age of scarcity, the unfettered economic rights of the individual have to become subservient to the larger economic needs of the group or else everyone will perish.

That is one major reason so much of the economic decision-making is moving from the marketplace into the political arena. The growth of the public-service sector is part of the growing recognition that we are moving into an age which requires a public response to economic problems. It is no longer possible to allow individuals free reign to exploit human and natural resources with impunity, amass inordinate wealth and power, and pollute the environment—in the name of freedom, rugged individualism and growth. It is also no longer possible to survive as a society without providing an array of public services to secure the general welfare.

The expanding role of the public-service sector is an attempt by society to place curbs on the unrestrained economic activity of individual persons and enterprises and to provide vital economic services that cannot be bought and sold piecemeal in the marketplace.

It is likely that the notion of self-reliance and the centrality of the individual (which was so intimate a part of the Protestant ethic and the liberal ethos) will continue to lose its driving force as society makes its final transformation into a service economy and as increased economic scarcity places greater pressure on the public sector to serve as a forum for the resolution and advancement of collective economic needs.

There are two other aspects of the developing service economy which deserve some attention because of the effect they are having on the current evangelical movement and the Protestant ethic. The first has to do with an inherent conflict emerging within the economic structure itself; the second concerns the vulnerability of the primary economic assets of a service society.

To begin with, it should be made clear that the shift to a service economy does not imply that the manufacturing sector is becoming less important, any more than agriculture was after the Civil War. Like agriculture, the manufacturing sector has become capital-intensive. New technologies greatly increased productivity yields between the end of World War II and the late 1960s. Beginning in the early 1970s the energy crisis and overall resource depletion combined to slow down and, in some industries, even reverse, the process of increased productivity. Still, since the post–World War II period, the capital-intensive drive within the manufacturing sector freed millions of workers for the burgeoning new service sector. As a result, the shift from factory to service has been every bit as profound as the shift from farm to factory.

This shift to a service economy has put a tremendous burden on the manufacturing sector. Increases in the service sector are still dependent, to a large extent, on manufacturing productivity. When productivity declines, there is less surplus available for expanding services, both in the commercial sector and, more importantly, in the public sector. With the depletion of our resource base, the increase in the cost of energy, the declining productivity of capital-intensive industry and the corresponding downturn in return on investment, the manufacturing sector is shrinking right at the very time when the country has all but completed its shift into a service economy. Since the service sector owes its very existence and vitality to a strong, healthy capital-intensive manufacturing base, it's not hard to see why the economists are worried. The service economy is like a house of cards. With its base, the manufacturing sector, no longer secure, it threatens to topple in on itself at any time.

Nowhere is this threat more apparent than in the public-service sector which depends entirely on taxes. With the energy and ecological crisis continuing to fuel inflation and dampen manufacturing productivity and return on investment, there is less real disposable income to go around, and the average worker is, therefore, less willing to be taxed for public-sector goods and services. Thus the tax revolt. So, on the one hand, the American people have become utterly dependent upon public goods and services to satisfy a wide range of basic everyday needs; on the other, they are less willing to pay the price for these services.

At the root of the tax revolt is an attempt by many Americans to bring back the Protestant ethic of self-reliance. There is a widespread feeling that the collective—i.e., the government—has taken over too many important economic decisions and that the individual has lost control over his own economic fate. The often-expressed attitude is that the individual is better off keeping his hard-earned money and providing for his own needs, rather than giving it up to the government to service his needs instead. The problem, as already mentioned, is that many important needs can no longer be met by each individual operating as an autonomous force in the marketplace. In fact, as we move further along into a contracting, high-entropy economy, collective consumption needs will continue to escalate. The dilemma, once again, is that we continue to want to live by the rules of the old theological and philosophical construct with its emphasis on self-reliance, even though we know that our individual survival depends more and more on a collective response to the severe economic problems that face us. That is why the public opinion polls continue to show the contradiction between a public that is in favor of less government and fewer taxes and at the same time in favor of increases in public expenditures on such things as health care, environmental services, old age benefits, and education.

The extent to which this political schism is either widened or narrowed in the years ahead will determine, to a great extent, how well American society will be able to survive.

Ultimately, the resolution of this explosive conflict depends on the recognition that the laissez-faire philosophy of life extolled by Reformation theologians and liberal thinkers, while suited for an age of growth and expansion, is anathema in an age of scarcity and limits.

Finally, it's important to take a look at the new assets of the emerging service economy, assets which are already becoming a focal point for the evangelical movement. The service economy is characterized by an increasing reliance on science, information and communication technology just as our capital-intensive industrial society is dependent on machine technology and natural energy resources. The reason for the shift is not difficult to discern. America is becoming more and more a "rentier" economy. That is, the United States is fast becoming the home office for the giant multinationals who are beginning to relocate their production facilities overseas—especially in Third World countries. Increased labor and energy costs, antiquated production facilities, inadequate and run-down transportation grids, increased taxation and government regulation all combine to make domestic production less attractive. By shifting manufacturing sites abroad to Third World countries, the multinationals are able to take advantage of cheap nonunion labor pools, cooperative governments with little or no regulations or taxes, and more abundant energy supplies.

Coordinating a worldwide production and distribution system requires sophisticated communications and information technology. At the same time, keeping ahead of the competition means more research and development to find cheaper, more efficient technologies that can be shipped to production sites overseas. The communication and information technologies require a highly educated and technologized labor force, one that can still best be provided in the United States, with its extensive educational institutions and government research and development expenditures. In fact, a great deal of the research and development that are so vital to the development of a postindustrial science, information and communication economy are provided directly by the government through the American tax dollar. While 63 percent of industry's research and development are still financed with its own funds, nearly 37 percent of the money is given to it by the federal government.[9]

With increasing importance placed on science, information and communication technology, it is certain that more conflict will develop around the issue of control over these basic assets. Bell, in his book, *The Coming of Post-Industrial Society*, argues that in an industrial setting, the primary battle is a class battle between the workers and the owners of capital. His contention is that such battles will be of less concern as we move into a postindustrial economy, where communication, information and science, not production capital, will be the primary sources of economic power. Bell is probably wrong in assuming that the confrontation over productive capital will ease off; every indication is that it will increase in the years ahead, especially as union workers and Northern industrial states, trapped by the relocation of the manufacturing sector to other regions of the country and abroad, begin to exert their power over capital-allocation decisions in order to insure their own employment and the survival of their local economies. Still, Bell is probably right about the likelihood of increased confrontation over access to communications and information systems and regulation and control over science. While the class conflict between workers and managers of production will continue, the new battles between the people and the institutional elites who control the vast scientific infrastructure and communications webs will become more and more pronounced. Public hostility over the monopoly of information and communication control lodged in the upper echelons of both public and private service bureaucracies is already manifesting itself throughout the country. Every indication is that it will continue to escalate in the years just ahead.

Resentment of the invasion of science and technique into every aspect of human life is also beginning to surface. The antiscience mood is likely to grow, as the scientific establishment attempts to assert its influence over more of the social and cultural life of the country. At the same time, the increasing failure of technology to adequately resolve major social and economic questions will heighten popular discontent and undermine the long-standing faith that Americans have placed in science.

As we will see, the evidence seems to suggest that the

Charismatic renewal movement is, to some extent, an unconscious reaction to the increasing reliance on science, information and communication technology.

THE CONSUMPTION MODE

More than anything else, Calvin's ethic of work for work's sake and frugality provided the theological energy for the age of growth. Today, however, that ethic has been seriously compromised by the shift in materialism's focus from the production mode to the consumption mode. This shift is creating an entirely different economic personality, one directly at odds with the Reformation ethic.

"He's a completely different guy once you get him out of the office." How many times have we heard that line or been shocked to find that the person we work next to every single day seems so radically different when we bump into him at a bar or in a social setting after work? The fact is, most of us lead a kind of Jekyll-and-Hyde existence. During the office day we're reposed, efficient, neat and orderly and above all "businesslike." At night, we're casual, intimate, sensuous, fun-loving and above all "loose." The worse rebuke that can be handed someone seems to be: "Let your hair down, for God's sake, you act like you're still at the office." Or, "Quit being so uptight and businesslike, no one's going to tell the boss."

It used to be there were two distinct worlds, the kingdom of God and the secular world. Now there are three. The everyday world has itself become divided. Economic man and woman now live two completely separate lives, the life of a producer and the life of a consumer. These two levels of existence have become so diametrically opposed over the past twenty-five years that their continued tension now poses a major threat to the existence of the capitalist system. The life of the producer—the working part of each person's existence—requires an efficient, planned and linear personality. The key feature of modern production, whether it be manufacturing or service, is rational organization. Every aspect of production must be rigorously planned, all details calculated and calibrated in advance. The individual worker must be efficient, orderly and attentive. The entire process must be continually reassessed, upgraded and expanded. The principles of organization and the blueprint for success rest on a firm understanding of scientific methodology and technological application. The worker, whether he be part of management or of the labor force, is an integral part of the rational process of organization. This production mentality contrasts sharply with man and woman, "the consumer."

In the year 1979 alone, corporate America will spend over forty-seven billion dollars in advertising to break down the strict, orderly producer into a spontaneous, hedonistic consumer.[10] "You deserve a break today"; "Be part of the 'now' generation"; "If you've got it, flaunt it." The consumer is cajoled, manipulated, harassed and encouraged to "do it," to "act" and not to worry about the consequences. Responsibility and frugality are inimical to increased consumption. Installment credit is based on living now and paying later. Saving is taboo. The more one saves, the less one consumes. Therefore, enjoy now and let tomorrow take care of itself.

If frugality is enemy number one to Madison Avenue, then Puritan morality is a close second. The consumer mode depends on the proper nourishment of people's carnal appetites. The commercial exploitation of lust and sensuality is essential to increasing consumption. While the basis of mass advertising is the development and exploitation of mass consumer markets, the appeals are almost always subjective and emotional. If *conformity* to rationalized work processes is the basis for man and woman "the worker," then the feeling of uniqueness provides the seductive escape hatch for man and woman the "consumer." Of course, the uniqueness factor becomes a bit illusory and blurred when thousands of people buy a Plymouth Fury so they can be different. Still, the psychology works; consumer appetites grow, production expands, and life goes on, with man and woman the producer increasingly at odds with their other half, man and woman the consumer.

Here lies another one of the ironies of the system. Capitalism has, in fact, created its own worst enemy. The system must continue feeding the consumer personality or it will perish. On the other hand, the consumer continues to grow off the system until his own nonrational psycho-appetites begin to overwhelm the "proper" functioning of the system itself. "Watch it now, you're beginning to lose your grip." "You're just not yourself anymore." These are the little voices of the producer personality trying to keep the other half from creeping out to do mischief at the office. Or, "Why can't you ever relax and unwind just once in your life? Why is it you're always so unfeeling and mechanical? Can't you learn to be spontaneous; must you always analyze everything?" These are the little voices of the consumer personality reproaching their other half for bringing the office home with him.

The tensions between the rational, scientific, technological requisites of production and the spontaneous, subjective, emotional requisites of consumption are becoming more intense each day, as the economy continues to contract. On the one hand, the contraction is resulting in a desperate push to escalate consumer spending in hopes of increasing production. On the other hand, the contraction is requiring further "rationalizing" of the production process itself. There is more emphasis than ever on designing more efficient, streamlined organizations in order to increase both output and return on investment. With the cost of energy and other basic resources continuing to rise, the capitalist system must rely more and more on upgrading the two other basic ingredients in the production mix—labor and machine capital. This means getting more efficiency and output out of both. Ironically, the productivity of American labor and machine capital is now, for the first time, rising at a declining rate. According to one Gallup Poll, 57 percent of the public thought "they could produce more each day if they tried," and a Harvard Business School study found that industry frequently uses only 30 to 40 percent of the average worker's mental and physical ability.[11]

Probing into the reasons for this problem, an exhaustive report done by HEW found that "the discontentment of trapped, dehumanized workers is creating low productivity." The increasing alienation of the American work force, says the HEW study, is making itself felt in a number of ways from increased absenteeism to sabotage, alcoholism and a general decline in mental health. The effect upon productivity is staggering.[12] No wonder. The consumer part of people rebels against the attitudes required at the workplace. The system however, can do little to arrest the problem. The long-range economic contraction has forced the system to hot-wire the consumer mentality to push spending up. This, in turn, is continuing to create a mass hedonistic personality structure that is unwilling to conform to the ascetic requirements of more rationalized and efficient production.

This split between the producer and consumer personality affects capital formation. The system needs to improve machine capital if it is to remain at all competitive in a contracting economic environment. Yet, it cannot find the necessary capital to finance new machine technology. To a large extent, this is because the inducements to invest just aren't there. Increased production costs brought about by increased costs of energy and other diminishing resources have lowered the overall rate of return on investments. For these reasons, the numbers of Americans investing in the stock market declined by 5.7 million, or a whopping 18 percent between 1970 and 1975 alone.[13] This situation is further exacerbated by the very consumer mentality that the system promotes. People are encouraged to spend, not save, to enjoy now, rather than invest in the future. The concept of delayed gratification, which, for so long, provided an ascetic rationale for capital investment, has been largely destroyed by the Madison Avenue emphasis on living hedonistically, for the moment. The system's entire approach to the consumer undermines the notion of savings and investment for the future. Thus, at the very time when capitalist production needs both a more efficient labor force and more investment capital to survive the economic contractions brought about by resource scarcity, it finds itself without either—and it has no one to blame but itself.

The increasing emphasis on consumption as a way of life has all but destroyed the Protestant ethic of work for work's sake combined with frugality. As for the Reformation emphasis on self-reliance, it is ironic, indeed, that the corporate system and the society at large continue to herald its virtues, while systematically destroying all semblance of its original meaning.

Hard work, frugality and self-reliance go hand in hand with the notion of individualism, a term first popularized by Reformation theologians (and later by the liberal philosophers of the Enlightenment). The Protestant ethic of individualism, however, is very different from what parades under the banner of individualism today. For Calvin, individualism meant an individual's responsibility to serve the glory of God. Every individual had an obligation to be self-reliant and a duty to lead a personal life centered on a combination of hard work and frugality. Today, all that remains of Calvin's doctrine is the notion of hard work, and even this is beginning to break down. Individualism has lost the ascetic quality that Calvin preached, and along with it, that transcendent quality which called upon every person to be responsible to his maker. As Paul Vitz makes note in his book, *Psychology As Religion: The Cult of Self-Worship*, individualism today means freedom to "do one's own thing," uninhibited by moral restraints.[14] It means license to consume anything and everything with as little "responsibility" to either God or others as possible. The Puritan notion of covenant has been replaced with the modern notion of self-ism. Nurturing the self, promoting the self, experiencing the self, loving the self, living with the self, have become a prime value in our culture. We live an anonymous existence, our only common bond being the vast consumer fantasyland of indulgences from which we pick and choose our playthings. Our lives now revolve around the shopping center—the place where more people spend their leisure hours than anywhere else.

One doesn't need to be a sociologist to understand the social consequences of self-ism in contemporary America. Eliminating personal responsibility from the concept of individualism has produced not only a society of noblesse oblige hedonists, but also a collection of millions of childlike individuals who are increasingly in search of someone or something to take responsibility for them—to protect and take care of them.

Today, the marketplace is increasingly responsible for taking care of personal needs. It has also become the chief moral instructor for the individual. The government, in turn, has become the backup family of last resort. Together, the universal marketplace and the government are the new foster parents of society. They service our every need. The service economy and the service society continue to grow. But the notion of service is far removed from the notion advanced during the early years of the republic. Service then meant covenant with God and shared responsibility between individuals in society. Today, service means the commercial mothering of the marketplace and the benevolent mothering of the state.

CAPITALISM AND THE BREAKUP OF THE FAMILY

For Protestants and especially evangelicals, the home has traditionally served as the primary classroom for religious instruction. The family has long been revered as the institution most responsible for upholding the faith. Now the same economic forces that have run roughshod over the Protestant ethic in the workplace and in the marketplace are invading this last remaining sanctuary as well.

The family has become a source of controversy in America.

In the week of June 12, 1978, the Carter Administration officially postponed the White House Conference on Families which was supposed to take place in 1979. The reason, according to administration sources, was the worry that a conference held so close to the 1980 Presidential Election would become a virtual minefield for potentially explosive issues like abortion, gay rights, the Equal Rights Amendment and demands for increased public programs.[15]

With one out of three marriages ending in separation or divorce, and with women now comprising over 40 percent of the total labor force, some observers are questioning whether the family can survive, and if so, whether it still has a significant role to play in American life. Defenders of the family often point to lax sexual mores among adults and permissiveness with children as key reasons for the demise of the family. In particular, blame is heaped upon feminists and careerism, which take women away from the home; abortion and homosexuality, which it is believed weakens the traditional sexual relationship between male and female; and the influence of a permissive society, which it is contended undermines parental discipline over children.

While there is a germ of truth to some of these arguments as well as a great deal of false supposition, the underlying reasons for the demise of the family go much deeper—in fact, they go right to the heart of the vast economic changes that America has been experiencing at least since the end of World War II.

Most of us are used to thinking of the family unit as a revered institution as old as time itself. In fact, that's not the case, as John Lukacs points out in his book, *The Passing of the Modern Age*. The modern concept of family emerged with the age of capitalism and the Reformation. In medieval times, there were fewer boundary lines separating blood relations from neighbors.[16] Life itself, says Lukacs, was very much an external affair—interaction took place primarily out of doors, and children were more apt to be left free to their own wiles—just as they are in many poor Third World countries today. It was not until the fourteenth and fifteenth centuries that the modern notion of the family began to take shape. The development of trade, the clustering of people into cities and the emergence of primitive capitalism all had the effect of breaking up the communal nature of serf life that characterized the medieval era. As the bourgeois (man of the city) began to replace the serf, life itself began to move indoors. This was, first, because many of the guild trades of the new burgher class were best performed inside—whereas peasant life was intimately bound up with being out on the land. Secondly, life in the cities became specialized. Trades served to divide people into certain districts or quarters within cities. Living space was at a premium for the first time. Overcrowding further divided people into basic living units. Then, too, the Reformation theology had a profound effect on life. Calvinism's asceticism served to internalize life, to drive it further indoors. The carnal world of the flesh, the external world, was to be resisted by an internal and private life centered on holiness. The godly life was to be ordered, planned and systematic—all of these qualities favored the emergence of the private home, where each individual could build his own spiritual temple. The replacement of the Catholic Church with the notion of the universal priesthood also made the father figure, for the first time, responsible for passing on religious doctrine to his children.

Our modern concept of family and home, then, appeared alongside these other developments of the Reformation period. Up until the mid-nineteenth century, the family and the home changed very little; the family continued to be relatively self-sufficient on most levels. Spiritual guidance, education, health care, and most foodstuffs and household goods were provided for within the home. Even in the larger cities, until well into the nineteenth century, most families tended their own gardens and raised their own small flock of chickens and pigs. All of this began to change radically with the rise of modern industrial capitalism. Functions long provided for within the home were taken over, one by one, by the capitalist system. Machine-woven textiles replaced home-sewn garments; processed and canned foods replaced home-prepared cooking; professional doctors, clinics and hospitals replaced family care for the sick; public education took over for home instruction, and so on.[17]

The family as a basic unit of production disappeared. With it disappeared much of the shared or communal life that home economics required. The family, to be sure, has stayed together, but mainly as a consuming unit. The consuming function is, by its nature more of an individual and less of a shared or communal affair. As the capitalist system has developed newer and more sophisticated ways of promoting individual consumption habits, the process of self-ism has begun to take over for cooperation within the family. Shared tasks and responsibilities have become less important as a result of newer and cheaper consumer technologies. For the middle class at least, everyone can now have their own TV to watch in their own room, if they so choose. The dishes no longer have to be washed and dried by two family members standing over the sink together, one with the soap, the other with the towel. The automatic dishwasher takes care of the whole process. In fact, even the dishwasher is becoming increasingly irrelevant. The average American family is eating fewer meals at home. The Food and Beverage Trade estimates that within seven years, most American families will eat over half their meals at restaurants or fast-food outlets.[18]

It's not just in the realm of consumer goods, however, that the universal marketplace has taken over functions and prerogatives long held by the family. Both the private and public (government) service sectors have increasingly expropriated even the most private parts of family life onto themselves. If a family member is facing emotional problems, he or she is immediately sent to a professional psychologist. If the parents' sexual life is not what it could be, they are encouraged to seek "professional" help and instruction. If a child wants to learn to play tennis, he is signed up for instruction at a professional sports clinic. Parents are no longer guides or instructors, but merely monitors in the home. Their job is to keep tabs on potential need areas and then locate the right kind of service in the marketplace or government to deal with them.

A recent survey asked three-year-old children whom they liked best, Daddy or TV? Forty-four percent answered TV. It's not surprising. The average parent talks to his children an approximate total of three minutes per day. The TV, on the other hand, talks at children for an average of four to five hours a day. The home, which was once touted as the last sanctuary of privacy in an all too public world, is no longer. The TV invades even the smallest living spaces nonstop, with thousands of images and sounds bombarding the psyches of both adults and children alike. Corporate America spends billions of dollars a year on TV advertising and programming to instruct each person on how they should look, talk, act, and live in contemporary society. It is hard for anyone to compete with its overwhelming presence and authority.

Finally, it should be apparent that the removal of the woman from the home, which so many critics have used as a "whipping boy" for the demise of the family, is in reality only a secondary consequence of these other developments. The primary cause of the demise of the family is the takeover of family life by the universal marketplace of capitalism. Today, nearly half of the work force are women.[19] They work because they have to. As Christopher Lasch points out in his book, *Haven in a Heartless World: The Family Besieged*, there was little choice for women but to go to work within the capitalist system, after it stripped away the economic functions they had previously performed within the home.

> Work formerly carried on in the household could now be carried out more effectively in the factory. Even recreation and child rearing were being taken over by outside agencies . . . Women had no choice but to "follow their occupations or starve" . . . emotionally if not in literal fact. Confined to the family, women would become parasites, unproductive "consumers upon the state" as a feminist writer put it in 1910.[20]

The demise of the family and the rise of the universal marketplace has also produced another related cultural change of far-reaching significance. As the private and public service sectors began to take over and minister to the most intimate needs of family members—previously the function and responsibility of the parents—a new concept of people's essential relationship to their fellow human beings and society began to emerge. Within the traditional family, relationships and personal responsibilities had largely been defined in religious terms. Family members were inculcated with the Biblical principles of upholding God's commandments and resisting evil. Right and wrong behavior were cleary delineated. One was either sinful or good. Rewards and punishments, in turn, were bestowed or meted out in accordance with the principles of the Protestant ethic. This all began to change as both the private marketplace and the government moved into the field of personal behavior. The concepts of good and evil simply did not fit the scientific and technological orientation of the *service* sectors. Good and evil could not be quantified. The soul was unobservable. Therefore, as long as personal behavior was defined in spiritual terms, it could not be brought under the control or management of the universal market. As a result, another unconscious change in the definition of human behavior began to take shape. Behavior, previously defined in spiritual terms, and clearly demarcated as good or evil, began to be redefined by the service sectors more in terms of health, with the demarcation of "sick" versus "well."

According to Christopher Lasch, this new conception of behavior first took concrete shape in the juvenile court systems during the progressive era. Children committing crimes were reclassified. Juvenile offenders had previously been looked upon as "bad apples," or sinful by nature. The courts now claimed there were no bad children, just bad homes. The home was looked on as the source of juvenile crime. An unhealthy home environment, argued the court, produced unhealthy, emotionally disturbed children, which, in turn, produced crime. The answer, according to the courts, was to place the sick children in a healthier more therapeutic environment so they could be doctored back to health. As Lasch points out, the introduction of the concept of the courts as foster parents was a major incursion into family life—it was a statement by the government that it could better provide for the needs of these "problem" children than their own parents.[21] The concept of healthy or sick as opposed to innocent or guilty soon spread throughout the court and legal system. The question of whether a criminal is individually responsible for his crimes, in the Biblical sense of committing sinful acts, or whether he is merely a sick victim produced by an unhealthy environment, has become the single most controversial issue of our entire legal system.

Changes in public education also served to undermine the traditional authority of parents and substitute the notion of health for goodness. Using new "scientific" methods of instruction, teachers began to rely more on psychology in the classroom. If a child was a poor student or unresponsive, he was no longer misbehaving. Rather he was maladjusted. Instead of sending him to the principal for disciplinary action, he was now shunted off to the school psychologist for therapy. Like the courts, the public schools continued to enlarge their role as foster parents, taking on more of the functions previously provided in the home.

Today, the commercial and government service sectors have eliminated the traditional Christian notion of good and evil and personal responsibility, as well as much of the authority of the parents as moral instructors and disciplinarians in the home. The new instructors are the legions of professional technicians whose job it is to diagnose emotional and physical illness and apply therapy to make people well again. Personal responsibility has been relegated to a secondary status. When one is sick, he might well have contributed to the illness, but the primary cause still resides in an unhealthy environment. The key, then, for both physical and emotional ailments, is either to change the environment, or more often than not, find a way to immunize the patient against it—for emotional therapies, this is called adjustment, or "learning to cope."

Stripped of virtually all of their authority, parents have been largely reduced to the role of helpmates or even playmates. How many parents do you know whose children call them by their first name or who boast that they and their children are more friends and companions than anything else. The father, once the chief disciplinarian in the family, has indeed been replaced by the service sector as has the nurturing mother. The scientific and technological methods of industrial capitalism, which had successfully invaded every other aspect of life, also ended up invading the inner sanctum of personal beliefs as well. Biblical notions of good and evil and personal responsibility were scrapped in favor of the modern "scientific" approach to good health and proper therapy. For every personal problem or need there is now an appropriate "technique" that can be applied for the right price. The only responsibility a person has left is to earn enough money to be able to pay for it.

The radical changes in the way people work, the shift to a service economy, the nurturing of an insatiable consumption mentality, the cult of self-worship and the breakdown of the traditional family are all by-products of the liberal ethos and the age of growth. The tremendous strain that all of these forces exert on both the individual and the culture threatens to overwhelm the existing social order. Most scholars agree that the liberal superstructure is beginning to crack under the combined weight of continued economic disintegration and the destabilizing effect of these various changes. This dislodgement, in turn, is beginning to exert pressure on the Protestant ethic which has long served as the foundation of the American culture. The Christian community is responding to these jarring changes with the beginnings of a new liberating force and the elements of a new covenant vision.

10

THE CHARISMATICS: A NEW LIBERATING FORCE?

In his last book, *A Guide for the Perplexed*, E. F. Schumacher points out that periods of growth are generally characterized by the quest for freedom, while periods of decay are characterized by the search for order.[1] America is moving from a growth period to a decay period. With this economic shift has come a tremendous psychological and social dislocation resulting from the transformation of a culture based on freedom to one increasingly in search of order.

The evangelical-Charismatic movement is the single most visible and significant response to these changes going on in contemporary American life. Today's spiritual revival shares many of the characteristics of America's other two great awakenings. It is taking place during a major shift from one economic period to another; it is finding its expression within a contracting economic environment; it is, at least subconsciously, reacting to the authority of the existing order and at the same time groping for the elements of a new covenant vision. Still, the economic shift we are experiencing is unlike any of the past several hundred years. It is not merely a shift in degree, but in kind. What is being challenged is the concept of economic growth itself, the methodology of science and technology that underlies it, and the philosophy of liberalism that justifies it. In short, we are not just at the end of one period and the beginning of another, but between epochs.

If there is a common denominator that characterizes the

American psyche today, it is the word *anxiety*. We hear it used over and over again as an expression of the mood of modern America. Neuroses, anxiety attacks, hypertension are all synonymous with life in the popular culture. Our literature speaks of the isolated, lone individual, confused and manipulated by forces outside of his control or understanding, tossed to and fro amidst a bewildering array of fragmented experiences and subject to the whims of arbitrary, unresponsive and inaccessible bureaucracies which regulate his every activity.

Anxiety, both in the individual and the mass variety, is the by-product of loss of faith. Faith, of whatever kind, requires belief in a world view that answers "all" of one's most basic questions with complete certainty. It is that absolute certainty that breeds the confidence to act without fear or trepidation. As long as one's world view continues to "work," faith is maintained and confidence is upheld. When a particular world view begins to break down, when it can no longer adequately answer the basic questions to the satisfaction of its adherents, faith is broken, uncertainty and confusion set in, and the individual and the masses are cast adrift—exposed, unprotected and above all frightened. Today's world view is breaking down. Science and technology, the ultimate *truths* of the modern era, are no longer working adequately. Capitalism, the institution charged with translating those truths into our everyday lives, is proving to be less than invincible. Its operators, the technicians and professionals of the modern age, are proving to be fallible and often in error.

Of course, people are not running through the streets shouting epithets at science, capitalism and its engineers and technicians. Obviously, if we were able to identify what the real source of our anxieties was, we wouldn't be nearly as frightened as we are and nearly as desperate to locate some fixed point of reference and order. But, unfortunately, history doesn't work that way. As the age-old saying goes, when in the trees it's often impossible to see the forest. We are all, to a large extent, products of our culture. For that reason, it's difficult to simply jump out of it and take a dispassionate look at how it's affecting us. Still, our unconscious or intuitive side is doing that all the time. In very real demonstrable ways that is exactly what's happening right now, as we find ourselves trapped between the end of one age and the beginning of another. As our world view begins to crack, our institutions begin to erode, and our authority figures begin to stumble, we, in fact, have begun to react—and our unconscious or intuitive reactions have taken specific courses which zero in almost precisely on the major areas of dispute and change.

Nowhere is that reaction more acute than in the evangelical-Charismatic movements. But to understand how they are dealing with the mass anxiety wrought by the breakdown of the modern world view, and why they have chosen specific mannerisms and targets, it's helpful to look once again to the period of the Reformation, where the last great epochal transition in history spawned its own peculiar reactions within Christianity.

ECONOMICS, DISEASE AND FAITH

By the fourteenth century the old feudal order was already showing signs of decay, even as the new capitalist mode was just barely beginning to make its presence felt. While trade routes were opening up, cities were coming into their own, and a new burgher class of individual tradesman was beginning to emerge as an independent force; the feudal order of Western Europe was experiencing a serious economic contraction.

As historian William McNeill points out, by the fourteenth century, medieval agriculture began to experience a long-range decline.

> Many parts of Northwestern Europe had achieved a kind of saturation with humankind by the fourteenth century. The great frontier boom that began about 900 led to a replication of manors and fields across the face of the land until, at least in the most densely inhabited regions, scant forest remained. Since woodlands were vital for fuel and as a source of building materials, mounting shortages created severe problems for human occupancy. . . . On top of this, the climate worsened in the fourteenth century, so that crop failures and partial failures became commoner, especially in the northerly lands . . .[2]

The economic decline of the old system and the embryonic beginnings of the new created a sense of confusion and disorder that provided a sharp contrast with the more or less steady-state that Europe had been living under for over eight hundred years. The profound *anxiety* wrought by these turbulent economic changes found its most dramatic expression in the Reformation theology of Martin Luther and, more importantly, John Calvin. "Anxiety" was at the heart of Calvin's beliefs. As mentioned earlier, anxiety, for Calvin, was a sign of people's fallen nature. That anxiety, in turn, was continually fueled by chaos and disorder, which to Calvin's mind represented the forces of Satan himself. It is interesting to note that the anxiety Calvin talked of was of a special kind. As Walzer points out in his essay, "Puritanism as a Revoluntionary Ideology," Calvin's anxiety was not just the fear of death and damnation, but rather, the fear of sudden and violent death. To quote Calvin directly:

> Now, whither soever you turn, all the objects around you are not only unworthy of your confidence, but almost openly menace you and seem to threaten immediate death.[3]

Like theological scholars today, Calvin's own anxiety was unfocused. He could feel that the world around him was becoming increasingly menacing and disordered. But he did not wake up one morning with a revelation that the cause was indeed the tumultuous and unsettling transition between the old economic order and the new. In truth, it would probably be fair to say that such thoughts were far removed from his mind or absent altogether. But Calvin's anxiety was, nonetheless, a real reaction to those changes and the disorder they brought with them.

Many modern scholars, while recognizing the subconscious anxiety effects that the changing economic patterns must have had on both Calvin and Luther's thinking, are at a loss to explain how such a slow process of dissolution and almost imperceptible change could produce such a dramatic theological turnaround during the Reformation. They are even more puzzled as to how such radically new doctrines could have caught on so fast among the people. The fact is that during all great periods of epochal change, the submerged anxiety produced by the accompanying dislocations in cultural values, institutional arrangements and world views will often bubble up to the surface and explode around "specific" events or occurrences that are related to the larger changes going on. This is likely what happened during the Reformation.

Over the past few years a new field of scholarly research

has provided some important insights concerning the Reformation, which are beginning to more fully explain and account
for Luther and Calvin's thinking. Why was the mass of people
so willing, all of a sudden, to challenge the institutional authority of the Church, an authority which had remained secure
for over eleven centuries? Why, all of a sudden, was there
such a need for a theology stressing a personal communion
between the individual and God? Why, all of a sudden, did so
many people reject the notion of good works and sacraments
as the key to salvation and replace them with the notion of
faith alone? For that matter, why did faith overtake reason as
the motivating force for leading a transcendent life? And why
were people so willing to give up their rather slothful and casual
style of life, all of a sudden, in favor of a fanatic obsession
with unceasing work amidst a life of almost monastic asceticism.
It could not all be accounted for simply by the gnawing anxiety
created by the long-range economic changes going on; nor
could mere disenchantment with the unresponsiveness and corruption within the Church hierarchy account for it.

The new scholarship into the relationship of health, disease
patterns and history has begun to provide some compelling, if
not convincing, answers to these questions.

The opening up of trade routes with the East brought with
it an unexpected side effect, the spread of new and deadly
diseases from Asia to Europe. A series of devastating plagues
hit Western Europe between 1346 and the end of the seventeenth century. It is estimated that between 1346 and 1350
alone, nearly one-third of the entire population of Western
Europe was wiped out by the first great wave of plagues. These
plagues continued to recur throughout the continent for the next
300 years.[4] According to historians, previous to the first outbreak in the last fourteenth century, Europe had been free of
plagues for almost 600 years. The sheer devastating impact of
these plagues did more to create a sense of immediate chaos,
disorder and confusion than any other single factor of the period. It is not hard to understand why Calvin would feel such
anxiety over the prospect of sudden death. The plagues struck
without warning. Mass death often occurred within days of the
initial outbreak. The impact of the plagues on Christian theology was, no doubt, considerable. In a world suddenly characterized by unexplainable and uncontrollable death, the world
view of the Church no longer seemed capable of providing all
the answers. The Thomistic doctrine of reason and good works

as the basis for individual salvation no longer held up. Reason simply couldn't explain the arbitrary nature of the mass death and destruction that were devastating Europe. Good works seemed of equally little consequence, since the good and the bad were just as likely to be claimed by the plagues. Nor were the sacraments of the Church much help in protecting the individual from this violent death. In fact, the Church and the priests were completely powerless to explain or deal with the fear, anxiety and death that were everywhere. As McNeill, in *Plagues and Peoples,* points out:

> God's justice seemed far to seek in the way plague spared some, killed others; and the regular administration of God's grace through the sacraments was an entirely inadequate psychological counterpoise to the statistical vagaries of lethal infection and sudden death.[5]

Luther and Calvin's doctrine spoke directly to the disenchantment with the existing Church authority. The new Reformation doctrine seemed perfectly suited to answer the questions "plaguing" European man. First, faith replaced reason. What else could one bank on but faith, given that there was no other seeming explanation for the calamities. Secondly, the universal priesthood of believers replaced the priesthood of the Church. In times of tremendous uncertainty and fear, each person begins to realize that they, in fact, stand alone and therefore must deal with their God alone. The need for a personal, one-to-one experience with God was likely an overwhelming urge for people in search of protection from the ravages that might engulf them at any moment. Finally, the notion of preelection and hard work matched the temperament of a period where everything seemed inexplicable and uncertain. The concept that everything is predetermined by God erased the need to continue to search for explanations. The concept of unceasing hard work had two effects. First, it created a sense of personal *order* amid the disorder around one. Secondly, it kept one's mind off of the day-to-day world of cruel excesses and firmly ensconced the individual in the world of God and the kingdom of heaven.

No doubt the plagues influenced Reformation theology in other ways as well. For example, the emphasis on resisting temptations of the flesh and carnal knowledge could not help but arrest the spreading of infectious disease. Still, the most important point to bear in mind is that the plagues were an intimate part of the larger epochal changes going on during the thirteenth to the seventeenth centuries. Their introduction to Europe, after all, was a direct result of the opening up of trade and the beginnings of capitalist expansion. The ravaging of life on both the continent and England was also attributable to the conditions of the old economic order, especially overpopulation, which acted like a tinderbox for the spread of disease.

The plagues, then, were a specific series of occurrences which placed in dramatic focus all of the anxieties created by the larger changes going on in the transition from medieval life to the bourgeois age. Reformation theology can be viewed as both a response to that set of specific occurrences as well as a response to the overall changes occurring in the economic and cultural life of the period.

Even if we ignore the potential impact of the plagues altogether, there is no doubt that Reformation theology owed much of its success to external economic changes that were already challenging traditional Church authority. The new burgher class of the emerging port cities of Europe had little use for a Church hierarchy steeped in feudal political arrangements and unwilling to bend to the new priorities and needs of incipient capitalism. This independent force in European life was already beginning to flex its economic muscle and political clout when Luther and Calvin came along. Their theological perspectives, though not intended as a spiritual place mat for the burgher class, nonetheless served that purpose well.

Throughout the period of transition from feudalism to capitalism, one overriding feature remained constant. The mass anxiety of an uprooted and displaced people continued to manifest itself in a thousand and one different ways. A dance of life and death was being performed by millions of individual souls caught in the conflict between economic and religious ideologies. Their lives, like ours today, were caught up with day-to-day survival and with a search for ways to find meaning and purpose in the world. The Reformation theology provided meaning and restored a sense of personal confidence; it presented a new world view that answered, to many people's satisfaction, all of the important questions of life. Capitalism in turn provided the institutional mechanisms for translating these new truths into the secular world.

Today, the capitalist system serves much the same function as the Catholic Church did during the medieval era. More than any other set of institutions it is responsible (along with its junior partner, the state) for fashioning and prescribing the behavior, the activity and the values of each member in society. Its guiding truths are science and technology. Its priests are the technicians and professionals who translate scientific and technological truths into our daily lives. The capitalist church, like the Catholic Church of six centuries ago, is slowly losing its authority. Capitalism, which was long looked at as being invincible, unchallengeable and beyond reproach, is no longer so revered. The American public has become increasingly hostile to the economic system, a trend that will escalate as we move further and further into economic contraction between now and the turn of the century. The list of grievances has become almost endless: unsafe products permanently disable and kill tens of thousands of Americans each year, corporations bribe candidates and illegally buy elections, chemical companies pour deadly substances into rivers and lakes, and the system itself seems unwilling or unable to curb inflation or ease unemployment.

At the heart of the public loss of faith in the capitalist state is science and technology, the ultimate truths upon which the system functions. Public perception of the role of science and technology has radically changed. "A few years ago," says Phillip Handler, the president of the National Academy of Sciences, "people regarded science and technology as a huge cornucopia that was going to enrich everyone's life. Now many people feel that science and technology have done more harm than good."[6] The public has good reason to feel that way. Americans have become painfully aware of some of the effects of the new scientific and technological advances over the past twenty-five years. Military technology has brought us to the brink of nuclear holocaust; industrial technology has wrought irreversible damage to the natural environment; the technicalization of life in general has resulted in an increasingly impersonal and robotized culture. According to one opinion survey, over 57 percent of the public believes that science has made life change too fast, and nearly half now believe that science has become a disintegrating factor.

Then, too, there is the public perception of the effectiveness of technicians and scientists; the corporate priests, ranging from physicists and engineers to sociologists and psychologists, who run the machine and are responsible for translating these higher truths into workable answers for our individual lives. Between

1966 and 1973, public confidence in the people running the scientific community dropped nineteen percentile points to a low of 37 percent.[7]

The mass anxiety wrought by the steady breakdown of the present system and the emergence of a new and still undefined economic order is becoming more pronounced with each succeeding day. This anxiety is not yet manifesting itself in a frontal assault on capitalism, science, technology and the professional class. No modern-day Luther has come forward and nailed his treatise of particulars on the door of the New York Stock Exchange.

Still, like the Reformation period, the submerged anxieties produced by the shifting from one economic epoch to another are surfacing around specific occurrences that are related to the larger picture. As with the Reformation period, disease is, once again, beginning to provide dramatic focus for the expression of society's individually and collectively felt anxieties. Not surprisingly, the evangelical-Charismatic movements are turning their attention to this area of concern.

Cancer is the new plague. It strikes without warning and seemingly without reason. Over half a million Americans die of cancer every year. According to experts this is only the beginning of an epidemic that is expected to accelerate in the 1980s. It is predicted that at least one out of every four Americans alive today will die of cancer.[8] Like the plagues of 600 years ago, the survival rates for victims are not good. Only one out of every two victims will be restored to a semblance of full health.

Cancer, like the plagues, is a direct consequence of the changing economic period we're living in. Seventy to 90 percent of all cancer, according to government studies, is caused by the environment of industrial capitalism. Food additives, toxic substances at the workplace, air and water pollution, low-level microwave radiation and hundreds of other by-products of the final stages of industrial expansion cause cancer.[9] *No other aspect of contemporary American life creates as much personal anxiety as cancer.*

Just as the Catholic Church was unable to deal satisfactorily with the anxiety wrought by the arbitrary nature of the plague and its ruthless destruction of human life, today's capitalist establishment is also without answers. If there is one element that has shaken public confidence in science and technology more than any other it would be the ineptness of the commercial health establishment and government in dealing with cancer. In the early 1970s President Nixon announced the war on cancer. Today, with billions of dollars of tax money spent, a solution is no more in the offing than before. The reason is that the problem does not lend itself to a particular scientific cure. On the contrary, it is science itself that is responsible for cancer. Science created chemical pesticides, nuclear radiation, toxic substances and all of the other ingredients that cause the disease. Cancer is a direct reflection of the destruction of the natural ecosystem and its replacement with an artificial environment. Cancer represents the internalization of the high-entropy waste produced by modern science and technology. The external chaos caused by exponential industrial growth has now found its way into the human body. Cancer, after all, is an unrestrained and chaotic growth of cells, which eventually overwhelm the carrying capacity of the body. Cancer, then, is nature's way of signaling the end of the age of economic expansion and its unbridled use of science as a means of technologizing both nature and people.

For this reason, the technicians and professionals of the capitalist machine have no satisfactory answers to give, because their very approach to the problem is reflective of the problem itself. While it is conceivable that the medical establishment could find a new technological cure for cancer, it is more than likely that the cure itself would merely serve to create an even greater set of problems in human biology at some future date. Ultimately, the answer to the problem of cancer (and other more sophisticated diseases that might replace it) lies in the establishment of a new world view based on an ecologically balanced steady-state economic system. Only by slowing down the entropy process and restoring the natural balance and interplay of nature can the problem of cancer be ultimately put to rest. Until that realization sets in, the popular response to cancer and other future environmentally induced diseases is likely to be a mixture of public resentment and hostility toward the scientific medical establishment (which is justified) and a search for alternative cures. That search has already begun.

One of the central features of the Charismatic movement is faith healing. Millions of Americans are beginning to turn to faith healing because they no longer believe that science can provide the ultimate answers. This is a revolutionary gesture of major significance. The loss of faith in science and the corporate medical establishment and the movement back to faith in supernatural truths for health cures is as earth-shattering in portent as the turning away from Papal authority and the ecclesiastical truths of the Roman Church doctrine 600 years ago. Today, millions of Americans are professed adherents of faith healing as an alternative to medical science.[10] Cancer is certainly the most obvious manifestation of this transformation of loyalty from scientific to spiritual truths. The evidence suggests, however, that in the area of health generally, millions of Americans are beginning to turn not only to Charismatic renewal and faith healing for their cures, but also to other natural cures as well, including special diets and exercise, all in an attempt to restore a natural balance to their bodies. The public emphasis is increasingly away from curative treatment and toward preventative health. The former approach to health is a reflection of the existing order of science and technique and the latter a reflection of an emerging order based on natural balance and a steady-state existence.

SPECIAL GIFTS AND LIBERATION

Faith healing is one of several important spiritual responses to the dislocations and changes taking place in the economic sphere. The mass anxiety created by the contracting economics of the present order is manifesting itself in other profound and potentially revolutionary ways.

The last speaker at the mass Charismatic renewal rally in Kansas City in September 1977, Reverend Bob Mumford, spoke to the prevailing mood of the assembly when he lifted his Bible up into the air and said, "If you sneak a peek at the back of the book, Jesus wins!"[11] The crowd of 50,000 roared their approval with ten minutes of cheering and applause.

The Charismatics have found a new confidence amidst the anxiety and chaos of the modern world. They are optimistic that God, if not history, is on their side, and that the future will belong to the glory of the kingdom. That confidence is providing the liberating energy and the potential revolutionary power that could dislodge the existing order.

The basis of their confidence is to be found in the "special gifts" which include faith healing, speaking in tongues, prophesy, and so forth. These gifts represent a direct assault on the age of science and a materialist world view based on technique and horizontal expansion. While we've already caught a glimpse of the revolutionary potential in the shift of faith from medical science to faith healing, the full gravity of what's taking place only becomes apparent upon deeper examination of the underlying assumptions behind the Baptism of the Holy Spirit.

The Charismatics' proof of election or salvation is at direct odds with the Calvinist view. It is this difference which sets the stage for the crumbling of the old order and the emergence of the new. Calvin asserted that *unceasing physical work* was the individual's only sign or possible proof of election. This notion led directly to the idea of unlimited material accumulation, expansionary growth, efficiency, technique, and exploitation of physical and human resources. The Reformation person was grounded in the horizontal world of time, space and history. His only way of assuring himself that he had been chosen for passage to the other world was to keep on producing in this one. The more he produced the more he was able to overcome his anxiety about election, and the more he was able to develop a sense of confidence and faith in the Reformation's world view.

For the Charismatics, proof of election or salvation is supernatural, not materialistic. One becomes convinced that he is saved by the Baptism of the Holy Spirit. Like the Reformation person the Charismatic is in constant need of the observable proof that he has been saved. But, whereas for the Reformation person, proof was to be found in hard work and material accumulation, for the Charismatic, observable proof is to be found in special gifts. To the question, how do I know that God resides in me, the Charismatic answers with the Baptism of the Holy Spirit: "a powerful experience that *convinces* the recipient that God is real and that God is faithful to what he has promised."[12]

One of the important aspects of special gifts is that they are, in fact, observable and repeatable, just like scientific phenomena. Unlike science, however, their manifestations do not depend on what the individual does, but what God (through the Holy Spirit) does. The individual is no longer in "control" as with scientific truths. Instead, he becomes the faithful repository of supernatural truths. When a Charismatic "lays hands" on someone, and in so doing, cures them of an ailment by the special gift of faith healing, there is no doubt that the results of the procedure are often observable—as observable as the results of a medical operation. But it is not the special skills or knowledge of people that cures the victim, but the indwelling spirit of God working its supernatural powers through individuals.

The Charismatics have replaced the scientific method with supernatural power. They have replaced material accumulation (or remaking and improving the world) as proof of salvation with spiritual gifts. They have taken the human being from a horizontal perspective and converted him to a vertical one. They have attempted to resolve a central dilemma of Reformation theology. On the one hand, Christian doctrine holds that sin is man and woman's hubris, expressed in the belief that each person can remake the world better than it already is. On the other hand, Reformation theology (and its extension into liberal ideology) holds that each person has a responsibility to continue to remake the physical world, to produce, streamline, upgrade, rearrange and change it in order to serve God's glory. Thus, human beings are forever trapped. We're damned if we do and damned if we don't.

If to be revolutionary is to challenge the existing authority with a new vision, then to be revolutionary today is to challenge the authority of science and technology; these are the principle assumptions upon which modern industrial society rests. The Charismatics are doing just that. Their challenge to the existing order is profound and could well end up turning the world upside down, just as the Reformation theologians did a half a millennium ago. To begin with, vertical experience provides an ahistorical context. The Charismatics believe that God can speak to each person today just as authoritatively as he spoke to the apostles 2000 years ago. The Baptism of the Holy Spirit sets up a nonlinear frame of reference. There is no past, present or future when God and people commune. God is all present, all knowing; he interacts with history but is above and beyond it. He is not enslaved by time because he is time immemorial. He knows neither birth nor death, just total being. Thus, when he chooses to interact directly and personally through the Holy Spirit, he is taking man and woman outside of the rigid confines of human history. His revealed truths are timeless. When they reside in the individual human being and reveal themselves through special gifts, they act to liberate people from the limited world of life and death, past and future. During these moments man and woman become at one with God and the unity of his total Being.

While this might appear abstract, at first, it has very real consequences in everyday life. For example, one of the overriding themes of the age of expansion is "technique." Technique is the process by which people attempt to speed up the natural order of things, namely, to make things more efficient. The ultimate objective of technique is to overcome time and space limitations altogether and to produce an ideal, efficient state. Technique is humanity's way of trying to create a *timeless* world, a world of total unified being, omnipotent, all present and eternal. Technique is a horizontal race to a vertical finish line. Of course, human beings can never win the race; in fact, we can never even finish it. The more people apply technique, the more we reduce the components of life to their particulars and the further away we slide from the universality we're striving for. The age of expansion is characterized by the notion that people can overcome all limits. Time and space, however, are the very real limits imposed upon all life. By trying to overcome these limits, people try to become God; this failure is reflected in a world in shambles, destroyed largely by science, technique and our own hubris.

The Baptism of the Holy Spirit eliminates the need for efficiency and technique. In so doing, it sets up conditions for a return to a balanced ecosystem. With special gifts people can overcome this world's time and space limitations and become one with God directly, now. Humanity doesn't need to get sidetracked on a long and futile journey technologizing people and nature. These special gifts, in turn, are more powerful than any scientific technique human beings could ever invent. Speaking in tongues is a more powerful form of communication than any satellite network. It is direct communication from the source, God himself, and it is available to everyone. The gift of prophesy is more powerful than any computer information system. A computer can only plan for the future and predict on the basis of the rather scanty and fragmented evidence people provide. It is therefore fallible and imperfect. Prophesy, on the other hand, comes directly from God. Therefore, it is information that is more than reliable; it is providential and inerrant.

It is no accident that the Charismatic movement has emerged at the very time that our economy is moving from the industrial to the postindustrial age. The new service economy is becoming more and more dependent on science and on information and communication technologies. These three items, in turn, are becoming concentrated under the control of a small technological-professional elite lodged within giant corporate and state bureaucracies. The Charismatic movement is an unconscious reaction against this monopoly of science, information and communications. It is also a reaction to the institutions and the authorities that oversee them. The Catholic Church of the fifteenth century also enjoyed a monopoly over information (the monks were the only ones who could read and write) and over communications (the priests were the only ones who knew Latin, the language of the Church).

"Access" has become a popular new phrase in the political, cultural and economic life of the nation. People feel they are being denied access to information, to communications and to decision-making. Lack of access is a major contributor to the sense of mass anxiety. Millions of Americans feel they no longer have control over the decisions that affect their lives. Being "frozen out" means being denied information necessary to understand one's condition and one's options. Being "cut off" means being kept from communicating one's ideas, thoughts and needs with others. Denied access to information and communications, people are left in the dark. The resulting fear and confusion are what lead to the kind of mass anxiety being experienced today. That anxiety is fueled as economic dislocations and changes continue to bombard us from every side, what Alvin Toffler calls "future shock." We become like the lame and the blind, stumbling, groping and forever anxious, never knowing when the next dislocation will strike, why it is striking and what can be done to protect against it.

"He made the lame walk and the blind see." According to the Bible, these were God's signs that he, not people, was supreme. Special gifts, say the Charismatics, are God's signs. In a secular sense, they are indeed signs—signs of the anxiety and hostility being engendered by the emergence of the new postindustrial order. Imagine, for a moment, the significance of tongues. It is as contrary to the notion of postindustrial communications technologies as faith healing is to modern medicine. Every person utters a unique and different set of sounds when they speak in tongues, or glossolalia. Yet, together they are all speaking the same language, since glossolalia represents the unified and ultimate truths revealed by God through the Holy Spirit. Speaking in tongues contradicts all communications theory. Communications theory is based on the uniformity of sound. That is, a series of vocal utterances must mean the same thing to everyone talking and listening, or there can be no common understanding. If everyone spoke in tongues, it would be indecipherable according to communications logic. Yet millions of people are now doing just that. They are speaking in tongues and the evidence is that they are communicating more effectively with each other as a result. Rather than setting up barriers, speaking in tongues appears to be knocking down walls.

The language in our postindustrial communications society has become so specialized by professional disciplines and so fragmented and divorced of meaning as a result of advertising and political double-talk, that it's no wonder people have turned to speaking in tongues.

Anyone can speak in tongues; it provides the kind of access that people feel is denied them by those who hold a monopoly over communications in this society. Speaking in tongues requires no special training. It is a universal language available to all men and women. There are no experts. Everyone can communicate equally well without the help, intervention or interpretation of professionals, institutions or specialized technologies. Speaking in tongues is not a learned skill, but a gift from God. Speaking in tongues provides everyone with the "information" they need to understand the world and their role in it. It does not provide partial information, or inaccurate information, but the complete body of truths necessary for life. This is so because the truths are those revealed by God, and therefore all-inclusive.

A technician of the Scientific-Information-Communication society would find all of this more than baffling. Here, in the midst of the postindustrial age of computers and satellites, millions of Americans are beginning to turn to the gift of tongues to secure access to information and communications. It is an approach based on faith, not reason, on observable supernatural gifts, not scientific techniques. More importantly, people are finding a new confidence and optimism in this experience, one that threatens to undermine their long-standing faith in science and technology as the ultimate truths in governing people's relationship to the world in which they live.

It is also important to note the extreme nonrational anti-instititional nature of the Charismatic movement. It is, first and foremost, a movement of the heart over the mind, of personal experience over objective analysis. The very basis of the Charismatic renewal is nonrational and subjective. Its spontaneous, unstructured nature is at sharp odds with the methodical world-view of the scientific-technological establishment. The Charismatics mistrust complex structure and remote authority figures. Their success is largely attributable to their decentralized character and their open participatory style. Large impersonal institutions regulate much of our daily lives, and their political and economic authority is becoming more and more distant and centralized. The antibureaucratic, antonomous and democratic approach of the Charismatic movement represents not only a reaction to the larger changes in our social order, but also a potential challenge to them as well.

BUTTRESSING THE STATUS QUO

As a possible revolutionary movement, then, the Charismatic renewal must be reckoned with seriously. Still, there are as many reasons for believing it will end up accommodating itself to the existing technological society as there are for believing it will help overthrow it.

The Charismatic phenomenon is what Marshall McLuhan would call a cool medium. The experience itself is instant, spontaneous, subjective and emotional. It takes place sensuously and visually, not analytically and organically. Its "nowness" is more suited to the medium of TV than it is to a print culture. Print imposes a distance between subject and object. This distance creates time and space, past and future. With TV, space is eliminated. There is no distance between subject and object. Everything is immediate. So too with the Charismatic experience. Its vertical posture, its elimination of time and space, its unity between God and people and its emotional, experiential nature all reflect the TV culture. In fact, one of the main differences between the evangelicals and Charismatics is that the former are more closely attuned to a linear-print orientation. Their doctrines demonstrate distance between subject and object—God and people. They are more analytical, less experiential. They act more from the mind than from the heart. For all these reasons the evangelicals are more suited to develop the components of covenant. Their sense of time, past and future, provides them with the disposition that is required for the institutionalization of ideas and the laying of foundations.

The Charismatics, however, with their electronic orientation and their immediacy, spontaneity and raw emotions, embrace the essential ingredients for rebellion and liberation from authority. This same orientation is also conducive to absorption by the secular culture. If an advertising agent on Madison Avenue were to be asked to list all of the psychological qualities that make a good consumer mentality, he probably would list many of the characteristics of Charismatic renewal. In fact, some critics wonder how much the Charismatic movement is part of a great awakening and how much it is simply the newest consumer experience. Enlightenment games and therapies have been a boom industry for the capitalist service sector for nearly a decade. The quick, spontaneous, all-consuming quality of the Charismatic experience is remarkably similar to other consumer fads that have come and gone over the past few years. Each was tried, accepted and then cast off as fast as the system and the advertising and TV mediums could prepare new ones to take its place.

One indication that this "consumerizing" of Charismatic renewal may be occurring is its increased dependence on TV for spreading its appeal. In many important particulars, TV undermines some of the most salient features that have made Charismatic renewal unique and potentially threatening to the existing secular order. TV eliminates active involvement among the faithful. The participatory-group nature of the Charismatic process is eliminated. In its place is substituted a one-way communication between the TV studio and millions of isolated viewers. This segregation of each individual in his own living space, each vicariously sharing the Charismatic experience as an observer-spectator, replaces the interpersonal aspect of the phenomenon with its antithesis—technological hardware in the form of sophisticated communications systems. Likewise the unstructured, decentralized nonauthoritarian basis of the Charismatic experience is virtually inverted into its opposite with the predominance of TV as the prime "communicating" agent. Shows like the "700 Club" and "PTL" are highly structured, extremely centralized and rely on key authority figures like Pat Robertson and James Bakker. Above all, they are dependent on the very communications and information technology that the Charismatic phenomenon is reacting against. In fact, Bakker's and Robertson's fascination with satellite technology has become a near obsession—one might even say idolatry. They are forever talking about their own use of advanced satellite systems and communications grids, to the point where these items are often allotted more time than God.

Then, too, there exists the real possibility that what are now regarded as special gifts from God will fast become objects of examination, experimentation and exploitation by the scientific-technological establishment. Psychic phenomena are already receiving a great deal of attention in the Soviet Union, and there are suggestions that if such phenomena could be "properly" harnessed they could be made to work for the benefit of the economy. In fact, it could be convincingly argued that the new postindustrial information-communication society will increasingly require the technologizing of psychic phenomena in order to upgrade and streamline its operational systems. This mental upgrading could be as important to the new economic age as physical upgrading of resources, labor and machines has been to the industrial age. What are now perceived as supernatural gifts bestowed on people in order to serve God's glory could be secularized and made into technological skills to serve the postindustrial order. Why not? Calvin's asceticism was designed to serve God, and in the end, it merely served the needs of capital accumulation for the new bourgeois class. Unless the Charismatics are able to resist the temptations of the materialist culture, this could easily become the fate of the special gifts they proclaim. It is an unfortunate fact of modern life that the same person who speaks in tongues or performs faith healing during the evening is likely to be programming a computer the next morning at work. The irony is that we are both part of, yet alienated from, technological society. It is integral to our way of life, even as it has fragmented our humanity. Whether its grip has become so overwhelming that all other gods must be accommodated to it is still an open question. A lot will depend on whether the Charismatics (and evangelicals) are willing to give up some of the consumer security in a technological society in favor of a more spiritual and ascetic life.

The central theme of the mass Charismatic renewal in Kansas City in 1977 was resistance to the secular, materialist culture. The participants were urged to begin building an alternative Christian environment in which materialist values would be replaced by spiritual beliefs. As observer David Stump noted:

[the participants at Kansas City] were clearly seeing the years ahead as a time of struggle to determine if the future would be formed in a Christian image or in the image of secular materialism.[13]

While it's too early to tell which way the Charismatic movement will eventually lean, a great deal will depend on their understanding of the nature of our secular-materialist culture. If they see the problem simply as one of saving fallen individuals from an evil world, leaving the institutional basis of materialism untouched, then it is likely the existing world will change them, rather than they it. If, however, the evangelical participants in the new awakening are able to introduce the Biblical notion of fallen "powers and principalities" as a dual concern along with individual renewal, then this new awakening may, indeed, combine liberation with covenant and change the course of history.

THE EVANGELICALS:
A NEW COVENANT
VISION?

"You have to break a few eggs to make an omelet." This has been a popular slogan among all sorts of twentieth-century revolutionary leaders. It is a saying that has special meaning for the new spiritual revolution as well. If the Charismatics are beginning to break the eggs, it is the evangelicals who will have to make the omelet. A successful revolution requires more than rebellion. It also needs an alternative vision, if it is to succeed. Developing the components of that vision and putting theory into practice require a great deal of careful thought and planning and a vehicle for execution. The evangelicals have the structural base that is necessary to carry out this two-pronged process of conceptualization and implementation. Thousands of evangelical secondary schools, colleges and seminaries are just beginning to grapple with the tough question of developing Christian alternatives to challenge the secular culture. The churches and their outreach organizations and programs are likewise beginning to promote fragmented parts of an alternative Christian agenda. While their structure is impressive, there is no guarantee that the evangelical movement will find either the determination or the wherewithal to provide much more than another popular diversion, one easily absorbed and institutionalized within the larger secular culture. There are several good reasons to assume that this might be the case.

First, the evangelicals have always been uncomfortable

with the notion of power. Calvin's condemnation of church power and authority, the colonials' distrust of the monarchy and the present-day resentment toward government bureaucracies are all part of a deeply ingrained tradition within Protestantism. The notion that "power corrupts" and that "absolute power corrupts absolutely" is one of the central themes of evangelical Christianity. Power and evil are often synonomous in the evangelical mind. This is partly because the evangelicals have always felt themselves to be an "embattled minority" within a larger culture, and thus a target for victimization by the powers that be. Whether that's true or not is, of course, another question. But the important thing is that many evangelicals think it's true. Then, too, power has become associated in evangelical minds with the fallen world of the flesh and therefore with evil itself. As a result, American evangelicals exhibit an interesting duality in their approach to power. On the one hand, they are skeptical and distrustful of people and institutions that represent power. On the other, they are unwilling to assume the "responsibility" of either confronting that power or taking on power themselves for fear that it will corrupt them, as well. Evangelicals will often identify with populist outbursts against existing authority but seldom engage in either discussion or implementation of alternatives to that authority. Two notable exceptions are the first great awakening prior to the American Revolution and the second awakering prior to the Civil War. More often than not, evangelicals will deal with power by withdrawing altogether into a monastic "otherworldliness," concentrating on personal piety and holiness, but not on the "fallen powers and principalities."

Secondly, power has to do with masses of people and massive institutions. These configurations are often an anathema to evangelicals. There is an unconscious fear that, in dealing on the large macro level, the individual will be lost in the scuffle. The very appeal of the present evangelical-Charismatic renewal is anti-institutional and antimass. Millions of anxious, isolated, lonely and confused Americans are in search of personal solace and reconstruction. The impersonality of mass bureaucracies and masses of people are exactly what millions of individuals are turning away from. The evangelical emphasis on the individual is precisely why so many folks are turning toward Christian renewal. The natural inclination, then, is for the evangelical movement to remain reluctant to deal with power and alternative power, because to do so would mean fixing attention on big institutions and collectives, the very things individual Christians are attempting to escape from when they enter the evangelical sanctuary.

Thirdly, there is every reason to suspect that many evangelicals are reasonably content with the existing "powers and principalities"—fallen or otherwise. This is more likely to be the case in the burgeoning Sunbelt than in other regions of the country. Of course, Southern evangelicals are certainly not immune from the mass anxiety generated by the present workings of the system. They, too, are finding themselves objectified at the workplace and fragmented by the consumer mentality. Their families are falling victim to the universal marketplace, the commercial and government service sectors. Still, their anxieties are kept somewhat in check by the relative growth in material affluence of the Sunbelt vis-à-vis other parts of the country. Inflation and unemployment are not taking as big a toll south of the Mason-Dixon line, and this has had the effect of softening, somewhat, the anxieties and fears wrought by the larger economic decline being experienced by the country as a whole. At the same time, the dramatic rate of industrialization and technologization of the South, the immigration of population from the North and the influx of rural labor into burgeoning new Southern cities is no doubt exerting an equally important effect on the Southern psyche, creating new anxieties and strains even amidst partial affluence.

Regardless of the net effect of these counterbalancing tendencies on the Southern psychology, it is true that there is a renewed interest in evangelism within the South which is, no doubt, related to the upsurge in economic growth there. The South is the last remaining area of real expansion for the capitalist system within the United States. Along with it has come a sort of reversion back to the post–Civil War concept of rugged individualism and laissez-faire development. In many ways the South is existing within a kind of special time capsule. While the capitalist expansion is entering its final stages within the United States, it is doing so in this last remaining, untouched, and commercially unexploited region. The "old-time religion," for many, provides a nostalgic justification for the traditional capitalist virtues. The Southerner can use his evangelical theology to screen out the suffering around him and assuage both his individual and collective guilt for gobbling up the last remains of a system that has already abandoned millions of others to an uncertain fate. For him, the evangelism of Dwight Moody and Andrew Carnegie and their Gospel of Wealth provide the necessary succor he's looking for. This form of evangelism is quite prepared to leave the powers and principalities alone, at least as long as material prosperity continues.

It is also fair to say that part of the national interest in evangelism is attributable to the Sunbelt's rise to national prominence. Evangelicalism has always been culturally dominant in the South, and now that the South is exerting its dominance over the country, it's not surprising that its evangelical roots are branching out into other regions as well.

Many other reasons could be cited as evidence that the current spiritual revival will fail to exert itself as a powerful force in the years ahead. Yet, when all is said and done, one overriding consideration continues to suggest that this religious awakening might still play a key, if not decisive, role in the epochal changes taking place in the economic sphere. Many economists and ecologists are in agreement on at least one thing: that as the economy continues its long-range contractions, as vital resources continue to be depleted, as production continues to slow, as inflation and unemployment continue to rise and as cities and entire regions fall victim to breakdown and paralysis for want of adequate tax funds to provide for critical public services, *the need for imposing strict order over all key functions of society will become a practical necessity*. The question, then, is what form this imposition will take. Some, like economic historian Robert L. Heilbroner, argue that the control will be externally imposed by the state through a combination of manipulation and outright brute force, to wit, the authoritarian state.[1] Heilbroner may or may not be right. But, chances are that a second possibility is equally likely: that the external order imposed upon people by the state will combine with an internally imposed order, imposed by each individual upon himself. That internally imposed order may play either a secondary, adjunct role to the imposition of state authority or a primary role, with the state as an enforcer of last resort. The first combination will bear the earmarks of fascism, the second combination the features of a new revolutionary covenant.

EVANGELICALISM AND FASCISM

In 1936 Sinclair Lewis wrote a book called, *It Can't Happen Here*. It was a novel about fascism coming to America. The book didn't receive a great deal of attention in literary circles at the time, but it may yet claim a special place in American history. In the beginning of the novel Mr. Doremus Jessup, the hero, reflects on how fascism might develop here in this country. He argues that an American style of fascism would combine old-time Christian revivalism with conservative business interests to manipulate the mass psychology of the country.[2]

Fascism did not spread to America in the late 1930s. Political observers have offered many reasons to explain why it failed to materialize, and some of these reasons have merit. Still, there is an overriding reason that must be clearly appreciated in order to understand why fascism might well succeed today (in much the way Sinclair Lewis prophesied) where it did not in the 1930s.

The fascist movement in Germany was, at its core, a rebellion against the age of modernity. Germany was crippled by a humiliating defeat in World War I and an even more humiliating armistice agreement—the Versailles Treaty. The Weimar Republic of the 1920s was weak and compromising, thus adding to the public's loss of optimism and national self-confidence. At the same time, the grand promises and expectations of the modern age, which had captured the imagination of German society for nearly three decades, were simply not being met. Germany had become the center of modern European enlightenment. Its universities and economic and political institutions were overflowing with the best minds on the continent. Their scientific and technological expertise, however, proved impotent to deal with the deteriorating economic and political conditions of the late 1920s and early 1930s. Nothing seemed to work in Germany. The feeling that things were breaking down and that German society was grinding to a sputtering halt generated a kind of *mass anxiety* that led to a near hysterical obsession with the need to restore a sense of functioning order in the country. The fact that the best scientific and technological elite anywhere in the world was incapable of resolving this crisis served to further alienate the German people from both the prevailing institutions and the professional classes. That alienation also extended to the scientific, modernist world view of those in power. An unconscious rebellion against the age of modernity began to take shape. The liberal attitudes of the modernists were blamed for the breakdown of traditional cultural values, the demise of the family, and the erosion of accepted patterns of authority—all of which was somewhat true. The Jews were seen as the carriers and proselytizers of the new modernist doctrine. They made up a small but impressive part of the academic elite that was spreading new ideas in psychology, sociology, physics and philosophy throughout the world.

Into this psychological cauldron came the Nazi party. Its brilliance lay in its absolute mediocrity. Adolf Hitler and his cohorts were, more than anything else, an exaggerated example of the neuroses, fears and desires gripping the German people. Their rise to power was less Machiavellian than fortuitous. In them the German people found a vehicle to elevate their own image of themselves to national power. As is often the case in history, that reflection became increasingly less recognizable as the new Nazi elite settled into the corridors of authority.

The Nazis promised the one thing everyone so desperately craved: they promised to "act." Economic stagnation and the breakdown of German culture and society had increasingly been internalized in the form of cynicism, resentment and despair. The Nazis turned the cynicism into hope, the resentment into channeled hostility and the despair into a new missionary doctrine. The pent-up *anxieties* of the German people exploded onto the world with a force that swept up and engulfed the entire continent of Europe.

This new force was aimed at both challenging the age of modernity, and at the same time, reestablishing a sense of *order* in German society. The Nazis, however, never provided a new vision for this order. Theirs was a movement in rebellion against authority without a covenant to replace it. As a result, the rebellion turned in on itself from the very beginning. The unconscious drive against the age of science and modernity became a conscious drive to emulate its worst features. The new order became an extreme parody of the old. All of science and technology were ruthlessly harnessed by the state to serve the Third Reich. "The Nazis succeeded in making the trains run on time." They took the concepts of modern science and created a "master race" and a "master order" that was more precise, more streamlined, more technologized and more efficient than anything the world had ever seen.

However, from beginning to end, their efforts never deviated from their original intent. Theirs was the first war against the age of modernity. Their conceptual theories concerning blood ties and the super race were distinctly primeval in origin. Just before the fall of Paris, Reynaud, the French premier, remarked that if Hitler succeeded in winning the war: "It would be the Middle Ages again, but not illuminated by the Mercy of Christ."[3]

The Germans were determined to destroy every last vestige of the modern era by unconsciously turning the modern world against itself. Science and technology were no longer just tools to exploit for material gain. They were vehicles that the German people would climb aboard to make the final race to the end of history: the millennium was at hand. The master race would be the new gods. They would reign supreme for 1000 years. Their victory would not only be over the world, but over science and technology itself. They would finally become its masters, not its slaves. Yet, at the same time, science and technology were also to be used as the agents of mass destruction against the modern world the master race was in rebellion against. German tanks, rockets and bombs wreaked havoc across civilized Europe. The German experience, then, was nihilistic in the extreme. The Third Reich waged a two-pronged assault on the age of modernity. The Germans used science and technology in an attempt to both master the age of modernity and *destroy* it at the same time.

Today, America finds itself reeling in the throes of economic stagnation and the painful memories of its first humiliating military defeat. Governmental authority, once revered, now appears inept at best, and corrupt at worst. All of this, however, is of secondary importance to a deeper more fundamental change going on within the American psyche. For the first time in its entire history, the American people are beginning to lose faith in the scientific and technological world view that has made this country the most powerful nation on earth.

Nowhere is this loss of faith more manifest than in the Charismatic revival movement. The Charismatic phenomenon is, at its core, a reaction against the age of science, technology and the rationalism of the industrial age. It is also a movement in the first stages of rebellion against the existing order. As the economy continues to decline, and as our scientific and technological experts continue to prove impotent to resolve the crisis, the rebellion will continue to spread within both the

Charismatic renewal movement and the country at large. As in Germany, dislocations and disruptions in the national life of the country will further escalate mass anxiety and the desperate call for both *order* and *action* will become louder and more shrill. If, as was the case in Germany, a new covenant vision is not established, then there is every reason to believe that a succession of evangelical reactions in the 1980s will provide an ideal psychological vacuum for right-wing and capitalist interests to move into and exploit, just as Sinclair Lewis prophesied.

Even a thoughtful and respected evangelical theologian of the stature of Francis Schaeffer (a man not known for hyperbole) believes that fascism is a very real possibility for America in the troubled economic years that lie ahead. In reflecting on America's inability to find a solution to the problems of worsening inflation and recession cycles, Schaeffer concludes:

> I cannot get out of my mind the uncomfortable parallel to the German's loss of confidence in the Weimar Republic just before Hitler, which was caused by unacceptable inflation. History indicates that at a certain point of economic breakdown people cease being concerned with individual liberties and are ready to accept regimentation.[4]

Schaeffer is pessimistic about the prospects for America. He believes that the overriding value that Americans place on their own "personal peace and affluence" will likely lead to a fascist-type order as the economy continues to contract:

> I believe the majority . . . will sustain the loss of liberties without raising their voices as long as their own life styles are not threatened.[5]

What Schaeffer failed to say is that there are already many disturbing signs within the Charismatic and evangelical movements pointing to just such a possibility. For example, many middle-class evangelicals are more and more falling back on the old notion of the "Gospel of Wealth," equating Biblical doctrine with rugged individualism, free enterprise, and unlimited material accumulation. This kind of expansionary theology is still very much a dominant motif in American evangelicalism. The "Gospel of Wealth" theme will likely continue to be used by individual Christians to justify a lack of concern or involvement with the pressing economic crisis ahead—a crisis which will require a communal, not merely an individual or free-enterprise response. For these Christians, the evangelical community will serve as a sanctuary for withdrawal from the turmoil around them. If economic conditions become so bad that they begin to threaten even this last refuge of the middle class, chances are good that withdrawal will quickly translate into active support of right-wing and capitalist interests, even to the point of accepting whatever authoritarian measures are deemed necessary by the state to maintain social order. As Richard Viguerie, the mastermind and chief theoretician of the "new right," recently remarked: "The Evangelical community is the next major recruiting ground for new right politics in America."[6]

Much of the imagery of the present evangelical-Charismatic movement is, indeed, easily interchangeable with the political imagery of a prospective fascist movement. The agonizing pain and crucifixion of Christ conjures up the image of an American government made to suffer an agonizing defeat in Vietnam. Christ died to atone for humanity's sins just as American G.I.'s died to preserve the honor of the American government. Christ's resurrection signaled his ultimate victory, and a sign of the future coming of the kingdom. America's resurrection could signal a return to past glory and new conquests and victories throughout the world.

One of the most disquieting elements of the new spiritual revival is the heavy emphasis placed on premillennial eschatology. The notion that the world is destroying itself and that the final stages of history and the millennium are at hand could be translated into a mass nihilistic campaign to self-fulfill the prophesy. Science and technology, as in Germany, would then become an instrument to both speed up the journey to Armageddon as well as to obliterate the path leading up to it.

What is now a religious movement, at least in part unconsciously reacting to and challenging the expansionary ethos and the idolatry of scientific and technological truths, could, in fact, be turned into its opposite. Christian doctrine, made an adjunct to right-wing and capitalist policies, could provide the necessary self-imposed order that a fascist movement in America would require to maintain control over the country during a period of long-range economic decline.

Whether the Christian renewal movement becomes a pawn in the hands of a fascist regime, or a force for revolutionary change to a steady-state society, depends on whether or not the Christian community embraces the concept of a new covenant vision. The key elements that are necessary to give meaning to that alternative covenant vision are already distinguishable.

GENESIS, CREATION AND THE STEADY STATE

A major reformulation of Protestant doctrine is beginning to take shape. At its center is the story of creation from the Book of Genesis. This reformulation could set the stage for a third great awakening in America and a new covenant vision for a steady-state economic order. Not surprisingly, the theologians who are refocusing on the story of creation and redefining its central message are largely unaware of the profound revolutionary impact their theories could have upon America and the world. Nonetheless, their reconstruction of doctrine continues to ripple out into wider circles. If it becomes a tidal wave within the Christian community, then Luther and Calvin may well be retired to the theological archives to be replaced by the yet unnamed heretics of the second great reformation.

Many evangelical and mainline Protestant scholars are beginning to argue that a basic redefinition of the story of creation provides the only viable starting point for establishing a new ecologically sound approach to people's relationship to the world around them. Their arguments are compelling, if not convincing, especially when compared with the other possible alternatives being advanced.

In 1977, President Carter made a historic appeal to the American people in his energy address to the nation.[7] He said that the energy crisis had plunged us into a virtual state of siege, as threatening to our national security as any war we'd experienced. He called upon all Americans to band together and to make common sacrifices during this time of travail. Carter's message was somber and realistic. He warned that a lack of shared commitment to the principles of energy conservation could spell defeat and ruin for the United States in the years ahead. His appeal and his warnings went unheeded. Carter failed. He had appealed to a sense of public virtue that no longer exists. He had enjoined Americans to act as public citizens, and they simply turned away and continued on with business as usual. That business is the business of producing

and consuming within the capitalist mode. Its modus operandi
is not public virtue and public citzenship, but private self-ism,
competition and exploitation. In one moment in time, the President, rather naively one might say, was calling upon Americans to *transcend* the very belief system that allowed them to
survive day-to-day within modern American society in response
to some vague notion of serving the public good.

Carter's speech is reflective of the kind of mentality that
permeates the public interest movement in America. Ralph
Nader, Common Cause, environmentalists and others are forever berating the American public for not transcending their
selfish concerns and acting in consort for the common good.
But what is the common good? What are its guiding principles?
These are the hard questions that environmentalists and ecologists are now pondering. While they are all in agreement that
a new transcendent set of values is essential for acceptance of
a steady-state society, they are at a loss as to how to spell out
the particulars of that value system, and even more at a loss
as to how to get people to accept the particulars, assuming they
were spelled out in the first place.

Their problem has to do with their philosophical focus. By
and large, the public interest community is caught in an ideological trap. They continue to approach the problem of ecology
from a liberal perspective. But, the liberal ethos is the opposite
of *conservation*. It is an expansionary world view based on a
belief in relativism and growth. For the liberal public interest
advocate, the world is seen in dialectical terms. Life is constantly changing. Truth is partial and relative to time and cir-
cumstance. History is an "open-ended" system, and each moment
in time represents a partial truth in the process of evolving into
a new partial truth—the sum total of which never adds up to
the ultimate truth (that would mean the end of history) but only
to a more enlightened partial understanding of life, to wit:
"There is always something new to learn."

Ecology, on the other hand, is a "closed system." To conserve means neither to expand or contract, but to maintain.
Ecology starts not with a partial or relative truth but with an
absolute truth. Nature has an order to it. That order, in turn,
operates on an absolute principle. That principle is balance.
All living things in the natural order exist in an interdependent
relationship with each other. That relationship is designed to
reproduce itself. Balance is the self-regulating biological process which maintains the natural speed of the entropy process.

An ecologist would argue that while the entropy process is always at work in nature, its speed does not change dramatically unless the natural order or balance of nature is grossly interfered with. Interference, of course, generally means the intervention of human beings.

One cannot accept liberal ideology and ecology at the same time. If one accepts the idea that nature is a closed-end system based on a fixed order and guided by a set of absolute principles, and if one further accepts that this natural order is preferable to any other alternative order that one might design, then of what value is science, technology, the modern view of change and progress and the dialectical view of history that sees the human journey as a linear search to discover fragmented or partial truths?

In order to convince the public to accept a steady-state existence, the public interest advocate would need to abandon his dialectical perspective in favor of a set of absolute principles or truths that fit the absolute principles and truths of ecology itself. To summarize, the liberal ethos is by its nature expansionary not conservative. A committed liberal will tell you: "You can't stop progress." Human beings will always be in search of new truths and new ways of doing things better. After all, it's part of our nature. Is it, or is it part of our ideology? The liberal activist is now stuck. He can no longer satisfactorily answer his own guiding assumptions. For example, what is progress? What is the final goal of progress? How will we know what is progress and what is not? Or is all change simply progress, and therefore without any intrinsic value or purpose? What are the truths people are in search of? If we can never know the full truth, then how do we know that the partial truths are, in fact, partial truths? When we say that people will always seek new ways to do things better, what are we comparing the better to? If we are comparing it to the original way or natural way, are we saying that people can eventually design a better order than the one we come from? If so, how can that possibly be the case, when people can only know partial truths about the existing order?

The public interest activist is a person sandwiched between two competing ideologies—one liberal and expansionary, the other conservative and fixed. His *moral instincts* have led him to embrace ecology. His *reason,* however, continues to reject the notion of belief in and adherence to absolute unchangeable truths that can be fully known and lived by now. For him, discovery, not revelation, is still the dominant approach. Thus, enter the new evangelicals. They are developing a very different approach to ecology.

The new evangelicals acknowledge that the traditional Christian approach to nature has been a major contributing factor to ecological destruction.[8] While they differ as to whether the blame rests with Reformation theology or the Byzantine theology of the Medieval Catholic Church, they agree that the overemphasis on "otherworldliness" has led to disregard and even exploitation of the physical world.[9] This view holds that the only things of true value are those found in the heavenly world of God. This world, the world of people and nature and the flesh, is seen as low, depraved and unworthy, and therefore of little concern or consequence to those seeking to live a holy life. The natural world is merely a stopover on people's journey to the next. Therefore, the less attention placed on it and the more attention placed on God's kingdom, the better.

The other mistake in Christian doctrine, they admit, is the misinterpretation of the concept of dominion in the Genesis account of creation.

Be fruitful and multiply and fill the earth and subdue it; and have dominion over the fish of the sea and over the birds of the air and over every living thing that moves upon the earth.

The concept of *dominion* has been used by people to justify the ruthless manipulation and exploitation of nature. Now, for the first time, evangelical scholars are beginning to redefine the meaning of dominion, and in so doing, they are creating the theological foundations for a steady-state world view.[10]

The new interpretation of Genesis begins with the idea that since God created the heavens and the earth and everything in this world, all his creations take on importance and an instrinsic worth because they are of his making. Since this creation of God's has a purpose and order to it, that purpose and order are to be revered just as God's creation is to be revered. Finally, what God has created is fixed. The Lord created the world and *everything* in it, and then he rested, according to the creation story. If follows from this, argue the new evangelical scholars, that anything that exploits or harms God's creations is sinful and an act of rebellion against God himself. Likewise, anything that undermines the "fixed" purpose and order that God has given to the natural world is also sinful and an act of rebellion. This is no small theological point. The evangelicals contend that every other religious conviction flows from these central truths of creation. Either God created the world, or he didn't. Either God gave purpose and order to the world, or he didn't. If one believes in these truths, then one believes in God. If one doesn't believe in these truths, one can't possibly believe in God. This thesis is the beginning point for all Christian believers.

It follows, then, that sin consists in the hubris of believing that people can treat God's creations differently than God does— namely, manipulating and exploiting them for purposes other than what they were created for. It is also hubris to believe that people can reorder this world and redefine its purpose to suit their own whims and fancies. These acts, argue the evangelicals, bring chaos and disorder to the world. Chaos and disorder are synonymous with evil. The Christian life, then, must be one of conserving order over chaos, wholeness over fragmentation, balance over imbalance and harmony over disharmony. A Christian must love God's creation and treat it with respect, because God created it with love.[11]

Dominion, then, does not mean the right to exploit nature. Far from it, say the evangelicals. Dominion means stewardship over nature. Henlee H. Barnette, in his book, *The Church and the Ecological Crisis,* points out that the Biblical view of humankind "is that of a keeper, caretaker, custodian . . . of the household earth." Stewardship, says Barnette, is "the New Testament term for this role of human beings in relation to the natural order." The first requisite of a steward, according to Barnette, "is faithfulness, because he handles that which belongs to another."[12] The concept of stewardship leads directly to the Biblical notion of covenant. In Genesis, God says:

> I established my Covenant with you [mankind], and with
> your seed after you and with every living created thing.

God also gives specific instructions as to how this covenant is to be carried out. For example, in Exodus 23:10–11 and Leviticus 19:9 God tells people to leave the ground fallow every seventh year for the purpose of conservation and replenishment. Other passages of the Bible warn people to "defile not the land which ye shall inhabit, wherein I dwell." The Bible also is full of references to what happens when people break this special covenant with God. For example, in Isaiah 24:4–6, Isaiah says:

> The earth lies polluted under its inhabitants: for they have transgressed the laws, violated the statutes and broken the everlasting covenant.

God, then, has a covenant with humanity. Men and women are to act as his stewards on earth, preserving and protecting all of God's creations.

This covenant puts human beings in a special relationship to God. Since people are a creation of God, just like all of God's other creations, they are equal with them in their finite nature; only God is infinite. While all creations are equal in that they owe their existence to the same source—God—human beings are different in an essential way. The difference, as Francis Schaeffer points out in his book, *Pollution and the Death of Man,* is that human beings are made by God in his image and are given the responsibility to act as stewards over the rest of God's creation. Therefore, people are both part of nature—equal to and dependent on all other living and non-living things—and at the same time, separate from nature—with a responsibility to protect and take care of it. As long as people accept both relationships, they are faithful to God's purpose and are carrying out the covenant God made with them. When people take advantage of their special relationship by taking over God's creation as their own and using it for their own ends rather than God's glory, they have broken the covenant and are in rebellion against God. [13]

It is important to emphasize that this radical reinterpretation of God's first instruction to human beings in the book of Genesis has been so thoroughly accepted by all shades of Protestant theology within the past decade, that it is no longer necessary to cite particular authorities in defense of its underlying supposition. The fact is, the old conception of dominion has been completely discredited and now lies abandoned. The new definition of dominion, though popularly embraced, has not yet been formally consecrated as the theological foundation for a new Christian world view. If and when that happens, Protestantism will take an unalterable turn toward a second reformation.

Interestingly enough, the creation story directly parallels the two basic laws of thermodynamics. According to Genesis, God's order is fixed. He created everything that exists at one moment in time. Similarly, the first law of thermodynamics states that all matter and energy in the world are constant and fixed. That is, they can neither be created nor destroyed. The totality of matter and energy that exists today has existed from the beginning and will continue to exist to the end of time. Only its "form" changes, never its "essence."

In Genesis, Adam and Eve are seduced by the forces of evil into disobeying God's command by eating the fruit from the Tree of Knowledge. For their act of rebellion, God banishes them from the Garden saying: "Dust you are and to dust you shall return."

Evil is synonymous with the forces of chaos and disorder. History, in theological terms, is seen as a long and protracted war in which the forces of evil continually attempt to enlist the help of fallen individuals in their battle to spread chaos in God's world. The forces of evil win most of the battles, but ultimately lose the war. That is, with the help of sinful people, they succeed in creating more and more disorder in the world, until Christ's return once again to earth. God then triumphs over evil at this climactic moment of history, and the world, which the evil forces have turned into complete and utter chaos, is transformed back into God's kingdom.

The second law of thermodynamics posits a similar view of history. It states that all matter and energy were created, in this original state, with an order and value to them. That ordered state is continually being eroded by an irreversible natural process. According to the law of entropy, all matter and energy are constantly and without exception moving from an ordered to a disordered state.

The evangelical world view coincides in another important respect with the basic laws of thermodynamics. Evangelical theologians hold that human beings can never restore the world back to its original state before the fall. Only God, they argue, can usher in the perfect kingdom anew. This is also what the second law of thermodynamics says. That is, there is no way that people can ever reverse the law of entropy. All matter and energy move from a low- to a high-entropy state, that is, from an ordered to a chaotic condition. While human technology gives the appearance of reversing the process at any given moment in time, it is, on the contrary, doing the exact opposite. Technologies, after all, are designed to speed up the entropy process by more progressively using up the stock of available matter and energy in the world.

The average person in the street, while unversed in the laws of thermodynamics, intuitively understands their underlying principles. His own observation of the effects of introducing new technologies into the world has convinced him of one central fact: that whenever a new technology seems to be providing a semblance of order in one place, it is ultimately creating a greater amount of disorder somewhere else—even though it may be years before the effects of the secondary disorders are discovered.

In maintaining the illusion that technology can overcome the forces of disorder at work in the world—that is, reverse the process of entropy—human beings have committed the ultimate sin that evangelical theologians have long warned against. Regardless of how hard people try, they can never restore things to the original order or create a new order to take the place of the old. In the final analysis, science and technology only serve to speed up the inevitable process of decay. To believe otherwise is to disregard the laws of physics as we know them.

From a theological perspective, every person still has a choice to make even though the second law of thermodynamics and evangelical doctrine both say that the natural order is moving irrevocably toward a state of total chaos. The choice, put rather simply, is whether the individual will align himself with the forces responsible for speeding up the entropy process, or the forces attempting to preserve God's creation. Of course, it might well be asked what value there is in choosing to serve as a steward, when evangelical theology and the laws of physics acknowledge that, in the end, human beings alone cannot win out over the forces of disorder. The evangelicals would argue that while only God can usher in the kingdom—reverse the process of entropy and remake the world—each person still has a responsibility during his lifetime to serve as a witness to the coming of that kingdom. Serving witness means respecting and protecting God's created order to the fullest, even while knowing that all of one's efforts are ultimately insufficient to the task. This knowledge, understanding and commitment represent the final casting aside of ego, the supreme act of faith and the ultimate cross that all must bear if they are to surrender themselves fully and completely in service to God.

For each individual, then, the question boils down to: "What do I choose to do *now* in my lifetime?" This is the only proper question to ask, because in Biblical terms, there is no way of knowing when the end will come. God's timetable is neither knowable or amenable. As for the second law of thermodynamics, if people radically change their destructive approach to the world and adopt a more balanced and harmonious relationship to the ecology of the planet, the current entropy escalation can be dramatically reduced, extending the life of the world's ecosystem for millions of years into the future.

Christian doctrine and the laws of physics assert that our world, the world of matter and energy, operates within the confines of a finite span of existence. Still, both recognize that within those broad limits, there is a constant ebb and flow of life: birth, death and rebirth; energy input, energy output, rest and replenishment. The individual's day-to-day choice is whether to serve that life-force or work against it. That choice is set forth in the creation story in the Bible and by the ecologists, economists and social thinkers who are calling for a radical change in humanity's approach to the earth.

Many evangelicals are already beginning to accept the reinterpretation of the creation story that Christian scholars are putting forth. As it becomes more and more clear that the second law of thermodynamics reinforces much of the basic orthodoxy of evangelical doctrine, there will, no doubt, be a rush to embrace it as well.

Perhaps one of the main reasons the second law of thermodynamics has never, up to now, attracted much public attention is that there was no need or desire to do so. After all, the laws of thermodynamics, when broadly applied, challenge the entire conceptual basis of materialism and the expansionary world view of science and technology. The laws of thermodynamics are finally being rediscovered and redefined within a broader theological and philosophical context precisely because the world has now arrived at the "physical limits" of which they speak. These two laws of thermodynamics will no doubt become the philosophical and metaphysical focus for the new age of scarcity, just as the Newtonian world machine was for the age of expansion.

When combined with more orthodox evangelical theology, the new creation theory and the laws of thermodynamics set the tone for a reformulation of Christian doctrine and a covenant that is suited to the ecological prerequisites of a steady-state social order. Still, there remains one critical obstacle in the way of such a development. The current premillennial attitude prevalent among most evangelicals is at direct odds with some of the interpretations of the creation story that have been set forth.

The premillennialists view history in much the same way as the second law of thermodynamics. However, their over-riding preoccupation with arriving as quickly as possible at the end of history—God's return—precludes any serious service as stewards over God's created order. Their attention has become so riveted on anticipation of the coming of the kingdom and saving as many souls as possible in the remaining time, that they have left God's created order unguarded and unprotected. In not honoring their covenant to God to serve as stewards, the premillennialists are acting in direct rebellion. Secondly, by doing nothing to resist or slow down the ongoing forces of disorder and chaos, they are not only showing disrespect for God's creations, but they are also failing to bear their cross, that is, to act as witness to the glory of God's order and the future coming of his kingdom. In fact, many premillennialists actually take satisfaction in observing the escalating turmoil around them. It serves to reinforce their belief that the end and the new beginning are near. As a consequence, they remain passive in the midst of mounting disorder. In their noninvolvement, they are as guilty of disrespect for God's creation as those who exploit the earth directly.

The absolute truths posited by the creation doctrine fit the absolute principles of thermodynamics and a balanced ecosystem. Most of all, the creation doctrine provides an answer to the question: "Why should I take responsibility for caring for and preserving the natural order?" Because it is God's fixed order. God created it and God entrusted human beings with the responsibility to oversee it. It boils down to a question of serving God or rejecting him.

Some ecologists argue that there is another equally compelling reason to preserve the ecosystem, namely, survival. Since humanity is dependent on the proper functioning of the natural order, they contend, we should continue to preserve that order to insure our own survival. This approach still leaves the ultimate question unanswered. What, then, is the purpose of survival? If there is no intrinsic meaning or purpose to life, then survival becomes inconsequential or irrelevant. To survive without purpose is of no value whatsoever.

The new interpretation of the creation story is as theologically significant for the future steady-state society as Calvin's

Reformation doctrine was for the emergence of the expansionary era of capitalism.

For example, the creation doctrine establishes a new relationship between the individual and his neighbor and the rest of creation. It asserts that all of God's creations are each of intrinsic worth because God created them. All creations are also equal because "all things are equally created out of nothing . . . all things, including human beings, are equal in their origin, as far as creation is concerned."[14] However, not only are all creations of equal intrinsic worth, but they are all dependent on each other as well. God did not create a human being, or a monkey, or a rosebush or a fish to be autonomous. None of God's creations can stand alone and survive. They are each locked into an intricate and delicately balanced web of dependent relationships with each other. Those dependent relationships make up the order of God's creation. Therefore, while God's creations have self-worth and are equal, they are also mutually dependent on each other. In fact, their individual survival depends on their mutual dependence. God's order, then, is made up of a finely tuned give-and-take relationship between all creatures.

It is impossible, therefore, to deal with any of the individual parts of God's creation in isolation. Instead, all parts of creation must be dealt with as a holistic system. This approach to life poses a direct threat to the concept of the autonomous individual; the economic notion of private ownership and exploitation of resources; and the idea of reductionism, which is the basic principle behind science and technology.

Calvin perceived a world in which the lone, autonomous individual performed his personal calling for the glory of God. For him, unceasing work and unlimited personal accumulation were at the heart of each individual's role in life. Neither concept fits the creation doctrine. First, in the natural order, energy output never runs at optimal levels at all times. Instead, periods of energy release are followed by rest, during which time the organism is replenished by the absorption of new energy. This process is called balance. Balance is the self-regulating biological process which maintains the natural speed of the entropy process. In Calvin's world there was no rest, or allowance for replenishment. There was only an unrelenting battle to gobble up as much low-entropy matter and energy as possible. As a result, Calvin's Reformation man and woman created a great deal more high-entropy disorder in the world

than would be the case if the "natural entropy" process had
been left to operate at its own speed. Modern man and woman,
then, are forever violating their relationship to other beings,
other creatures and the earth's resources, by disregarding the
need for rest and replenishment. They do this whenever they
try to harness energy (their own as well as of other creations)
at maximum, unceasing levels in order to enhance their own
accumulations. In the process, they not only short-circuit the
natural order of energy release, rest and energy replenishment,
but also place themselves at the center of that energy transfer—
a place previously reserved for God.

Then, there is the question of unlimited accumulation of
wealth (another Calvinist doctrine). Since there is no wealth
beyond what God has created, the accumulation of God's bounty
into private hands is a second major violation of the creation
doctrine. According to creation theology all things have intrinsic worth and are equal and mutually dependent. Humanity's special role is to preserve that intrinsic worth and equality
by acting as God's caretaker. This is its covenant. Nowhere in
the creation story does it say that some men and women have
a greater responsibility than others to take care of God's creations. On the contrary, the Bible makes it clear that this is a
shared responsibility that must be taken up *equally* by all human
beings. Therefore, if some individuals take more of God's
creation onto themselves, they are, in effect, denying other
people their responsibility as God's custodians. In fact, since
stewardship assumes that humankind is merely a caretaker of
a creation that belongs only to God, then the entire concept of
private ownership of land and resources is an act of rebellion.
God did not give individuals the right to expropriate parts of
his creation in order to exploit it for private gain. This too
constitutes an act of rebellion. When a person claims that a
certain piece of land and the oil under it belong to him, and
profits off that claim, he is asserting his sovereignty over that
oil against God's. In so doing, he is violating God's covenant
and his relationship with the rest of creation.[15]

In Biblical terms, restoring the covenant with God and with
the rest of creation is most often expressed by the notion of
economic justice. The Bible speaks concretely of the need for
a jubilee every fiftieth year, when the rich shall redistribute
their wealth in order to bring harmony back to human relationships and restore the covenant between people and God.

The Biblical principle of economic justice finds its counterpart in the principle of balance in nature. Whenever one element of an ecosystem multiplies or grows out of proportion to its proper functioning relationship with the rest of the elements in the system, it threatens the vitality and continued existence of the entire system. This is also the case in human society. When one or more individuals amass an inordinate amount of wealth and power, they threaten the economic existence and survival of everyone else. Nature relies on self-regulating biological laws to restore balance. Society, on the other hand, must rely on agreed upon principles of justice to achieve these ends. The Bible prescribes those principles of justice and the covenant of stewardship between human beings and God is the self-regulating mechanism of enforcement.

Finally, the creation doctrine postulates a holistic world view. It rejects the concept of autonomy. Nothing can exist alone (all creations are dependent on all other creations for their survival). Therefore, it is foolish to attempt to reduce the world to a collection of autonomous parts, either as a way of understanding the overall picture, or as a way of reconstructing or upgrading those parts to perform independently and more efficiently than the surrounding natural order. In the final analysis, this approach—the scientific method—ends up creating even greater dislocation and chaos in God's created order.

Evangelical theologians and ecologists argue that the scientific method is based on a faulty premise, to wit, that the whole is always equal to the sum of its parts. This view has become an axiom of modern science. If the whole is equal to the sum of its parts, as scientists claim, then it's logical to assume that by studying and understanding the function of the parts, one at a time, in isolation, the fragmented information obtained can eventually be assembled in such a way as to enable the researcher to understand the whole organism, mechanism or system those parts make up.

Both ecologists and Christian doctrine argue otherwise. They assert that the whole is always greater than the sum of its parts. For that reason scientific reductionism can never provide more than an intuitive partial picture of the whole. For the evangelicals, the gap between the larger whole and the sum of its parts is God's love—the spiritual essence that God imbues in and among all his creations. For the ecologist, the difference or gap between the whole and the parts is a nonquantifiable bonding or interrelationship that exists with all life. Both evangelicals and ecologists assume then that there are aspects to life that can never be measured. These aspects, they claim, are the most important, and are always overlooked in the scientific approach. Because the primal essence of all phenomena is beyond human reach, we can never hope to fully understand, control or reduplicate the world around us. In trying to do so, we end up creating even greater dislocation and chaos.

Like the reductionists', the holistic view of nature is partially intuitive, but its premise leads to a very different outlook on life. The understanding that there is a nonquantifiable aspect to all life that is beyond human reach creates a reverence or respect toward creation. That reverence is essential if people are to fulfill God's covenant as stewards and live by the rules of the natural ecosystem. In its absence, people will continue to exhibit that hubris that comes of believing that they can know all, and thus can manipulate and control all as well.

The scientific method, then, is a crude measurement of partially observable phenomena which people have transformed into a set of absolute truths governing the world. These scientific "truths" provide people with the false hope that they can redesign the natural order and make it better than it is, even though they are never privy to the detailed blueprint of God's original plan. When man and woman, the caretakers, begin to assume the role of sovereign architect, God's covenant is broken and all creation suffers.

If the new interpretation of the creation story is "religiously" applied, it will challenge the entire range of assumptions and relationships of the present expansionary ethos.

THE CREATION DOCTRINE AND WORK

As mentioned earlier, there are many similarities between the pre-Reformation Church and today's capitalist machine. Nowhere is this more evident than in the production process. Like the sixteenth-century Catholic Church, corporate management attempts to take away from the individual all *independent* thought. Under scientific management, every aspect of the worker's behavior and activity is rigidly prescribed and codified in advance. The "sacraments" of the workplace are to be faithfully executed without challenge or question of management's authority. The management priests, in turn, not only provide all of the important answers for questions that might arise, but also dispense rewards (dispensations and blessings) and punishments (excommunication) in the form of promotions and firings.

The principles of scientific management are designed to divide the human being into two distinct parts, mind and body— the former being placed in the hands of management, the latter being left to the workers. This separation of *conception* from *execution* violates a basic proposition that is essential to the creation doctrine. The evangelicals believe that the human being is at the same time equal to and different from all God's creations. In that he is finite and created by the same God that created all other creatures and phenomena, he is an equal in creation. He is different in that God created him in his image so that he could serve as a caretaker or steward over God's creation. For this task the human being was blessed with the ability to conceptualize and think rationally—something no other creature can do. As long as people retain their ability to conceptualize as well as execute, they can continue to faithfully carry out their covenant to serve as a steward for God on earth.

Scientific management expropriates the conceptual side of the worker's identity. In so doing, it deprives him of the wherewithal to carry out his covenant with God. A person without a mind is no different from all of the other creations. He has "consciousness" but not "self-awareness," as E. F. Schumacher would put it. Without his conceptual faculty he can *perform,* but he can not watch over the earth, because he is without the ability to abstract himself from his milieu. Scientific management fragments the wholeness of the human being and makes him different from what God created him to be. If God had meant some persons to be pure machines and other persons to be pure minds, he would have created two different types of beings. In changing the nature of people, the scientific management of capitalism has rebelled against God and broken his covenant. As Francis Schaeffer points out:

God is going to deal with them [His creations] as He made them. He will always deal with a plant as a plant, with an animal as an animal, with a machine as a machine and with man as a man, not violating the orders of creation. He will not ask the machine to behave like a man, neither will He deal with man as though he were a machine. Thus God treats His creations with integrity; each thing in its own order, each thing the way He made it. If God treats His creation in that way, should we not treat our fellow creatures with a similar integrity? If God treats the tree like a tree, the machine like a machine, the man like a man, shouldn't I, as a fellow creation, do the same, treating each thing with integrity in its own order?[16]

While evangelical scholars have begun to apply the newly defined creation doctrine to ecology in general, they have barely begun to understand its relationship to human ecology. There is much talk about the exploitation of natural resources and upsetting God's natural order, but little discussion of the way the system exploits human resources. Yet the very same principles that apply to natural resources and other creations apply to people as well. Some of those principles have already been discussed.

One in particular, however, deserves closer attention. God's order, say the evangelicals, works on the principle of interdependence and balance. That balance and interdependence rest on an important principle of energy transfer. All living things receive energy and expend it. That process is itself finely calibrated. Anything that attempts to bypass any of the key aspects of the process—energy release, rest and replenishment—throws the rest of the system into imbalance. Many ecologists, and even evangelicals, are beginning to understand this basic proposition when it comes to energy resources, land cultivation and the protection of various types of wildlife. For example, the value of land is continually eroding as a result of the natural entropy process. However, this very slow process of decay is dramatically speeded up when people ignore the need for rest and replenishment. What they have not yet seen is that the same principles hold for *workers* in the production process.

The entire concept of productivity in the modern industrial mode is based on bypassing the essential rest and replenishment cycle of the natural order. Management is in constant need of finding new ways to maximize labor's output by reducing input. The less it costs to service a worker in relationship to what he produces, the more profit will accrue to the system. This is the very basis of capitalist production. It is also the opposite of the principles of the ecological steady state and the newly defined creation doctrine. The key is to remember the basic underlying principle of capitalist productivity: Increase the value of output while decreasing the cost of input. In other words, try to get more and more energy out of the worker relative to what is necessary to put back into the worker by technologizing his behavior and performance and making him more efficient than he would normally be in a natural environment. The difference is what profit is all about.

Of course, the results of this process of bypassing the natural order are beginning to manifest themselves with human resources just as with natural resources. In both cases, productivity is increasing at a decreasing rate. Diminishing returns are setting in because it's impossible to continue to use up more energy without replenishment. Eventually the resource slows down and either burns out or is used up. This is exactly what is happening with human and physical resources. This resource depletion, in turn, has been a major contributing factor to the increased cost of production, lower rates of return on investment and slowdown in the economy. With human resources, as opposed to natural resources, the manifestations differ, but not the results. When human resources begin to burn out we attach neat antiseptic phrases like "worker alienation" to explain the slowdown in productivity. The real explanation is that the wholeness of the worker has been destroyed. He has been reduced to an objective resource factor in the production mix; his human resources have been speeded up and technologized beyond their natural entropy state; he is not provided with nourishment commensurate with the speedup of his energy output; he continues to use up energy at a faster rate of speed; the system profits while he is used up, wasted and eventually discarded because he no longer has resource value. Today, there are millions of older American workers who understand this process intimately. While they may not have intellectualized it or thought it through in terms of nature and the exploitation of resources, they nonetheless feel the results of what has happened to them in a very real and personal way. In exploiting human resources in this manner, in creating imbalance in the natural order, in expropriating to themselves the profits derived from the depletion of other people's energy, the owners and controllers of the capitalist system are, then, acting in rebellion against God's covenant.

THE CREATION DOCTRINE AND CONSUMPTION

The consumption mode of the present expansionary economic order is also at direct odds with the creation doctrine and the prerequisites of a steady-state order. The modern consumption mentality, fostered by tens of billions of dollars in capitalist advertising each year, assumes that there is an unlimited supply of resources and experiences that can be consumed, as well as an insatiable public appetite to consume them. This mentality leads inexorably to the wholesale waste and depletion of God's creation. At the same time the self-ism generated by the advertising industry works against the notion of stewardship and covenant—that is, personal responsibility for preserving nature's bounty. The ideas of frugality and conservation are inimical to the demands of a consumption economy. As with natural resources and human labor, however, there is a point of diminishing returns. The more one consumes, the less satisfaction one gets, requiring even greater consumption—the principle is the same as that with any "addiction." In the end, instead of consumption serving the user, the user begins to serve it. In other words, the consumer invests more energy than he gets back. Of course, this is exactly the mentality that Madison Avenue tries to establish. Creating mass consumer addiction is the sine qua non of the marketing world view.

Like other addicts, consumers are beginning to experience withdrawal symptoms as the contracting economy dries up their supply and inflation eats away at their ability to maintain their habit.

Various therapies, cults and even part of the evangelical movement have begun to play off this sense of loss in a fashion that only prolongs the agony. Many people become hooked on numerous psychological and spiritual encounter groups and games in a desperate attempt to renew their energy, so they can continue to service their consumer habits. *The Power of Positive Thinking; I'm OK, You're OK; How to Win Through Intimidation;* and a multiplicity of other books, programs, ideologies and religious experiences are designed to restore one's sense of personal confidence in the notion that material success can indeed be maintained (with the proper outlook), even in a period of increasing scarcity. The irony is that such psychic energy infusions only act as temporary adrenaline, allowing the individual to overcome his personal alienation and mental fatigue just long enough to put out that extra push needed to maintain his consumption fix. The vicious cycle continues to work against the user because he ends up expending much more energy on his fix than he gets back from it. Consumption, which should serve the function of replenishment and maintenance, becomes its opposite. Consumption becomes a matter of greater waste and depletion. We use up goods and services without truly absorbing or recycling them. In so doing we litter the mind, pollute the body, exhaust our own energy and the energy around us, speed up the natural entropy process, and act in open defiance of God's covenant to serve as stewards.

There is both an individual and an institutional cause for this problem. The evangelicals argue that the liberal theory that people are basically good is to blame for much of the consumer fix. The "people are good" theory, they contend, has served as a blank check to justify anything and everything people want to experience. If people are good, then any experience they consume must likewise be good, or if it is not good, at least educational or informative. While they obviously overstate the case, there is no doubt that there is an element of truth to their claim. We have all become at least partially aware of the psychological dimensions of the so-called "permissive society," even as we continue to enmesh ourselves in it.

"How do you know if you'll like it or not, until you've tried it?" "The least you can do is give it a try." "If it isn't your cup of tea, then you can always try something else. After all the worst thing is not to try at all."

The evangelicals say that only by starting with the belief that human beings are basically evil—not good—is it possible to put the brakes on the runaway consumer mentality. They reason that, as long as one believes that people are good by nature, there will never be enough restraints or limits put on their behavior—either by themselves or society—since to do so would be to undermine their unlimited right to have good experiences.

If one starts with the idea that human beings are fallen, however, then it is necessary to impose limits on their activity in order to curb potential evil or the temptation of evil. "Limits," of course, are essential factors in both God's created order and in a steady-state society. There are very real limits to the natural order. It is a finite reality. Therefore, all creatures within that finite reality have very real limits placed on them as well. With all other creatures, those limits are imposed biologically. Only humans have the capability to overcome their self-imposed biological limits. Their power to reason and conceptualize provides them with a special power which can be used either to serve God as his steward on earth, or which can be used to tear down the *limits* imposed by God's order and sow disorder and chaos in the world. When humans attempt to disregard limits, they are attempting to seize sovereignty over the world and claim *unlimited* omnipotence for themselves. But only God has *no* limits—he is infinite, all else is finite. Fallen people, say the evangelicals, are people who refuse to accept the real limits placed upon them by God's order and creation. By reasserting the belief that human beings are fallen, and by placing self-imposed limits on what they can do and what they can't do—those limits being prescribed in the Bible as God's revealed truths and commandments—the evangelicals say that a semblance of order and discipline can be restored to the world and God's natural order.

Sex is a good example of the conflict between those who argue for unlimited consumer experience and those who call for restraints. The sexual revolution of the past twenty years has done a great deal to liberate men and women from the unnatural inhibitions imposed by the Puritanism of orthodox Christian dogma. At the same time, the universal marketplace of capitalism has moved in and effectively transformed this essentially positive phenomenon into just one more consumer experience. Today, the commercial sexual revolution is without boundaries. Madison Avenue has created a multibillion-dollar industry which feeds off the sexual exploitation of millions of Americans. The consequence of packaging sex has been profound. Today technique and efficiency have largely replaced love and emotion in sexual relations. Like other consumer experiences, sex has become so overused and objectified in our society that it is losing much of its intrinsic value. Diminishing returns are setting in as individual consumers find themselves spending more energy serving their sex habit than they are getting back in sexual rewards. After all, perpetual shopping for the right clothes, the right cosmetics, the right personality and the right techniques can be so exhausting that little is left for the actual sexual experience itself. Then, too, by the time the moment arrives, chances are fair to good that any positive subjective energy that might have transpired between two people has been all but lost to the commercial technicalization of the process.

The new interpretation of the creation doctrine would hold that sex is something to enjoy and appreciate. The new evangelicals say that, if the Creator had meant for sex to be painful and unenjoyable, he would have made the experience just that. While sex, then, is to be enjoyed because God intended it to be a pleasurable experience, it does not follow that it should be consumed without responsibility. The fact is, that like all other biological resources, sex conforms to the law of energy release, rest and replenishment. Conservation and balance are as important to the maintenance and preservation of sexual energy as they are to all other resources. Placing limits on sexual experiences, then, should no longer be viewed, in the "old-fashioned" sense, as an act of disapproval of sex, but rather as an act of appreciation for the joy it brings to life. At the same time, argue the new evangelicals, sex should be entered into on the basis of mutual respect for the intrinsic self-worth and equality of both man and woman, since both sexes are equal in God's eyes, and since every being has intrinsic self-worth because each is God's creature.

Any behavior, therefore, that undermines the natural pleasure of sex, overconsumes sexual activity and fails to respect the intrinsic self-worth and sexual equality of others is an act of rebellion against God and God's created order.

Evangelicals are quick to point to people's fallen nature and the need for each individual to place limits on himself. They are less quick to realize that there is also an institutional base, a set of economic arrangements, if you will, that consciously promote the mentality of *unlimited* consumer experience. It is not just a matter of resisting the "permissive society," a vague catchall phrase that connotes the idea that some sort of undefined murky force is out there luring each individual into Satan's hands. The fact is, there are real economic institutions out there, spending tens of billions of dollars to promote that "permissive society." Until there is a recognition that the capitalist system with its advertising and marketing programs is as much responsible for the consumer fix as one's personal nature, the overriding problem will never adequately be addressed. This means, as the Sojourners and other more radical evangelicals have asserted, equal attention must be placed on changing the powers and principalities to bring them in line with the principle of God's order and the steady-state society.

THE FAMILY AND THE CREATION DOCTRINE

It is no coincidence that when we think of the family and family values or family arrangements, the terms conserve or protect come to mind first. The family has always been intimately involved with these functions. It has been looked to as the conservator and protector of the culture and the species.

In many ways the traditional family combined the salient features of both the new creation doctrine and the steady-state social order. In theory at least, all members of the family were considered equal and of intrinsic self-worth in the same sense that each was created by the same source—their biological parents. The family, then, served as a microcosm of the larger natural order where God was the parent of all things. Not only did all family members have an intrinsic self-worth, equal because of their common biological creators, but traditionally, the members of the family were also mutually dependent on each other for survival. Each played an important role in a sort of understood covenant relationship. The father was responsible for providing a roof over everyone's head and food for the table, while the mother and children, in turn, were responsible for doing the chores (a word that has disappeared from the American vocabulary) and taking care of the house. In other words, they served in a stewardship role. The home itself served as a place of rest and replenishment, as well as a center of productive activity. To have an "orderly home" was the highest compliment one could be paid. It usually meant that the relationships and responsibilities between family members were being faithfully performed and that the proper balance of give-and-take had been achieved. A harmonious family was a family that was in synchronization with itself. In this regard, the traditional family reflected many of the basic principles of both the creation doctrine and the steady-state doctrine.

Today the order and balance of the traditional family have been nearly decimated by the encroachment of the commercial and government service sectors. With many of the former responsibilities of the family taken on by the universal market-place, there is little cement to tie family members together in a shared covenant. The family, which once served as a relatively self-sufficient living habitat, has been picked away at, until each of its component parts has been dislodged, expropriated and finally exploited by the universal marketplace. The ruthless takeover and exploitation of the family by the capitalist system is really not very different, in many ways, from its takeover and exploitation of other natural habitats in the biological system.

Evangelicals are beginning to reemphasize the importance of reestablishing the family. When they talk of conserving family values, they are, in a vague way, trying to reassert a kind of order and balance to the world around them. The creation doctrine and the doctrine of the steady-state economy provide a compelling macrorationale for their efforts. But it should also be understood that a few basic characteristics of the traditional family no longer hold; new adjustments are in *order* if the family is to play a significant role in the new era into which we are moving.

First, the role of the woman has changed, and that change is irreversible. Today, women make up nearly half of the labor force. They work because they have to. If they don't, their families would not be adequately provided for. The American family can no longer survive with just a male wage earner. The fact is both parents now share equally in both their biological role as the creators of family and in their productive-work role as providers for their families. For this reason, the *covenant* relationship in any reconstruction of the family would have to be based on this equality, or it would fail, not only because it would be morally wrong, but because it would not accurately represent the new relationships of interdependence between family members. A covenant, whether it be God's covenant of creation or the steady-state covenant, or a family covenant, has to be truthful to the relationships it is ordering. Any attempt to force the relationship of women in the work world back into the older family covenant is bound to fail, for the simple economic reason that the woman's new role in the workplace is not going to be eliminated.

This raises the second major change in the external world which will force an adjustment in the conception of a reconstructed family. The family no longer serves as an independent production unit. The universal marketplace has taken over that function, and in so doing, has relegated the family to the role of consumer—and even here, each family member has been decompartmentalized by the advertising and marketing process, thus further dividing family members from one another. While the family's role as producer has been expropriated, that very process has, in turn, led to a new and unique set of circumstances requiring a new role for the family. The capitalist system has now reached a critical impasse where public consumption needs are taking an increasing priority over private consumption needs. Yet, no transcendent value system has yet emerged to replace the Calvinist-capitalist world view of autonomous rugged individualism with a steady-state spiritual doctrine based on the concept of shared responsibility and interdependence. The creation doctrine does just that, while at the same time respecting the intrinsic self-worth and equality of every individual.

The reconstructed family could well end up playing a new role—one of caretaker or steward over public decisions concerning the allocation and distribution of production and consumption. It is clear that in order to move from an exploitative, capitalist ethos to a decentralized, participatory steady-state ethos, power over decisions will have to be transferred from the present professional and financial elites to the people themselves. The family has traditionally served as the primary regulator and enforcer of the shared cultural and social norms of society. There is every reason to suggest, then, that the reconstructed family may be ideally suited to serve as the primary regulator and enforcer of the communal economic norms of a steady-state society.

Of course, as with the production and consumption roles, whether the family takes on a new reconstructed role depends largely on whether the evangelical community becomes aware of the institutional as well as personal causes behind its demise. If they fail to deal head-on with the "powers and principalities" of the universal marketplace of capitalism, then the family will continue to remain a broken remnant of the existing order. There are, however, signs that the evangelical community might well respond to the larger problems challenging the family. The Christian school movement, with its dependence on parental supervision, is one sign of the family reclaiming responsibilities that the service sector had previously expropriated. Another sign is the movement, within the evangelical community, against TV violence and sexual exploitation. The Na-

tional Association of Religious Broadcasters, the Southern
Baptist Convention and several other large mainline Protestant
denominations have spearheaded a family crusade against large
corporate advertisers and the three TV networks to take violence
and sex exploiting programming off the air. They have launched
this campaign because they feel that the commercial sector has
invaded their homes and their children's minds with messages
that are inimical to Christian values. This may signal the opening battle of a larger war with the service sector over other
basic issues of concern to the preservation and reconstruction
of the family in America.

STEWARDSHIP AND DISARMAMENT

At the present time the new stewardship doctrine is finding
its most concrete expression in a growing evangelical movement against the nuclear arms race. Like the mainline Protestant
denominations and the Catholic Church, many evangelical
church leaders are beginning to focus in on the grave dangers
posed by the escalating worldwide armaments race.

According to the most recent government figures, the United
States now has enough nuclear warheads stashed in underground silos, on nuclear submarines and in sophisticated jets
around the globe to launch an all-out attack which would kill
every man, woman and child in the world twelve times over.
The Pentagon says that if a total nuclear war did break out,
between 95 million and 120 million Americans would die immediately in the exchange, with millions upon millions of others dying in the days and weeks following the holocaust. Despite
the insanity of maintaining a nuclear arsenal of over 30,000
warheads, our government continues to build three new warheads every twenty-four hours. Worldwide expenditures on
armaments now amount to a staggering 400 billion dollars a
year—most of it being spent by the two superpowers.[17]

In 1978 over a hundred religious leaders, most of them
evangelicals, issued a tough, uncompromising public statement
in opposition to the proliferation of nuclear arms. This dramatic
declaration by evangelical leaders would have been simply
unthinkable ten years ago, when the evangelical community
was still looked on as the bedrock of popular support for the military establishment. The statement itself, entitled "A Call to

Faithfulness," begins with the admonition that "the Church bears the Biblical responsibility for stewardship of the whole creation." With the new stewardship doctrine as a focus, the declaration boldly proclaims a commitment to the total abolition of nuclear weapons. In language reminiscent of the early "ban the bomb" movement of the 1950s, the evangelicals declare that:

> There can be no qualifying or conditioning word. We, the signers of this declaration, commit ourselves to non-cooperation with our country's preparations for nuclear war. On all levels—research, development, testing, production, deployment and actual use of nuclear weapons—we commit ourselves to resist in the name of Jesus Christ.

Other major evangelical groupings have joined in with their own disarmament resolutions. At their one hundred thirty-third annual convention some 22,000 delegates of the Southern Baptist Convention passed a resolution urging the federal government to seek international agreements to slow the arms race and shift funds from "nuclear weapons to basic human needs."[18] Even the generally staid and noncommittal National Association of Evangelicals urged "Christians everywhere to acknowledge that their trust is in a sovereign God rather than in superior armaments."[19]

The first real "public" awareness of this extraordinary shift in evangelical attitude regarding the arms race surfaced in a historic interview with Billy Graham on the CBS television network on March 29, 1979. Graham, who is now preaching against the "insanity and madness" of the proliferating arms race, says that he detects a vast change taking place in the evangelical community.

> I don't think that they [evangelicals] were aware of the potential horror of what a nuclear war with present weapons could do to the human race. And I think that they're awakening to the fact that they have a responsibility to speak out.

This is a far different Billy Graham from the one a decade earlier who was preaching to the faithful that America had to maintain a military superiority in the world regardless of the costs. Graham acknowledged in the interview that he had come to his new conviction rather late in life, but that he was now convinced that active opposition to all nuclear arms is "the teaching of the Bible." Late or not, Graham's turnaround is perhaps the best single barometer of the changes taking place within the evangelical community—changes that reflect the thinking of a new generation of theologians, ministers and lay leaders who perceive their role as stewards over God's creation.

It is quite possible that growing opposition to the nuclear arms race will provide many evangelicals with an entry point for a broader activist commitment to stewardship, just as the abolitionist cause did during America's second great awakening in the nineteenth century.

TOWARD A SECOND PROTESTANT REFORMATION

The new stewardship doctrine turns the modern world view upside down. The rules and relationships that are used to exploit nature are diametrically opposite to those that are necessary to conserve nature.

Terms and concepts positively associated with the age of expansion become negative factors in an age of conservation. Private ownership of resources; increased centralization of power; the elimination of diversity; greater reliance on science and technology; the refusal to set limits on production and consumption; the fragmentation of human labor into separate and autonomous spheres of operation; the reductionist approach to understanding life and the interrelationships between phenomena; the concept of progress as a process of continually transforming the natural world into a more valuable and more ordered human-made environment have long been considered as valid pursuits and goals in the modern world. Every single one of these items, and scores of others that make up the operating assumptions of the age of growth, are inimical to the principles of ecology, a steady-state economic framework, and more importantly, the newly defined creation doctrine.

Stewardship requires that humankind respect and conserve the "natural" workings of God's order. The natural order works on the principles of diversity, interdependence and decentralization. Maintenance replaces the notion of progress, steward-ship replaced ownership and nurturing replaces engineering. Biological limits to both production and consumption are acknowledged; the principle of balanced distribution is accepted; and the concept of wholeness becomes the essential guideline for measuring all relationships and phenomena.

In reality, then, the new stewardship doctrine represents a fundamental shift in humanity's frame of reference. It establishes a new set of governing principles for how human beings should behave and act in the world. As a world view, the stewardship doctrine demands of the faithful an uncompromising adherence. As a way of life, however, it will likely come to accept the many qualifications that humanity has always placed on all of its theological prescriptions. It is these very qualifications which allow humanity to reject one world view in favor of another while, at the same time, incorporating essential aspects of the old order into the new. So, while many of the distinguishing features of the prevailing ethic will remain a part of the new order, their role and their importance will be completely redefined within the context of a new set of assumptions about people's relationship to the world around them.

It is impossible to separate the Protestant ethic from the unique economic period in which it has flourished. It is obvious that the age of material growth could not possibly have coexisted for nearly 500 years alongside a theological world view that was inimical to its basic suppositions. The fact is, the Reformation theology, as refined by the Enlightenment and the liberal ethos, has provided enough of an expansionary value system to both justify and encourage the expansionary economic era. Now that the age of growth is coming to an end, the elements of a new Reformation theology are just beginning to surface.

The Charismatics' emphasis on supernatural gifts over unceasing physical activity as proof of salvation represents a radical break from the traditional Protestant ethic. Scientific truths and concepts like technological efficiency, specialization and material accumulation begin to lose their religious justification when the signs of faith are suddenly transformed from "doing" to "being."

Today's Charismatics are providing the most significant challenge to the truths of the expansionary era yet mounted. Faith healing, speaking in tongues and prophesying are, indeed, weapons of rebellion against the authority of the modern age.

Similarly, by radically redefining humanity's relationship to the rest of God's creation, contemporary evangelical scholars are thrusting a theological dagger directly into the heart of the expansionary epoch. The new concept is that dominion is stewardship rather than ownership and conservation rather than exploitation. This belief is at loggerheads with both the Reformation and the materialist world view of the past several hundred years. By refocusing the story of creation and humanity's purpose in the world, evangelical theologians have committed an act of open rebellion against their own Reformation roots. The Calvinist individual who for hundreds of years sought salvation through productivity and the exploitation of nature is now being challenged by a Christian person who seeks salvation by conserving and protecting God's creation. *The Protestant "work" ethic is being replaced by the Protestant "conservation" ethic.* This new emphasis on stewardship is providing the foundation for the emergence of a second Protestant reformation and a new covenant vision for society.

Taken together, then, the Charismatic and evangelical movements are beginning to establish a radically new theological prescription for a nongrowth, steady-state ecological future.

Of one thing there is little doubt: the Protestant Reformation theology of Luther and Calvin and the liberal ethos which grew out of it will not outlive the age of material growth with which it has been so intricately bound up.

A new economic order is emerging in the world. It calls for a second Protestant reformation. The historical moment has arrived.

Notes

CHAPTER 1: AN ESTABLISHMENT IN CRISIS

1. *The New York Times*, January 23, 1976, p. 1.; February 10, 1976, p. 22.
2. Press Release, U.S. Department of Labor: 77–771, Bureau of Labor Statistics, Labor Day Weekend, 1977.
3. Bill Peterson, "Rallying Cry for Liberals," *Washington Post*, June 18, 1978, p. A6.
4. "Ben Wattenberg's Paean to America," *Washington Post*, August 7, 1978, p. A8.
5. Peterson, op. cit., p. A6.
6. David Broder, *The Party's Over* (New York: Harper & Row, 1972).
7. "Ben Wattenberg," op. cit., p. A8.
8. David Broder, "60's Activists in Quest of a Consensus," *Washington Post*, July 19, 1978.

CHAPTER 2: THE LIBERAL ETHOS AND THE AGE OF EXPANSION

*For various analyses of the historical progression of liberalism, the following books are helpful: Harry K. Girvetz, *The Evolution of Liberalism* (New York: Collier Books, 1967); Dante L. Germino, *Modern Western Political Thought* (Chicago: Rand McNally, 1972); John Herman Randall, *The Mak-*

ing of the Modern Mind (New York: Columbia University Press, 1976); William Theodore Bluhm, *Ideologies and Attitudes* (Englewood Cliffs, NJ: Prentice-Hall, 1974).

1. Ewart Lewis, ed., *Medieval Political Ideas* (New York: Alfred A. Knopf, 1954), I, 225.

2. R. H. Tawney, *Religion and the Rise of Capitalism* (New York: Harcourt, Brace & Co., 1926), p. 61.

3. Martin E. Marty, *A Short History of Christianity* (New York: Collins, World, 1959), p. 211.

4. Francis A. Schaeffer, *How Should We Then Live?* (Old Tappan, NJ: Fleming Revell Co., 1976), p. 80.

5. John H. Gerstner, "The Theological Boundaries of Evangelical Faith," in David F. Wells and John D. Woodbridge, eds., *The Evangelicals* (Nashville: Abingdon Press, 1975), p. 23. See also, Marty, op. cit., p. 215.

6. Schaeffer, op. cit., p. 81.

7. Marty, op. cit., p. 215.

8. Lester DeKoster, "Keep the Church Out of What?" *The Christian Century*, vol. 84, March 29, 1967, p. 404.

9. Marty, op. cit., p. 220.

10. Ibid., p. 223.

11. Max Weber, *The Protestant Ethic and the Spirit of Capitalism* (New York: Charles Scribner's Sons, 1958), p. 105.

12. Ibid., pp. 104–105, 116–117.

13. Ibid., p. 108.

14. Lester DeKoster, op. cit., p. 405.

15. As quoted in Bertrand de Jouvenel, "Essai sur la Politique de Rousseau," *Du contrat social* (Geneva: Cheval Aile, 1947), pp. 25, 26, in Dante L. Germino, *Modern Western Political Thought* (Chicago: Rand McNally, 1972), p. 11.

16. Quoted by Judith Serrin, "Science Finding New Ways to Make Babies," *Detroit Free Press*, July 27, 1978, p. 3.

17. Francis Bacon, *Novum Organum*, Book I, Aphorism 71.

18. Ibid., Book I, Aphorism 2.

19. Ibid.

20. Jean Houston, "Prometheus Rebound: An Inquiry into Technological Growth and Psychological Change," *Alternatives to Growth—I*, Dennis Meadows, ed. (Cambridge, MA: Ballinger, 1977), p. 274.

21. Ibid., p. 274.

22. Bacon, op. cit.

23. Ibid., I, 83.

24. Descartes, *Discourse on Method*, part 6.
25. Voltaire, *Lettres Philosophiques*, quoted in John Herman Randall, *The Making of the Modern Mind* (New York: Columbia University Press, 1976), p. 311.
26. Leo Strauss, *Natural Right and History* (Chicago: University of Chicago Press, 1953), pp. 250, 251.
27. Ibid., p. 258.
28. John Locke, "Second Treatise," in *John Locke, Two Treatises of Government*, Peter Laslett, ed. (Cambridge: Cambridge University Press, 1967), p. 315.
29. Ibid.
30. Ibid.
31. Ibid., p. 312.
32. Ibid.
33. Ibid.
34. Adam Smith, *An Inquiry Into the Nature and Causes of the Wealth of Nations*, Edwin Cannan, ed. (London: Methuen & Co., 1961), I, 475.
35. Jeremy Bentham, *Principles of Morals and Legislation* (1780).
36. Peoples Bicentennial Commission, *Voices of the American Revolution* (New York: Bantam Books, 1975), p. 160.
37. Statistics on U.S. economic growth and change reported here are from Robert L. Heilbroner, *The Economic Transformation of America* (New York: Harcourt Brace Jovanovich, 1977), p. 27.
38. William Ophuls, *Ecology and the Politics of Scarcity* (San Francisco: W. H. Freeman & Co., 1977), p. 185.
39. Marquis de Condorcet, *Outline of an Historical View of the Progress of the Human Mind*, in John Hallowell, *Main Currents in Modern Political Thought* (New York: Holt, Rinehart & Winston, 1950), p. 132.

CHAPTER 3: LIMITS TO GROWTH

1. Fred C. Allvine and Fred A. Tarpley, Jr., "The New State of the Economy: The Challenging Prospect," *U. S. Economic Growth From 1976 to 1986: Prospects, Problems and Patterns*, studies for the Joint Economic Committee of the U. S. Congress (Washington, D. C.: GPO, 1976), p. 58.
2. Lester R. Brown, *The Twenty-Ninth Day*, A Worldwatch

Institute Book (New York: W. W. Norton & Co., 1978), pp. 99–100.

3. Lee Schipper, "Energy: Global Prospects 1985–2000," *Bulletin of the Atomic Scientists,* March 1978, p. 58.

4. Hobart Rowan, "Oil Supply Adequate, Possibly to 1990s, Trilateral Commission Study Concludes," *Washington Post,* June 14, 1978, p. D9.

5. Emile Benoit, "The Coming Age of Shortages, Part I," *Bulletin of the Atomic Scientists,* January 1976, p. 9.

6. Brown, op. cit., pp. 104–105.

7. William Ophuls, *Ecology and the Politics of Scarcity* (San Francisco: W. H. Freeman & Co., 1977), p. 87.

8. Benoit, op. cit., p. 11.

9. Julian McCaull, "Wringing Out the West," *Environment,* vol. 16, no. 7, 1974, p. 10.

10. National Academy of Sciences, *Energy and Climate* (Washington, DC: Government Printing Office, 1977).

11. Ibid.

12. Worldwatch Institute, "The Global Environment and Basic Human Needs," report to the U.S. Council on Environmental Quality, 1978, p. 36.

13. Benoit, op. cit., p. 11.

14. Worldwatch Institute report to C.E.Q., 1978, op. cit., p. 33.

15. David Dickson, "Nuclear Power Uneconomic Says Congressional Committee," *Nature,* May 11, 1978, p. 91.

16. Benoit, op. cit., p. 31.

17. Luther J. Carter, "Radioactive Wastes: Some Urgent Unfinished Business," *Science,* February 18, 1977, p. 661.

18. Ibid., p. 661.

19. Ibid., p. 662.

20. "Surveying the Radioactive Waste Dilemma—An Overview," Critical Mass Energy Project, August 1978, p. 5.

21. *Nuclear Power Costs,* report of the Subcommittee on Energy, Environment and Natural Resources of the Committee on Government Operations, U.S. House of Representatives (Washington, DC: US GPO, April 1978). The Critical Mass Energy Project in Washington, DC, points out that because of the radioactivity of the nickel components in nuclear reactors the danger period for a nuclear power site may be as long as 1.5 million years.

22. Ophuls, op. cit., p. 100.

23. Benoit, op, cit., p. 14.

24. Ophuls, op. cit., pp. 103–104.

25. Ibid., p. 102.

26. Benoit, op. cit., p. 14.

27. Sam Love, "The New Look of the Future," *The Futurist,* vol. XI, no. 2, April 1977, p. 80.

28. Richard England and Barry Bluestone, "Ecology and Social Conflict," *Toward a Steady-State Economy,* Herman E. Daly, ed. (San Francisco: W. H. Freeman & Co., 1973), p. 196.

29. Preston Cloud, "Mineral Resources in Fact and Fancy," in Daly, op. cit., p. 68.

30. *U.S. Long-Term Economic Growth Prospects: Entering a New Era,* studies for the Joint Economic Committee of the U.S. Congress (Washington, DC: Government Printing Office, January 25, 1978), p. 73.

31. Cloud, op. cit., p. 74.

32. *Growth Prospects,* J.E.C., 1978, p. 75.

33. Ophuls, op. cit., p. 212.

34. Benoit, op. cit., p. 16.

35. Ibid., p. 15.

36. Ophuls, op. cit., p. 68.

37. Ibid., p. 71.

38. Erik Eckholm, "Disappearing Species: The Social Challenge," Worldwatch Paper 22 (Washington DC: Worldwatch Institute, June 1978), p. 6.

39. Ibid., p. 7.

40. Ibid.

41. Birth and death statistics from Frank H. Oram, Associate Director, World Population Society, Washington, DC, August 1978.

42. Worldwatch Institute report to C.E.Q., 1978, op. cit., p. 1.

43. Ophuls, op. cit., p. 48.

44. Senator Dick Clark, "Food and Development," *Finite Resources and the Human Future,* Ian G. Barbour, ed. (Minneapolis: Augsburg Publishing House, 1976), pp. 95–96.

45. Brown, op. cit., p. 137.

46. Edward Goldsmith, "Settlements and Social Stability," *Alternatives to Growth—I,* Dennis L. Meadows, ed. (Cambridge, MA: Ballinger, 1977), p. 331.

47. Ibid., p. 333.

48. According to the Overseas Development Council (ODC), 0.7 billion people are "destitute" or starving in the world and another 0.5 billion are surviving barely above that level caught in the cycle of malnourishment, disease, infant mortality and short life expectancy. John W. Sewell and the ODC Staff, *The*

U.S. and World Development Agenda 1977 (New York: Praeger, 1977), pp. 60–61.

49. Donella Meadows, "The World Food Problem: Growth Models and Nongrowth Solutions," *Alternatives to Growth—I*, Dennis L. Meadows, ed. (Cambridge, MA: Ballinger, 1977), p. 331.

50. Ian G. Barbour, *Finite Resources and the Human Future* (Minneapolis: Augsburg Publishing House, 1976), p. 24.

51. Brown, op. cit., p. 46.

52. Ibid., p. 48.

53. Mary Margaret Pignone, S.N.D., "Concentrated Ownership of Land," *The Earth Is the Lord's*, Mary Evelyn Jegen, Bruno Manno, eds. (New York: Paulist Press, 1978), p. 119.

54. Brown, op. cit., p. 163.

55. Pignone, op. cit., p. 117.

56. "Soil Erosion: The Problem Persists Despite the Billions Spent on It," *Science*, April 22, 1977.

57. Worldwatch Institute report to C.E.Q., 1978, op. cit., p. 7.

58. Brown, op. cit., p. 28.

59. U.N. Conference on Desertification, *Desertification: An Overview*, Nairobi, August 29–September 9, 1977.

60. Worldwatch report to C.E.Q., 1978, op. cit., pp. 8, 9.

61. Ibid., p. 10.

62. Ophuls, op. cit., p. 52.

63. John Strohm, "An Open Letter to Colleen," *International Wildlife*, vol. 8, no. 5, September–October 1978, p. 16.

64. Depletion of domestic forests statistics from National Wildlife Federation report, 1978.

65. Worldwatch Institute report to C.E.Q., 1978, op. cit., p. 30.

66. Ibid., pp. 31, 32.

67. Joan Davis and Samuel Mauch, "Strategies for Societal Development," *Alternatives to Growth—I*, Dennis L. Meadows, ed. (Cambridge, MA: Ballinger, 1977), p. 232.

68. Michael Fox, *Science*, vol. 201, July 7, 1978, p. 35.

69. Erik Eckholm, op. cit., p. 13.

70. Eugene P. Odum, *Fundamentals of Ecology*, 3rd ed. (Philadelphia: Saunders, 1971), p. 412.

71. Ophuls, op. cit., p. 52.

72. Strohm, op. cit., p. 16.

73. Barry Commoner, *The Poverty of Power* (New York: Bantam Books, 1977), p. 25.

74. *Growth Prospects*, J.E.C., 1978, p. 83.

75. Herman E. Daly, "The Transition to a Steady-State Econ-

omy," *U.S. Economic Growth From 1976 to 1986: Prospects, Problems, and Patterns,* studies for the Joint Economic Committee of the U.S. Congress (Washington, DC: Government Printing Office, 1976), p. 20.

76. *Growth Prospects,* J.E.C., 1978, p. 84.

77. Commoner, op. cit., pp. 21, 22.

78. Nicholas Georgescu-Roegen, "The Entropy Law and the Economic Problem," *Toward a Steady-State Economy,* Herman E. Daly, ed. (San Francisco: W. H. Freeman & Co., 1973), p. 39.

79. Daly, "Transition," *Growth 1976–1986,* J.E.C., 1976, p. 21.

80. Georgescu-Roegen, 1973, op. cit., pp. 41, 42.

81. *Environment Magazine,* vol 20, no. 2, p. 19.

82. According to the USDA's *Pesticide Review 1978,* Lee Fowler, ed., the U.S. in 1977 produced 1,387,519,000 pounds of synthetic organic chemicals valued at over $3.1 billion. Pesticides produced in 1940 were of an estimated $35 million according to *Pesticide Review 1953.* In a television program examining Rachel Carson's *Silent Spring,* CBS News estimated that about 200 million pounds of pesticides were produced following WWII. (*CBS Reports,* April 3, 1963, transcript, p. 4).

83. Commoner, op. cit., p. 187.

84. Ophuls, op. cit., p. 23.

85. Harry Rothman, *Murderous Providence: A Study of Pollution in Industrial Societies* (New York: Bobbs-Merrill Co., 1972), p. 64.

86. "Costs of Municipal Waste Disposal," *Conservation News,* July 15, 1977.

87. "Hazards of Wastes at Dumping Sites," *U.S. News & World Report,* August 21, 1978, p. 37.

88. "The Mob Cashes in on Pollution," *East West Journal,* March 1978, p. 16.

89. National Wildlife Federation, Annual Report, 1978.

90. "Fine Particles in the Atmosphere," *NRDC Newsletter,* vol. 7, nos. 2, 3, March 1978–June 1978, Natural Resources Defense Council, p. 13.

91. Ward Sinclair, "Studies Warn About Menace of 'Acid Rain,'" *Washington Post,* June 2, 1978, p. A18.

92. Albert Rosenfeld, "Forecast: Poisonous Rain," *Saturday Review,* September 2, 1978, p. 18.

93. *NRDC Newsletter,* "Fine Particles," op. cit., p. 8.

94. Sinclair, op. cit., p. A18.

95. "Acid Rains," *East West Journal*, October 1977, p. 23.

96. Worldwatch Institute report to C.E.Q., 1978, op. cit., p. 42.

97. Rufus E. Miles, Jr., *Awakening from the American Dream* (New York: Universe Books, 1976), pp. 200, 201.

98. Michael J. Conlon, "EPA Cites U.S. Environment As a Leading Death Cause," *Washington Post*, August 27, 1978.

99. Council on Environmental Quality, *Carcinogens in the Environment*, December 1975, p. 8; and *United States Chartbook, Health 1976–77*, HEW, National Center for Health Statistics, DHEW No. (HRA) 77–1233, pp. 1, 5.

100. Emile Benoît, "A Dynamic Equilibrium Economy," *Bulletin of the Atomic Scientists*, February 1976, p. 48.

101. National Wildlife Federation, Annual Report, 1978.

102. *East West Journal*, August 1977, p. 13.

103. Ophuls, op. cit., p. 79.

104. England, Bluestone, "Ecology and Conflict," in Daly, 1973, op. cit., p. 194.

CHAPTER 4: PROSPECTS FOR THE AMERICAN ECONOMY

1. Robert L. Heilbroner, "Boom and Crash," *The New Yorker*, August 28, 1978, p. 70.

2. William Ophuls, "The Scarcity Society," *Skeptic*, July/August 1974, pp. 50, 51.

3. Robert L. Heilbroner, *An Inquiry Into the Human Prospect* (New York: W. W. Norton & Co., 1974), pp. 47, 48.

4. Carl H. Madden, "Toward a New Concept of Growth: Capital Needs of a Post-Industrial Society," *Growth 1976 to 1986*, J.E.C., vol. 8: *Capital Formation*, 1977, p. 17.

5. William Ophuls, *Ecology and the Politics of Scarcity* (San Francisco: W. H. Freeman & Co., 1977), p. 132.

6. Sanford Rose, "The Global Slowdown Won't Last Forever," *Fortune*, August 14, 1978, p. 93.

7. Edward Renshaw, *Long-Term Economic Growth*, Hearings before Joint Economic Committee of the U.S. Congress (Washington, DC: Government Printing Office, 1976), p. 192.

8. Sylvia Porter, "Acid of Inflation Erodes Nation's Moral Values," *Washington Post*, September 11, 1978, p. B6.

9. Ophuls, *Ecology*, op. cit., p. 114.

10. Barry Commoner, *The Poverty of Power* (New York: Bantam Books, 1977), pp. 200, 201.

11. Ibid., p. 207.

12. Ibid., pp. 208, 209.

13. Michael Harrington, *The Twilight of Capitalism* (New York: Simon & Schuster, 1976), p. 261.

14. New York Stock Exchange, Inc., *The Capital Needs and Savings Potential of the U.S. Economy, Projections through 1985*, September 1974.

15. Lester R. Brown, *The Twenty-Ninth Day* (New York: W. W. Norton & Co., 1978), p. 178.

16. Perry Pascarella, "Goodbye Technology; Farewell Future," *Industry Week*, vol. 194, no. 6., September 12, 1977, p. 86.

17. Fred C. Allvine and Fred A. Tarpley, Jr., "The New State of the Economy: The Challenging Prospect," *Growth 1976 to 1986*, J.E.C., vol. 7: *Limits to Growth*, 1976, pp. 57, 58.

18. "Productivity and Technological Change," *Growth Prospects*, J.E.C., 1978, p. 94.

19. Pascarella, op. cit., p. 91.

20. Ophuls, *Ecology*, op. cit., p. 118.

21. Bradley Graham, "U.S. Productivity: Golden Days Over," *Washington Post*, September 10, 1978, p. F1.

22. Jay W. Forrester, *Long-Term Economic Growth*, Hearings before J.E.C., November 10, 1976, p. 46.

23. "Productivity and Technological Change," *Growth Prospects*, J.E.C., 1978, p. 110.

24. Rufus E. Miles, Jr., *Awakening from the American Dream* (New York: Universe Books, 1976), p. 48.

25. Fifteen to 20 percent of the work force is employed in the automotive sector of the economy according to estimates of the Washington office of the American Automobile Association. (Telephone confirmation December 1978.)

26. Heilbroner, 1974, op. cit., p. 86.

27. "Poor vs. Rich: A Global Struggle," *U.S. News & World Report*, July 31, 1978, p. 55.

28. George S. Siudy, Jr., "Stewardship and World Poverty," *The Earth Is the Lord's*, Mary Evelyn Jegen, Bruno Manno, eds. (New York: Paulist Press, 1978), p. 149.

29. Miles, op. cit., pp. 163, 164.

30. John Strohm, "An Open Letter to Colleen," *International Wildlife*, September–October 1978, p. 18.

31. "The Global Environment and Basic Human Needs," World-

watch Institute report to the U.S. Council on Environmental Quality, 1978, p. 15.
32. Brown, op. cit., p. 207.
33. Ibid., p. 208.
34. Ibid., p. 222.
35. *Growth Prospects,* J.E.C., 1978, p. 112.
36. Ophuls, *Ecology,* op. cit., p. 148.
37. Arnold Toynbee, "After the Age of Affluence," *Skeptic,* July/August 1974, p. 38.
38. Brown, op. cit., p. 323.
39. Ibid., p. 272.

CHAPTER 5: AMERICA'S NEW SPIRITUAL AWAKENING

1. The Gallup Opinion Index, "Religion in America," 1977–1978, p. 2.
2. "Back to that Oldtime Religion," *Time,* vol. 110, December 26, 1977, pp. 52, 58.
3. Richard Quebedeaux, *The Worldly Evangelicals* (New York: Harper & Row, 1978), p. 52.
4. Richard Quebedeaux, *The Young Evangelicals* (New York: Harper & Row, 1974), pp. 3, 4.
5. "Religious Climate Remains Strong in the U.S.," *1977–1978 Gallup Poll,* p. 12.
6. Lowell D. Streiker and Gerald S. Strober, *Religion and the New Majority* (New York: Association Press, 1972), p. 125.
7. The Gallup Opinion Index, 1977–1978, p. 41.
8. Dean M. Kelley, *Why Conservative Churches Are Growing* (New York: Harper & Row, 1977), p. 1.
9. "Back to that Oldtime Religion," op. cit., pp. 52–58.
10. Kelley, op. cit., p. 21.
11. "Back to that Oldtime Religion," op. cit., pp. 52–58.
12. "Here's Life, World," *Christianity Today,* December 9, 1977, p. 52.
13. National Religious Broadcasters statistics reported by Religious News Service, August 8, 1978.
14. Phil McCombs, "Born-Again Celebrities to Star at Broadcaster's Meeting," *Washington Post,* January 22, 1978, p. A7.
15. *PTL Television Network,* press release from PTL, Charlotte, NC, 1978, p. 2.

16. "The Lord's Network," *Newsweek,* March 20, 1978, pp. 80–82.

17. *PTL Television Network,* op. cit., p. 1; "The Lord's Network," op. cit., pp. 80, 81.

18. PTL Club publicity packet, Fall 1978.

19. Ibid.

20. *PTL Television Network,* op. cit., p. 3.

21. Frank M. Roberts, "CBN—the Fourth Network," *Logos Journal,* September/October 1977, pp. 11–12; also William Martin, "Video Evangelism," *Washington Post Magazine,* June 4, 1978, p. 44.

22. Ibid., pp. 37, 39.

23. Roberts, op. cit., p. 11.

24. Wayne King, "Praise The Lord Club Brings Gospel to TV," *The New York Times,* August 30, 1976, p. 25.

25. Ibid., p. 43.

26. "The Lord's Network," op. cit., pp. 80–82.

27. Ed Zuckerman, "Born-Again Broadcasts Come to Boston," *The Real Paper,* May 6, 1978, p. 18.

28. Martin, op. cit., p. 39.

29. "The Lord's Network," op. cit., pp. 80–82.

30. Martin, op. cit., p. 41.

31. Ibid., p. 39.

32. Ibid., p. 37.

33. Zuckerman, op. cit., p. 18.

34. Ibid., p. 15.

35. Ibid.

36. "Christian Groups Battle for Cable TV Audience," *National Courier,* February 18, 1977, p. 29.

37. Janis Johnson, "Religious Broadcasting Limit Urged; Californians Seek Restriction to Commercial Radio," *Washington Post,* February 28, 1975, p. B16.

38. Tom Berry, "Cable TV: Channel of Blessing," *Logos Journal,* p. 25.

39. "The Selling of Jesus," *Newsweek,* February 28, 1978.

40. "CBS Reports: Born Again," July 14, 1977, p. 6.

41. "Here's Life, World," op. cit., p. 52.

42. Evangelical Press News Service, July 23, 1977.

43. Religious News Service, press release, July 19, 1977.

44. James Feron, "Growing Publishing Empire Is Built on Religion," *The New York Times,* November 6, 1977, Section XXII, p. 2.

45. Paul Baker, "Rock of Ages," *The Saturday Evening Post*, April 1978, pp. 28–30.

46. "Mass Media and Church Reform," *Christianity Today*, Editorial, vol. 14, October 24, 1969, p. 28.

47. Avery Dulles, S.J., "The Church as Multimedia," *New Catholic World*, vol. 215, January 1972, p. 23.

48. Ibid., p. 44.

49. Sherwood E. Wirt, "Moving Upon the Media," *Christianity Today*, May 22, 1970, p. 6.

50. Streiker and Strober, op. cit., p. 139.

51. Elmer L. Towns, "Trends Among Fundamentals," *Christianity Today*, vol. 17, July 6, 1973, p. 19.

52. Cindy Kadonaga, "Reborn Nightclub on Coast Shuns Glitter, Now Rocks to a Gospel Beat," *The New York Times*, June 6, 1977, p. 18.

53. Joann S. Lublin, "New Clubs Put Faith in Making a Profit on Song and Prayer," *Wall Street Journal*, March 30, 1978, p. 1.

54. Ibid., p. 26.

55. Dwayne Walls, "Born Again Bigotry," *Washington Post*, November 13, 1977, pp. C1, C3.

56. "'Christian-Only' Ads Charged With Bias," "Suits by B'nai B'rith Group Assert Business Directories Practice Religious Discrimination," *The New York Times*, September 7, 1977, Section II, p. 14.

57. Walls, op. cit., pp. C1, C3.

58. "Tribulations for Christian Ads," *Business Week*, September 19, 1977, p. 148.

59. "'Christian-Only' Ads Charged With Bias," op. cit., p. 14.

60. "Tribulations for Christian Ads," op. cit., p. 148.

61. Michael C. Jensen, "Clergymen Find Call in Industry," *The New York Times*, August 9, 1976, p. 31.

62. Quebedeaux, *Worldly Evangelicals*, op. cit., 1978, p. 74.

63. "Bill Gothard's Institute," *Christianity Today*, May 25, 1973, pp. 44, 45.

64. C. Peter Wagner, "How Christian Is America," *Christianity Today*, December 3, 1976, p. 12.

65. "God's Muscle," *Time*, vol. 101, May 21, 1973, p. 66.

66. "The Christian Woodstock," *Newsweek*, vol. 79, June 26, 1972, p. 52.

67. Edward E. Plowman, "Campus Crusade: Into All The World," *Christianity Today*, vol. 16, June 9, 1972, p. 38.

68. Quebedeaux, *Worldly Evangelicals*, op. cit., pp. 101–102.

69. *Christianity Today*, February 27, 1970.
70. Quebedeaux, *Worldly Evangelicals*, op. cit., p. 104.
71. B. Drummond Ayers, Jr., "Private Schools Providing Church-State Conflict," *The New York Times*, April 28, 1978, p. A1.
72. Towns, op. cit., p. 13.
73. Ayers, op. cit., p. A23.
74. Calvin Goddard Zon, "Christian Schools Find Phenomenal Growth," *Washington Star*, June 11, 1978.
75. Information from the Council for American Private Education, paper, n.d., by Dr. Lamborn, provided September 1978.
76. Zon, op. cit.
77. Towns, op. cit., pp. 13–14.
78. *The Organization of the Parental Christian School*, Pamphlet of the National Union of Christian Schools, Grand Rapids, MI, n.d., p. 1.
79. Dr. Robert Siemens, "Integrating Bible with School's Programs," *Christian Teacher*, vol. 15, no. 2, May/April 1978, p. 8.
80. "Social Studies from a Christian Perspective," Curriculum Guideline #3, Association for Bible Curriculum Development, Pasadena, CA.
81. Siemens, op. cit., p. 9.
82. Ibid., p. 9.

CHAPTER 6: EVANGELICALISM AND AMERICA: THE FIRST TWO CENTURIES

1. Richard V. Pierard, *The Unequal Yoke* (Philadelphia: J. B. Lippincott Co., 1970), p. 121.
2. John Locke, "Second Treatise," in *John Locke, Two Treatises of Government*, Peter Laslett, ed. (Cambridge: Cambridge University Press, 1967.)
3. Robert T. Handy, "The American Messianic Consciousness: the Concept of the Chosen People and Manifest Destiny," *Review and Expositor*, vol. 73, no. 1, Winter 1976, p. 48.
4. Ibid., p. 55.
5. *Winthrop Papers*, vol. II (Boston: The Massachusetts Historical Society, 1931), pp. 294, 295.
6. Penrose S. Amant, "The Impact of Religion in Shaping American Values," *Review and Expositor*, op. cit., p. 61.

7. Robert N. Bellah, *The Broken Covenant* (New York: The Seabury Press, 1975), pp. 17–18.

8. Ibid., p. 62.

9. Ibid., p. 34.

10. Winthrop S. Hudson, *Religion in America* (New York: Charles Scribner's Sons, 1973), pp. 62–71.

11. Ibid., p. 71.

12. Richard Hofstadter, *Anti-Intellectualism in American Life* (New York: Random House, 1962), p. 70.

13. Ibid., p. 74.

14. Hudson, op. cit., p. 76.

15. William Warren Sweet, *Revivalism in America* (New York: Charles Scribner's Sons, 1944), p. 41.

16. Peoples Bicentennial Commission, *Early American Almanac* (New York: Bantam, 1975), p. 13.

17. Hudson, op. cit., p. 92.

18. Ibid., p. 137.

19. Ibid., p. 138.

20. Hofstadter, op. cit., p. 89.

21. Ibid., pp. 95–97.

22. Ibid., p. 104.

23. H. Shelton Smith, Robert T. Handy, Lefferts A. Loetscher, eds., *American Christianity: An Historical Interpretation with Representative Documents*, vol. II (New York; Charles Scribner's Sons, 1960–1963), pp. 19–24.

24. Hofstadter, op. cit., p. 92.

25. Erling Jorstad, *That New-Time Religion* (Minneapolis: Augsburg Publishing House, 1972), p. 21.

26. Donald W. Dayton, *Discovering an Evangelical Heritage* (New York: Harper & Row, 1976), pp. 17–18.

27. Ibid., p. 21.

28. Sweet, op. cit., p. 157.

29. Ibid., p. 157.

30. Dayton, op. cit., p. 25.

31. Sweet, op. cit., p. 154.

32. Ibid., p. 156.

33. Dayton, op. cit., p. 76.

34. Ibid., pp. 88–89.

35. Ibid., pp. 89, 91.

36. Ibid., pp. 91, 93.

37. Ibid., pp. 94–95.

38. Sweet, op. cit., p. 149.

39. Hudson, op. cit., pp. 150–152.

CHAPTER 7: MODERN EVANGELICAL HISTORY

1. Donald W. Dayton, *Discovering an Evangelical Heritage* (New York: Harper & Row, 1976), pp. 125–126.
2. Ibid., p. 126.
3. Richard V. Pierard, *The Unequal Yoke* (Philadelphia: J. B. Lippincott Co., 1970), p. 33.
4. Dayton, op. cit., p. 126.
5. Richard Hofstadter, *Anti-Intellectualism in American Life* (New York: Random House, 1962), p. 107.
6. Ibid., pp. 109–111.
7. Ibid., p. 111.
8. Pierard, op. cit., p. 31.
9. Carnegie's "Wealth" is reprinted in *The Gospel of Wealth and Other Essays*, Edward C. Kirkland, ed. (Cambridge, MA: Folcroft, 1962).
10. Ibid., p. 302.
11. Dayton, op. cit., pp. 99–100.
12. William Warren Sweet, *Revivalism in America* (New York: Charles Scribner's Sons, 1944), p. 179.
13. Pierard, op. cit., pp. 29–30.
14. Winthrop S. Hudson, *Religion in America* (New York: Charles Scribner's Sons, 1973), pp. 272–274.
15. Dayton, op. cit., p. 99.
16. Peoples Bicentennial Commission, *Voices of the American Revolution* (New York: Bantam Books, 1975), p. 207.
17. Norman F. Furniss, *The Fundamentalist Controversy, 1918–1931* (Hamden, CT: Archon Books, 1963), p. 4.
18. Lowell D. Streiker and Gerald S. Strober, *Religion and the New Majority* (New York: Association Press, 1972), p. 88.
19. Ibid., p. 89.
20. Richard Quebedeaux, *The Young Evangelicals* (New York: Harper & Row, 1974), pp. 8–9.
21. J. Gresham Machen, *Christianity and Liberalism* (New York: Eerdmans Publishing Co., 1923).
22. Quebedeaux, *Young Evangelicals,* op. cit., p. 8.
23. Hudson, op. cit., pp. 370–371.
24. Ibid., pp. 377–378.
25. Quebedeaux, *Young Evangelicals,* op. cit., p. 23.
26. Martin E. Marty, *A Nation of Behavers* (Chicago: University of Chicago Press, 1976), p. 86.
27. Quebedeaux, *Young Evangelicals,* op. cit., p. 12.

28. Ibid., p. 29.
29. Carl F. H. Henry, *The Uneasy Conscience of Modern Fundamentalism* (Grand Rapids: Eerdmans Publishing Co., 1947), pp. 23, 84.
30. Klaas Runia, "Evangelical Responsibility in a Secularized World," *Christianity Today,* June 19, 1970, p. 11.
31. William G. McLoughlin, Jr., *Modern Revivalism* (New York: Harper & Row, 1959), pp. 505–512.
32. Streiker and Strober, op. cit., p. 30.
33. "The Preaching and the Power," *Newsweek,* July 20, 1970, p. 54.

CHAPTER 8: TODAY'S CHARISMATICS AND
EVANGELICALS: A TWO-PART THEOLOGICAL
MOVEMENT

1. Donald G. Bloesch, *The Evangelical Renaissance* (Grand Rapids: Eerdmans Publishing Co., 1973), pp. 35, 55–58. See also Richard Quebedeaux, *The Young Evangelicals* (New York: Harper & Row, 1974), pp. 37–38.
2. Bloesch, op. cit., pp. 52–54.
3. Ibid., pp. 59–60.
4. Ibid., pp. 63–65.
5. Ibid., p. 63.
6. Ibid., p. 62.
7. Ibid., p. 69.
8. Lowell D. Streiker and Gerald S. Strober, *Religion and the New Majority* (New York: Association Press, 1972), p. 103.
9. Bloesch, op. cit., p. 71.
10. Samuel H. Moffett, "What Is Evangelism?" *Christianity Today,* August 22, 1969, p. 5; see also Quebedeaux, *Young Evangelicals,* op. cit., pp. 98–102; Ronald J. Sider, "Evangelism or Social Justice: Eliminating the Options," *Christianity Today,* October 8, 1976, pp. 26–29.
11. Jim Wallis, *Agenda for Biblical People* (New York: Harper & Row, 1976), pp. 88–89.
12. Ibid., p. 9.
13. Ibid., pp. 67–68.
14. Kenneth A. Briggs, "Charismatic Christians Seek to Infuse the Faith With Their Joyous Spirit," *The New York Times,* July 22, 1977, Section II, p. 1.

15. Ibid.; see also "The New Healers," *Newsweek,* July 17, 1978, p. 60.
16. Martin E. Marty, *A Nation of Behavers* (Chicago: University of Chicago Press, 1976), p. 107.
17. Richard Quebedeaux, *The New Charismatics* (Garden City: Doubleday & Co., 1976), p. 55.
18. Ibid., pp. 64–65.
19. Briggs, op. cit., p. 1.
20. Marty, op. cit., pp. 112–113.
21. Briggs, op. cit., p. 1.
22. Ibid.

CHAPTER 9: THE PROTESTANT ETHIC AND ECONOMIC CHANGE

1. K. J. W. Kraik, *British Journal of Psychiatry,* vol. 38, pp. 56–61, 142–48.
2. Harry Braverman, *Labor and Monopoly Capital* (New York: Monthly Review Press, 1974), p. 88.
3. Ibid., p. 97.
4. Ibid.
5. Ibid., p. 171.
6. Ibid., p. 241.
7. Daniel Bell, *The Coming of Post-Industrial Society* (New York: Basic Books, 1973), p. 129.
8. Bureau of Labor Statistics, November 1978.
9. National Science Foundation, *R & D in Industry, 1974* (NSF 76–322), p. 2.
10. U.S. Department of Commerce, Industry and Trade Administration estimates that in 1979 advertising expenditures will reach $47.23 billion, press release ITA 79–1, January 3, 1979.
11. Sam Zagovia, "Search for Meaning in Work," *Washington Post,* February 6, 1972, p. B4.
12. U.S. Department of Health, Education and Welfare, *Work in America* (Cambridge, MA: MIT Press, 1973), p. 1.
13. James Roscow, "How We've Been Turning Off Investors," *Pension World,* February 1976; see also, James W. Davant, "The Wall Street Dropouts," *The New York Times,* November 30, 1977.
14. Paul C. Vitz, *Psychology As Religion: The Cult of Self-Worship* (Grand Rapids, MI: Eerdmans Publishing Co., 1977).

15. *Washington Post,* June 24, 1978.
16. John Lukacs, *The Passing of the Modern Age* (New York: Harper Torchbooks, 1970), pp. 200, 201.
17. Christopher Lasch, *Haven in a Heartless World: The Family Besieged* (New York: Basic Books, 1977), pp. xiv–xv. See also Braverman, op. cit., p. 272.
18. Information provided by telephone, Food Beverage Trades, AFL-CIO, Washington, DC, August 1978.
19. The National Organization of Women, Washington, DC, reports that 41 percent of the work force currently are women. Telephone communication, November 1978.
20. Lasch, op. cit., p. 9.
21. Ibid., pp. 15–16, 170.

CHAPTER 10: THE CHARISMATICS: A NEW LIBERATING FORCE?

1. E. F. Schumacher, *A Guide for the Perplexed* (New York: Harper & Row, 1977), p. 127.
2. William McNeill, *Plagues and Peoples* (New York: Anchor/Doubleday, 1976), p. 147.
3. S. N. Eisenstadt, *The Protestant Ethic and Modernization* (New York: Basic Books, 1968), p. 121.
4. McNeill, op. cit., pp. 149–150.
5. Ibid., pp. 163–164.
6. Robert Nisbet, "Knowledge Dethroned," *The New York Times Magazine,* September 8, 1975, p. 34.
7. Amitai Etzioni and Clyde Nunn, "The Public Appreciation of Science in Contemporary America," *Daedalus,* Summer 1974, pp. 191–205.
8. Larry Agran, *The Cancer Connection* (Boston: Houghton Mifflin Co., 1977), p. xvi.
9. Samuel S. Epstein, *The Politics of Cancer* (San Francisco: Sierra Club Books, 1978), p. 23.
10. "The New Healers," *Newsweek,* July 17, 1978, p. 60.
11. David X. Stump, "Charismatic Renewal: Up to Date in Kansas City," *America,* September 24, 1977, p. 166.
12. Richard Quebedeaux, *The New Charismatics* (Garden City, NY: Doubleday & Co., 1976), p. 2.
13. Stump, op. cit., p. 166.

CHAPTER 11: THE EVANGELICALS: A NEW COVENANT VISION?

1. Robert L. Heilbroner, *An Inquiry Into the Human Prospect* (New York: W. W. Norton & Co., 1974), p. 91.
2. Sinclair Lewis, *It Can't Happen Here* (New York: New American Library, Signet, 1970), see especially pp. 27–30.
3. John Lukacs, *The Passing of the Modern Age* (New York: Harper Torchbooks, 1970), p. 181.
4. Francis A. Schaeffer, *How Should We Then Live?* (Old Tappan, NJ: Fleming Revell Co., 1976).
5. Ibid., p. 227.
6. Quoted in "The Plan to Save America," by Jim Wallis and Wes Michaelson, *Sojourners Magazine,* April 1976.
7. "Report to the Nation on Energy," President James E. Carter, April 18, 1977.
8. Richard Quebedeaux, *The Young Evangelicals* (New York: Harper & Row, 1974), pp. 127–128.
9. Henlee H. Barnett, *The Church and the Ecological Crisis* (Grand Rapids, MI: Eerdmans Publishing Co., 1972), p. 69; see also Francis A. Schaeffer, *Pollution and the Death of Man: The Christian View of Ecology* (Wheaton, IL: Tyndale House Publishers, 1970), p. 37.
10. Barnett, op. cit., pp. 78–79.
11. Schaefer, *Pollution,* op. cit., pp. 91–92.
12. Barnett, op. cit., p. 81.
13. Schaeffer, *Pollution,* op. cit., pp. 49, 50.
14. Ibid., p. 48.
15. Ibid., pp. 69, 70.
16. Ibid., pp. 56, 57.
17. Sid Lens, "Mobilizing for Survival," *Washington Watch,* vol. 5, no. 47, December 2, 1977.
18. "Southern Baptists Call for Arms Limit," *The New York Times,* June 15, 1978.
19. "U.S. Churches Turn to Arms Race," *The New York Times,* March 25, 1979, p. 1.

BIBLIOGRAPHY

Adler, Mortimer, ed. *Great Books of the Western World,* vol. 30, *Novum Organum of Francis Bacon.* Chicago: Encyclopaedia Britannica, Inc., 1952.

Agran, Larry. *The Cancer Connection.* Boston: Houghton Mifflin Co., 1977.

Ahlstrom, Sydney E. *A Religious History of the American People.* New Haven: Yale University Press, 1972.

Barber, William J. *A History of Economic Thought.* New York: Penguin Books, 1967.

Barbour, Ian G., ed. *Finite Resources and the Human Future.* Minneapolis: Augsburg Publishing House, 1976.

Barnett, Henlee H. *The Church and the Ecological Crisis.* Grand Rapids: Eerdmans Publishing Co., 1972.

Beckerman, Wilfred. *Two Cheers for the Affluent Society.* New York: St. Martin's Press, 1974.

Bell, Daniel. *The Coming of Post-Industrial Society.* New York: Basic Books, 1973.

Bellah, Robert N. *The Broken Covenant.* New York: The Seabury Press, 1975.

Bentham, Jeremy. *Principles of Morals and Legislation.* 1780.

Berger, Peter L., and Neuhaus, Richard J. *Against the World for the World.* New York: The Seabury Press, 1976.

Billington, Ray Allen. *The Protestant Crusade.* New York: Quadrangle Books, 1964.

Blessitt, Arthur, with Walter Wagner. *Turned On to Jesus.* New York: Hawthorne Books, 1971.

Bloesch, Donald G. *The Evangelical Renaissance.* Grand Rapids: Eerdmans Publishing Co., 1973.

277

Bluhm, William Theodore. *Ideologies and Attitudes*. Englewood Cliffs, NJ: Prentice-Hall, 1974.

Bookchin, Murray. *Post-Scarcity Anarchism*. Berkeley: Ramparts Press, 1971.

Boulding, Kenneth. *Beyond Economics: Essays on Society, Religion and Ethics*. Ann Arbor, MI: Michigan University Press, 1970.

Braverman, Harry. *Labor and Monopoly Capital*. New York: Monthly Review Press, 1974.

Broder, David. *The Party's Over*. New York: Harper & Row, 1972.

Brown, Lester R. *The Twenty-Ninth Day*, a Worldwatch Institute Book. New York: W. W. Norton & Co., 1978.

Burlingame, Roger. *The Sixth Column*. New York: J. B. Lippincott Co., 1962.

Bury, J. B. *The Idea of Progress: An Inquiry Into Its Origin and Growth*. New York: Dover, 1955.

Caldwell, Taylor. *Great Lion of God*. Garden City, NY: Doubleday & Co., 1970.

Callenbach, Ernest. *Ecotopia*. New York: Bantam Books, 1977.

Campbell, Will D., and Holloway, James Y. *Up to Our Steeples in Politics*. New York: Paulist Press, 1970.

Clabaugh, Gary K. *Thunder on the Right: The Protestant Fundamentalist*. Chicago: Nelson-Hall, 1974.

Clouse, Robert G., et al. *The Cross and the Flag*. Carol Stream, IL: Creation House, 1972.

Cochran, Thomas C., and Miller, William. *The Age of Enterprise*. New York: Harper & Row, 1961.

Coleman, Robert E. *The Master Plan of Evangelism*. Old Tappan, NJ: Spire, 1963.

Commoner, Barry. *The Poverty of Power*. New York: Bantam Books, 1977.

Cornuelle, Richard C. *Reclaiming the American Dream*. New York: Random House, 1965.

Cuddihy, John Murray. *No Offense: Civil Religion and Protestant Taste*. New York: The Seabury Press, 1978.

Daly, Herman E., ed. *Toward a Steady-State Economy*. San Francisco: W. H. Freeman & Co., 1973.

Dayton, Donald. *Discovering an Evangelical Heritage*. New York: Harper & Row, 1976.

Dollar, George W. *A History of Fundamentalism in America*. Greenville, SC: Bob Jones University Press, 1973.

Douglas, Jack D. *The Technological Threat*. Englewood Cliffs: Prentice-Hall, 1971.

Ehrlich, Paul R. *The End of Affluence*. New York: Ballantine Books, 1974.

Eiselen, Frederick Carl, ed. *The Abingdon Bible Commentary*. New York: Abingdon-Cokesbury Press, 1929.

Eisenstadt, S. N. *The Protestant Ethic and Modernization*. New York: Basic Books, 1968.

Ellul, Jacques. *The Technological Society*. New York: Vintage Books, 1964.

Ellwood, Robert S., Jr. *One Way: The Jesus Movement and Its Meaning*. Englewood Cliffs: Prentice-Hall, 1973.

Epstein, Benjamin R. *The Radical Right*. New York: Vintage Books, 1967.

Epstein, Samuel S. *The Politics of Cancer*. San Francisco: Sierra Club Books, 1978.

Falk, Richard A. *This Endangered Planet*. New York: Vintage Books, 1971.

Fant, Clyde E. *Bonhoeffer: Worldly Preaching*. Nashville: Thomas Nelson, 1975.

Ferkiss, Victor. *The Future of Technological Civilization*. New York: Braziller, 1974.

————. *Technological Man: The Myth and the Reality*. New York: Braziller, 1969.

Furniss, Norman F. *The Fundamentalist Controversy, 1918–1931*. Hamden, CT: Archon Books, 1963.

Gasper, Louis. *The Fundamentalist Movement*. The Hague: Mouton & Co., N.V., 1963.

Germino, Dante L. *Modern Western Political Thought*. Chicago: Rand McNally, 1972.

Girvetz, Harry K. *The Evolution of Liberalism*. New York: Collier Books, 1967.

Gish, Arthur G. *The New Left and Christian Radicalism*. Grand Rapids, MI: Eerdmans Publishing Co., 1970.

Grounds, Vernon C. *Revolution and the Christian Faith*. Philadelphia: J. B. Lippincott Co., 1971.

Hallowell, John. *Main Currents in Modern Political Thought*. New York: Holt, Rinehart & Winston, 1950.

Hamilton, Michael P. *The Charismatic Movement*. Grand Rapids, MI: Eerdmans Publishing Co., 1975.

Hampshire, Stuart, ed. *The Age of Reason*. New York: Mentor Books, 1956.

Harrington, Michael. *The Twilight of Capitalism*. New York: Simon & Schuster, 1976.

Hartz, Louis. *The Liberal Tradition in America*. New York: Harcourt Brace Jovanovich, 1955.

Heilbroner, Robert L., with Aaron Singer. *The Economic Transformation of America*. New York: Harcourt Brace Jovanovich, 1977.

————. *An Inquiry Into the Human Prospect*. New York: W. W. Norton & Co., 1974.

————. *The Worldly Philosophers*. New York: Simon and Schuster, 1967.

Henderson, Hazel. *Creating Alternative Futures*. New York: Berkley Winhover, 1978.

Henry, Carl F. H. *Contemporary Evangelical Thought: A Survey*. Grand Rapids, MI: Baker Book House, 1968.

————. *The Uneasy Conscience of Modern Fundamentalism*. Grand Rapids, MI: Eerdmans Publishing Co., 1947.

Henry, Paul B. *Politics for Evangelicals*. Valley Forge, PA: Judson Press, 1974.

Hill, Harold. *How Did It All Begin*. Plainfield, NJ: Logos, 1976.

Hirsch, Fred. *Social Limits to Growth*. Cambridge, MA: Harvard University Press, 1978.

Hofstadter, Richard. *The Paranoid Style in American Politics*. New York: Alfred A. Knopf, 1965.

————. *Anti-Intellectualism in American Life*. New York: Random House, 1962.

Howard, Ted, and Rifkin, Jeremy. The Peoples Business Commission. *Who Should Play God?* New York: Dell, 1977.

Hudson, Winthrop S. *Religion in America*. New York: Charles Scribner's Sons, 1973.

Jegen, Mary Evelyn, and Manno, Bruno. *The Earth Is the Lord's*. New York: Paulist Press, 1978.

Jorstad, Erling. *That New-Time Religion*. Minneapolis: Augsburg Publishing House, 1972.

Kariel, Henry S. *Beyond Liberalism: Where Relations Grow*. New York: Harper & Row, 1978.

Kelley, Dean M. *Why Conservative Churches Are Growing*. New York: Harper & Row, 1977.

Kuhn, Thomas S. *The Structure of Scientific Revolutions*. Chicago: University of Chicago Press, 1962.

Lasch, Christopher. *Haven in a Heartless World: The Family Besieged*. New York: Basic Books, 1977.

Laslett, Peter, ed. *John Locke, Two Treatises of Government*. Cambridge: Cambridge University Press, 1967.

Lewis, Ewart, ed. *Medieval Political Ideas*. New York: Alfred A. Knopf, 1954.

Lewis, Sinclair. *It Can't Happen Here*. New York: New American Library, Signet, 1970.

Lipset, Seymour Martin, and Rabb, Earl. *The Politics of Unreason: Right-Wing Extremism in America*. New York: Harper & Row, 1970.

Lovins, Armory B. *Soft Energy Paths*. Cambridge, MA: Ballinger, 1977.

Lukacs, John. *The Passing of the Modern Age*. New York: Harper Torchbooks, 1970.

McLoughlin, William G., ed. *The American Evangelicals, 1800–1900*. New York: Harper & Row, 1968.

———. *Modern Revivalism*. New York: Harper & Row, 1959.

McLuhan, Marshall. *The Gutenberg Galaxy*. New York: Mentor Books, 1969.

———. and Fiore, Quentin. *The Medium Is the Message*. New York: Bantam Books, 1967.

McNeill, William. *Plagues and Peoples*. New York: Anchor/Doubleday, 1976.

Magnuson, Norris. *Salvation in the Slums: Evangelical Social Work, 1865–1920*. Metuchen, NJ: The Scarecrow Press, 1977.

Marcuse, Herbert. *One Dimensional Man*. Boston: Beacon Press, 1964.

Marty, Martin E. *A Nation of Behavers*. Chicago: University of Chicago Press, 1976.

———. *A Short History of Christianity*. New York: Collins, World, 1959.

Mathews, Donald G. *Religion in the Old South*. Chicago: University of Chicago Press, 1977.

Maury, Philippe. *Politics and Evangelism*. Garden City, NY: Doubleday & Co., 1959.

Meadows, Dennis L., ed. *Alternatives to Growth—I*. Cambridge, MA: Ballinger, 1977.

Meadows, Donella H., et al. *The Limits to Growth*. New York: New American Library, 1972.

Menendez, Albert J. *Religion at the Polls*. Philadelphia: Westminster Press, 1977.

Mesarovic, Mihajlo, and Pestel, Eduard. *Mankind at the Turning Point*. New York: New American Library, 1974.

Miles, Rufus E., Jr. *Awakening from the American Dream*. New York: Universe Books, 1976.

Mill, John S. *Principles of Political Economy*, vol. 2, 3, *John Stuart Mill's Collected Works*. Toronto: University of Toronto Press, 1963.

Mishan, E. J. *The Economic Growth Debate*. London: Allen and Unwin, 1977.

Moberg, David O. *The Great Reversal*. Philadelphia: J. B. Lippincott Co., 1972.

Mouw, Richard J. *Political Evangelism*. Grand Rapids, MI: Eerdmans Publishing Co., 1973.

Muehl, William. *Politics for Christians*. New York: Haddam House, 1956.

Mumford, Lewis. *Technics and Civilization*. New York: Harcourt, Brace and World, 1934.

National Academy of Sciences. *Energy and Climate*. Washington, DC, 1977.

Niebuhr, Reinhold. *A Nation So Conceived*. New York: Charles Scribner's Sons, 1963.

————. *The Godly and the Ungodly*. London: Faber and Faber, 1958.

————. *Christianity and Power Politics*. New York: Charles Scribner's Sons, 1952.

————. *The Irony of American History*. New York: Charles Scribner's Sons, 1952.

Niebuhr, H. Richard. *The Kingdom of God in America*. Hamden, CT: The Shoe String Press, 1956.

Nisbet, Robert. *Twilight of Authority*. New York: Oxford University Press, 1975.

Odum, Eugene P. *Fundamentals of Ecology*. 3rd ed. Philadelphia: Saunders, 1971.

Olson, Mancur, Jr. *The No-Growth Society*. New York: W. W. Norton & Co., 1973.

Oltmans, Willem L., ed. *On Growth I*. New York: G. P. Putnam, 1973.

————. *On Growth II*. New York: G. P. Putnam, 1975.

Ophuls, William. *Ecology and the Politics of Scarcity*. San Francisco: W. H. Freeman & Co., 1977.

Oursler, Will. *Protestant Power and the Coming Revolution*. New York: Doubleday & Co., 1971.

Peoples Bicentennial Commission. *Voices of the American Revolution*. New York: Bantam Books, 1975.

Pierard, Richard V. *The Unequal Yoke*. Philadelphia: J. B. Lippincott Co., 1970.

Plowman, Edward E. *The Jesus Movement in America*. New York: Pyramid, 1971.

Quebedeaux, Richard. *The Worldly Evangelicals*. New York: Harper & Row, 1978.

———. *The New Charismatics*. Garden City, NY: Doubleday & Co., 1976.

———. *The Young Evangelicals*. New York: Harper & Row, 1974.

Ramm, Bernard. *The Evangelical Heritage*. Waco, TX: Word Books, 1973.

Ramsey, Paul, ed. *Faith and Ethics: The Theology of Niebuhr*. New York: Harper & Brothers, 1957.

———. *Who Speaks for the Church?* Nashville: Abingdon Press, 1967.

Randall, John Herman. *The Making of the Modern Mind*. New York: Columbia University Press, 1976.

Rasmussen, Larry L. *Dietrich Bonhoeffer: Reality and Resistance*. Nashville: Abingdon Press, 1972.

Richardson, Herbert W. *Toward an American Theology*. New York: Harper & Row, 1967.

Rifkin, Jeremy. *Own Your Own Job*. New York: Bantam Books, 1977.

———, and Barber, Randy. *The North Will Rise Again: Pensions, Politics and Power in the 1980s*. Boston: Beacon, 1978.

Rosten, Leo, ed. *Religions of America*. New York: Simon & Schuster, 1975.

Roszak, Theodore. *Where the Wasteland Ends*. Garden City, NY: Anchor, 1973.

Rothman, Harry. *Murderous Providence: A Study of Pollution in Industrial Societies*. New York: Bobbs-Merrill, 1972.

Sandeen, Ernest R. *The Origins of Fundamentalism*. Philadelphia: Fortress Press, 1968.

Schaeffer, Francis A. *How Should We Then Live?* Old Tappan, NJ: Fleming Revell Co., 1976.

———. *Pollution and the Death of Man: The Christian View of Ecology*. Wheaton, IL: Tyndale House, 1970.

Schrag, Peter. *The End of the American Future*. New York: Simon & Schuster, 1973.

Schumacher, E. F. *A Guide for the Perplexed*. New York: Harper & Row, 1977.

———. *Small Is Beautiful*. New York: Harper & Row, 1973.

Sears, Jack Wood. *Conflict and Harmony in Science and the Bible*. Grand Rapids, MI: Baker Book House, 1969.

Sewell, John W., and the Overseas Development Council Staff. *The U.S. and World Development Agenda 1977*. New York: Praeger, 1977.

Sherrill, John. *They Speak With Other Tongues*. Old Tappan, NJ: Spire, 1977.

Sherwin, Mark. *The Extremists*. New York: St. Martin's Press, 1963.

Slater, Philip. *The Pursuit of Loneliness*. Boston: Beacon, 1976.

Smith, Adam. *An Inquiry Into the Nature and Causes of the Wealth of Nations*. Edwin Cannan, ed. London: Methuen & Co., 1961.

Smith, Page. *A New Age Now Begins*. New York: McGraw-Hill, 1976.

Smith, Timothy L. *Revivalism and Social Reform*. New York: Harper & Row, 1957.

Stent, Gunther S. *The Coming of the Golden Age: A View of the End of Progress*. New York: Natural History Press, 1969.

Stevick, Daniel B. *Beyond Fundamentalism*. Richmond: John Knox Press, 1964.

Streiker, Lowell D., and Strober, Gerald S. *Religion and the New Majority*. New York: Association Press, 1972.

Stringfellow, William. *A Private and Public Faith*. Grand Rapids, MI: Eerdmans Publishing Co., 1962.

————. *Dissenter in a Great Society*. New York: Holt, Rinehart and Winston, 1966.

Sweazey, George E. *Effective Evangelism*. New York: Harper & Row, 1976.

Sweet, William Warren. *Revivalism in America*. New York: Charles Scribner's Sons, 1944.

Tawney, R. H. *Religion and the Rise of Capitalism*. New York: Harcourt, Brace & Co., 1926.

Teich, Albert H., ed. *Technology and Man's Future*. New York: St. Martin's Press, 1972.

Thompson, William Irwin. *Darkness and Scattered Light*. Garden City, NY: Anchor, 1978.

Tillich, Paul. *A History of Christian Thought*. New York: Simon & Schuster, 1967.

Toynbee, Arnold J. *Civilization on Trial and The World and the West*. New York: Meridian Books, 1958.

Tyler, Gus. *Scarcity*. New York: Quadrangle Books, 1976.

The Peoples Business Commission is an educational organization dedicated to the examination of major ideas and issues of importance to the future of American society. Jeremy Rifkin and Ted Howard of the Peoples Business Commission would like to hear from you. If you have something to communicate, would like to become involved or just want more information, write to:

> Peoples Business Commission
> 1346 Connecticut Avenue, N.W.
> Washington, D.C. 20036
> (202) 466–2823

* * * * * * * * * * * * * * * * * * *
ABOUT THE AUTHORS

Jeremy Rifkin founded the Peoples Bicentennial Commission
in 1971 and served as its director until 1976. He is currently
co-director of the Peoples Business Commission in Washington. He has written several books, including COMMONSENSE
II and OWN YOUR OWN JOB, and with Ted Howard has
coauthored ENTROPY, WHO SHOULD PLAY GOD, and
THE NORTH WILL RISE AGAIN. As a result of THE
EMERGING ORDER, Jeremy Rifkin has become a major com-
mentator on the religious scene in America, in demand as a
speaker and writer. He lives in Washington, D.C.

Ted Howard was co-director of the Peoples Bicentennial Com-
mission from 1972 to 1976 and is now co-director of the Peoples
Business Commission. He is the author of AMERICA'S
BIRTHDAY and VOICES OF THE AMERICAN REVOLU-
TION, and also lives in Washington, D.C.

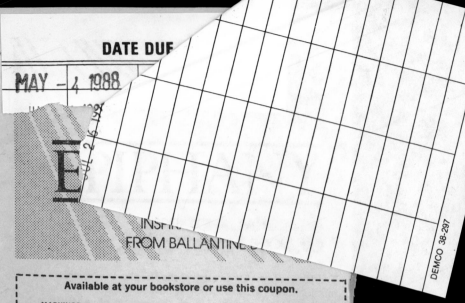

INSPIR
FROM BALLANTINE

Available at your bookstore or use this coupon.

____**MARKINGS**, Dag Hammarskjold   30699   2.95
The remarkable record of the spiritual life of Dag Hammarskjold, his personal diaries reveal his inner strength and his commitment to Christ.

____**MY PERSONAL PRAYER DIARY**, Catherine Marshall
& Leonard Le Sourd   30612   3.95
Three hundred sixty-five prayers and related scripture passages provide guidance for daily devotions.

____**TEST YOUR BIBLE POWER**, Jerome B. Agel & Stanley Shank
(Gen Ed)   30663   1.95
Nearly 300 games, puzzles, quiz questions and other brain teasers. Great for Sunday School classes and Bible Scholars!

____**THE COURAGE TO BELIEVE**, Craig Morton & Robert Berger   30564   2.75
Eleven famous athletes who have committed their lives to Christ including: Morton himself, Terry Bradshaw, Roger Staubach and many others.

 BALLANTINE MAIL SALES
Dept. TA, 201 E. 50th St., New York, N.Y. 10022

Please send me the BALLANTINE or DEL REY BOOKS I have checked above. I am enclosing $. . . . . (add 50¢ per copy to cover postage and handling). Send check or money order — no cash or C.O.D.'s please. Prices and numbers are subject to change without notice.

Name_____

Address_____

City_____ State_____ Zip Code_____
17   Allow at least 4 weeks for delivery.   TA-53